COLLECTIVE BARGAINING AND PRODUCTIVITY

A Contribution from the Research Program of the Institute of Industrial Relations, University of California, Berkeley

COLLECTIVE BARGAINING AND PRODUCTIVITY

THE LONGSHORE MECHANIZATION AGREEMENT

PAUL T. HARTMAN

UNIVERSITY OF CALIFORNIA PRESS

BERKELEY AND LOS ANGELES 1969

University of California Press

Berkeley and Los Angeles, California

University of California Press, Ltd.

London, England

Copyright © 1969, by The Regents of the University of California

Library of Congress Catalog Card Number: 69-16506

Standard Book Number: 520-01485-5

Designed by Dave Comstock

Printed in the United States of America

The Port of Los Angeles and the Pacific Maritime Association

made archive photos available to the author,

who wishes to acknowledge their use,

as well as to thank the Port of Seattle,

the Port of Astoria,

and the Port of Long Beach

for the use of photos lent under PMA aegis.

TO MY PARENTS

ACKNOWLEDGMENTS

This study never could have been completed without the help of many people in the union, the employers' association, and the universities. Lloyd Ulman of the University of California at Berkeley provided constant encouragement and a forum for testing ideas and airing problems. He read several drafts of the entire manuscript and made numerous useful suggestions. He, more than any other, goaded the study to completion and publication. Margaret S. Gordon, Van Kennedy, and Benjamin Ward, all of Berkeley, not only read the manuscript and suggested revisions but also gave advice and support from my first year as a graduate student.

At other universities, Professors George Hildebrand and Harold Levinson read the manuscript and offered suggestions and encouragement. Martin Wagner, Director of the Institute of Labor and Industrial Relations, and John Due, Chairman of the Department of Economics, both of the University of Illinois, provided financial support for computer time, data processing, computational assistance, and manuscript preparation.

I am especially indebted to Lincoln Fairley, the Research Director of the ILWU until his retirement in 1967, for his patience, courtesy, and generosity in answering questions, making available the union's records and files of data, arranging interviews, and much other help. Dr. Fairley read the manuscript and suggested scores of corrections and revisions. Pres Lancaster, Manager of the Contract Data Department of the PMA, provided all the data essential to the estimates of productivity, as well as other material and helpful insights. He read the manuscript and offered many suggestions and corrections.

Within the union, Barry Silverman, Research Director since early 1968, read the study, suggested corrections, and provided a friendly environment in which to work. I am also indebted for guidance in the union's records and on the waterfront to Margery Canright, Evey Wakefield, the late L. B. Thomas, Willie Christenson,

Bob Rohatch, and, for permission to do all this, to Harry Bridges, the union's president.

In the industry and the Pacific Maritime Association, I am grateful for insights and permission to use data to Wayne Horvitz, the late J. Paul St. Sure, and Rocco Siciliano, the current president of the PMA. Dr. Max Kossoris, Director of the Western Regional Office of the U.S. Bureau of Labor Statistics read the manuscript and was especially helpful with the background and data of the Pacific Maritime Association productivity studies.

Valuable programming or computational assistance were provided by Marian Frobish, Dennis Hickey, and Keith Kakacek. Typing and retyping of the various drafts was done by Mimi Hawkins, Anice Duncan, Julie Metzger, Pat Burcham, Sandra Marshall, Betty Wolfe, and others.

Through it all, my wife and children were compassionate and understanding.

PAUL T. HARTMAN

Urbana, Illinois
August, 1968

FOREWORD

This analysis of the influence — first negative and later positive — of unionism and collective bargaining on productivity in the longshore industry on the Pacific Coast is written in a vien of quiet brilliance. Therefore, it is the pleasant task of this Foreword to alert the reader to some of the important and original contributions to analysis and scholarship that lie ahead.

One might begin with two contributions to the body of knowledge concerning the formation of restrictive work rules. The first deals with the propensity on the part of trade unionists to invest bargaining power in such rules. This propensity was interpreted by Selig Perlman as a manifestation of a uniquely high degree of "scarcity consciousness" and aversion to risk which he assigned to the proletarian mentality. Contrasting with Perlman's "organic labor mentality" is what might be termed the John L. Lewis mentality: raise wages high enough to induce the employer to exchange jobs for machines and then take still more wages out of the machines. After the International Longshoremen's and Warehousemen's Union agreed to surrender work rules for money, its leadership moved closer to the Lewis end of the spectrum. Moreover, as Professor Hartman observes, although the union leaders who were instrumental in the abandonment of restrictive practices after 1960 were the same ones who had helped to install them originally, Harry Bridges and his colleagues never did conform to the Perlmanian ideal type of business unionist. The ILWU experience should not be taken to deny that the desire to protect relatively good jobs can stimulate the development of restrictive work practices. But it also shows that it is not impossible for union leaders of radical political persuasion to function effectively as business unionists. More important, a recent phase of that experience — the negotiation of the Mechanization and Modernization Agreement of 1960 — shows that it is possible under certain conditions for effective leadership to help the members to change their minds sufficiently to overcome stubborn habits. And this was hardly Lewis's way.

Professor Hartman's second contribution is an important supplement to our knowledge of environmental conditions surrounding the development of restrictive work practices. Slichter and his associates traced the origin of makework rules to technological change which, combined with union intransigeance, converted what had originally been economically innocuous practices into restraints on economic efficiency. Hartman finds that in Pacific Coast longshoring "almost all of the practices were restrictive at the outset" and that they were either negotiated by the parties or grew out of "job action" or wildcat strikes by the rank and file. Moreover, he points out that in industries like longshoring and construction, a high degree of inter-firm competition and brief job duration have tended to create casual labor forces with characteristically wide dispersions of earnings. Such labor market conditions may suffice (in the absence of marked technological change) to generate work rules designed to equalize earnings and effort among the workers and unit labor costs among the employers after the union (or legislative authority) has succeeded in "decasualizing" the work force. Uniformity in working practices, however, requires a considerable degree of control by the national union; in fact the industry-wide Mechanization and Modernization Agreement resulted in part from the intensification of interport competition on the West Coast to which local union autonomy and diversity of rules and practices had contributed. (One nevertheless wonders whether some part of the greater uniformity in costs attributable to the coastwide agreement of 1960 might have reflected simply the desire on the part of the leadership to increase the degree of centralization within the union, as in the case of the trucking industry.)

One of the outstanding innovations in this book consists in the quantitative estimates of the impact on productivity of the abandonment and relaxation of restrictive practices under the 1960 agreement, which appear in Chapters IV and V and in Appendix B. This pioneering effort produced highly interesting, and sometimes startling results. By implication these estimates also reveal the degree to which such practices had previously depressed productivity. In the first place, longshoring productivity increased sharply after the 1960 Agreement; by 1965, it was up by a third, following a decade of stagnation. In the second place, nearly all of the increases in productivity on dockwork were due to the abandonment of work rules, notably multiple handling and excessive manning scales, and not to increased mechanization. This was contrary to the expectations of the union negotiators and also to their hopes; they wanted machines to replace the "casuals" (nonmembers) and to lighten the effort of their members who remained attached to the industry. Finally, the retirement bonus provided under the agreement proved unexpectedly effective in inducing withdrawals from the elderly work force in longshoring; this, combined with an unanticipated increase in tonnage, resulted in acute shortages of manpower (despite the greatly increased productivity). These shortages, however, were easily filled; if some union benefits were effective in inducing retirements, others were equally efficient in attracting potential new entries far in excess of demand.

The finding that great increases could occur with no induced change in the quantity of fixed capital cannot be readily squared with either of the two categories of work rule most frequently analyzed in the literature: the requirement of a fixed proportion of labor to capital or the requirement that an absolute minimum amount of labor be hired. Abandonment of a rule of the former variety could induce an increase in fixed capital per unit of output; abandonment of the latter could result in the employment of less capital as well as less labor. But Professor Hartman, while accepting the generic definition of a makework rule as a device to require the employer to hire more labor than otherwise desired at the going wage rate, finds that the West Coast Longshoremen have tended to negotiate or impose rules permitting variations in the proportions of labor to capital in order to take advantage of different or changing conditions of demand. This important category of work rule is named "the negotiated production function" by the author, and its theoretical attributes are developed systematically in Appendix A. Among these attributes is the possibility that the elimination of such rules may result "for a given output level, in reductions in employment and costs and increases in productivity, with no significant increase in investment." This conclusion is confirmed impressively by the author's statistical evidence. It might also be concluded that neither the wage and benefit increases which the union had negotiated in exchange for the abandonment or relaxation of its negotiated production functions nor the pre-existing levels of compensation were sufficiently great to induce increased ratios of capital to output after the restrictive practices had been eliminated and the production function shifted. Indeed, Hartman finds that the post-1960 wage increases were not especially large, either by historic standards in this industry or in comparison with increases granted elsewhere at the same time; and he observes that employer contributions to the benefit funds established under the agreement "were the equivalent of only a modest wage increase."

Although Professor Hartman agrees with the view that few other unions in this country "have so much to give up" as the ILWU had in 1960, the appearance of this work coincides with the upsurge of what is known as "productivity bargaining" in Great Britain, a country where unions generally have a great deal to give up indeed. Some of the most successful examples of productivity bargaining have occurred in highly concentrated and capital-intensive industries — environments quite different from that provided by West Coast longshoring. This is true partly because in such industries work-sharing (as distinguished from makework) devices or restriction of output under piecework can depress labor productivity by restraining the productivity of capital instead of forcing up the ratio of labor to capital. And, just as the abandonment of makework rules in the American longshore industry resulted in increased productivity with less labor and virtually no more capital, so some British productivity agreements have resulted in increased productivity with less capital per unit of output and even with lower proportions of capital, to labor. (Diagramatically, this type of situation might be depicted by making the technologically optimal isoquant q_1 tangent to the lower cost boundary above employment $(x_1)_2$, instead of $(x_1)_1$ in Figure 3 of Appendix A.)

But such differences are of limited relevance to the conditions required for the successful negotiation of "pay and productivity deals," and the British reader is respectfully invited to consult those passages in Chapter III which deal with the role of the national union in educating the local representatives, with the willingness of the national union officers and the industry negotiators to conduct lengthy negotiations in the presence of these representatives, and with the provision in the agreement which contemplates temporary cessation of employer contributions to the special fund in the event of illegal stoppages, disregard of arbitration decisions, or failure to abide by the terms of the agreement. But these cannot be regarded as more

than necessary conditions of success; the recent refusal by the longshoremen to abide by an arbitration decision awarding the off-dock
loading of large containers to the Teamsters is evidence that even
such hallmarks of American collective bargaining cannot insure success. Thus, in addition to the historical, empirical, and analytic interest which Professor Hartman's book holds for his professional peers,
this volume holds policy implications for collective bargainers and
others in lands considerably removed from the docksides where the
author observed and analyzed his lively subjects.

LLOYD ULMAN

March 14, 1969

CONTENTS

TEXT TABLES

APPENDIX TABLES

INTRODUCTION

On October 18, 1960, after more than four years of study, negotiation, and resolution of disputes within their respective constituencies, representatives of the Pacific Maritime Association (PMA) and the International Longshoremen's and Warehousemen's Union (ILWU) signed a new memorandum of agreement. The employers agreed to contribute five million dollars each year for the five and a half years beginning January 1, 1961, to a fund to be jointly administered with the union. The money was to provide a bonus to retiring longshoremen, with provisions for retirement as early as age sixty-two, and a fund to maintain a wage floor at the equivalent of thirty-five hours weekly pay at the basic straight-time hourly rate. In exchange the union agreed to give up all work rules that required multiple handling of goods or employment of redundant men or that otherwise imposed limits to increased productivity or lower labor costs. Both parties expected increased investment, higher productivity per unit of labor employed, lower costs, and decreased employment in the industry.

The understanding was referred to by the parties themselves as the mechanization and modernization agreement. Mechanization was anticipated in the form of adoption of new machines and new techniques of cargo handling. Modernization referred to the elimination of "obsolete" work rules and practices.

The 1960 agreement was widely publicized during negotiations and its first year or so in force. Some observers disapproved. They regarded the agreement as an unfortunate recognition by management of the workers' "property rights" in the jobs; the rights had been given up only temporarily by management, and ought to have been recoverable without recourse to purchase or a multi-million-dollar annual "bribe." Other negative views construed the agreement as an unforgivable concession by the union in that it surrendered for a pittance the rights and favorable working conditions gained through years of arduous struggle. Most observers, however, saw the agreement as an intelligent accommodation to changing conditions. In this view the union's implicit policy of resistance to technical change and the employers' tolerance of the policy were institutional fossils ill-suited to a dynamic economy. Abandonment of the policy by the union was a rational response to the employers' rational offer of monetary benefits. Almost all writers and speakers — union officials, employer spokesmen, disinterested scholars and journalists — whether or not they approved, regarded the ILWU-PMA arrangements essentially as devices to cope with mechanization and technical change. Indeed, many believed the 1960 agreement to be a pioneering attempt, useful as a guide to other industries, to mitigate the effects of accelerated replacement of men by machines.

In part the publicity and the views of most observers were misleading. The 1960 agreement was not an automation agreement; in fact it had little to do directly with technical change. It was instead a drastic modification by the union of work rules and practices that imposed production inefficiencies at a given level of capital input and technology. Over the decades the ILWU had acquired a high degree of job control, probably more than any other union in the United States. Work rules and restrictive practices were many, varied, and ubiquitous. Unlike the typical union with one or a few rules, the ILWU required redundant manning, extensive makework, formal and informal output restriction, specified methods of production, and a wide variety of paid idle time. The industry and its post-1960 changes are not at all less interesting from this view. Indeed, the rapid and largely voluntary abandonment of restrictive work rules is a much rarer and more interesting phenomenon than mere adaptation to technical change. Scores of unions in the United States have accommodated to sharply modified techniques and massive changes in capital input, but few have had the opportunity, and almost none the inclination, to give up substantial control over the speed and efficiency of production.

The ILWU is also exceptionally interesting for the study of work rules because of its unique position in the history of labor relations. Most American scholars have believed job control to be a hallmark, if not the essence, of conservative "business unionism." But the ILWU, far from being a typical business union, is the strongest survivor among the unions expelled from the CIO in 1949 and 1950 for alleged Communist domination. Its leaders clearly have long had a political and social orientation far removed from the "bread and butter" outlook of the typical AFL craft union. For this reason the union provides a severe test for some of the hypotheses concerning motivation underlying the quest for job control. In addition, the union and its job control are relatively new. The usual leading illustrations of restrictive work practices are drawn from old unions and are rooted in circumstances of perhaps sixty, seventy, or even more years ago. The ILWU, on the other hand, was less than thirty years old in 1960. Even more interesting, the leaders and men who brought about the rules were generally the same men who later negotiated their abandonment.

Further, as a by-product of the negotiations leading to the agreement, the PMA gathered data that made possible the measurement of the effects of work-rule elimination. For this industry, at least, an approximate answer may be given to the question of how restrictive are, or were, the rules. This study exploits the unusual opportunity provided by the 1960 agreement and the subsequent behavior of the PMA and ILWU to describe and, more important, to analyze and measure the effects of the imposition and elimination of a highly developed, comprehensive system of union or worker control over the production processes of an important industry.

I | THE INDUSTRY AND THE UNION

The Pacific Coast longshore industry, as defined for this study, includes only the cargo handling for ships in ocean commerce and is geographically limited to the several dozen ports on the Pacific Coast of the continental United States, excluding Alaska.

Four major harbors handle nearly all the foreign trade and most of the nonspecialized general cargo in domestic oceanborne commerce of the Pacific Coast. Seattle is the northernmost. South of Seattle are Portland and Vancouver, which are adjacent cities, although their port areas are six miles apart. San Francisco Bay is about 600 miles south of Portland. San Francisco's harbor area begins just inside the Bay entrance and extends along the west side of the Bay. The Oakland harbor is about four miles from the center of the San Francisco waterfront on the east side of the Bay. Los Angeles and Long Beach harbors are nearly contiguous, and their extreme reaches are no more than eight miles apart. This double port is on San Pedro Bay, about 400 miles southeast of San Francisco.

In addition to the major ports there are more than forty cities and towns through which at least some oceanborne commerce passes each year. Most of these are specialized ports, shipping or receiving only one or a few commodities related to their principal natural resource or industry.

The hinterland of the Pacific ports is the area lying west of the Rocky Mountains. The region covers about one million square miles, including all of Montana and Wyoming. By far the most important part of the hinterland consists of the three coastal states. In the 300,000 square miles of California, Oregon, and Washington are all the large cities, more than 80 percent of the people, and most of the production of goods entering interstate and foreign commerce. The 700,000 square miles of the intermountain and Rocky Mountain areas are sparsely settled and contain few developed resources.

About 110 to 125 million tons of oceanborne goods were loaded or discharged at U.S. mainland Pacific ports each year in the early

1960s. This is about 15 percent of the country's total oceanborne trade. The value of the annual flow of goods across the Pacific port docks is, very approximately, six billion dollars.[1] Longshoremen handle only the dry cargo — goods in cartons, bales, sacks, pieces, and the like. Tanker cargoes are usually handled outside the main harbor areas by specialized industrial employees. Pacific port dry-cargo tonnage, foreign and domestic commerce combined, amounted to about thirty to forty million tons each year in the decade ending in 1966.

The dry-cargo goods moved by longshoremen reflect the natural resources and comparative advantages of the Pacific regions. The chief outbound goods are cotton, rice, fresh and processed fruits, iron ore, potash, iron and steel scrap, hides and tallow, machinery, vehicles, and some miscellaneous manufactured goods from California, and wheat, logs, lumber, and paper from the Northwest. The principal inbound cargoes are bananas, coffee, copra, sugar, iron and steel mill products, nonferrous ores, vehicles, machinery, jute products, and, in southern California, lumber. About 70 percent of the goods movement is in foreign trade. Almost half of that involves shipments to and from Japan. The domestic commerce handled by longshoremen consists, in about equal parts, of general cargo trade with Alaska and Hawaii, lumber and iron and steel mill products exchanged with the U.S. Atlantic Coast ports, and lumber carried in Pacific coastwise trade.[2]

THE STRUCTURE OF THE INDUSTRY

The most important firms in the industry are the ship-operating companies. They not only carry the goods but are also responsible for most of the investment, gross revenues, and decisions bearing on time, place, pace, and methods of work in handling and moving ocean cargoes. The ship operators have invested directly in some terminals and other shoreside facilities, and by commitment to long-term leases they have stimulated other investment by port authorities. Their ships are an equally important part of industry investment.

1. *The tonnage data is the sum of the tonnages reported, by port and type of commerce, in U.S. Army, Corps of Engineers,* Waterborne Commerce of the United States, *Part 4 (Washington, various annual issues). The value figure is the sum of values reported by Custom officials for foreign commerce and my estimates of the value of goods moved in domestic ocean commerce.*
2. *For an excellent study of the trade, its composition and changes over time, see Wytze Gorter and George H. Hildebrand,* The Pacific Coast Maritime Shipping Industry, 1930–1948 *(2 vols., Berkeley, 1952, 1954).*

Ship operators, or their agents, negotiate or decide the routes and ports to be used, arrange for berths and terminal facilities, contract with stevedoring companies for loading and unloading, and exercise control or supervision over nearly the whole of the goods movement.

The number of ship-operating firms, and the number of ships in the U.S. Pacific Coast trade is variable; it may change quickly as existing firms divert ships from a route in one part of the world to another, and as firms enter and leave the industry. Nevertheless, a reasonably close estimate for recent years would be that about 200 companies sail about 800 dry-cargo ships in thousands of arrivals and departures each year to and from Pacific ports (see Table 1).

The foreign companies are, by most criteria, very important. They carry slightly more than half of all dry-cargo tonnage, own about two thirds of the ships, and make up about three fourths of the companies involved in the trade. Japan furnishes the largest single foreign national contingent, with about one third of the foreign-flag ships in recent years. More than thirty Japanese companies sail regular routes involving U.S. Pacific ports, and ships from a still larger number call during any given year. The Scandinavian countries together have slightly fewer ships in the Pacific Coast trade than Japan has. Nearly thirty Norwegian companies provide about 15 percent of the foreign ships; about fifteen Swedish and Danish companies together furnish 10 percent. Another forty or so companies from Great Britain, Germany, and the Netherlands together provide a bit more than 20 percent of the ships in the trade, and some fifty companies from more than twenty countries contribute the remaining 20 percent of the shipping under foreign flags.

Although many foreign companies are large, no one firm is prominent in the carrying of goods to and from U.S. Pacific ports. Mitsui O.S.K. Lines, Nippon Yusen Kaisha, the Japan Line, Yamashita Shinnihon, Wilhelmsen, North German Lloyd, the Hamburg-Amerika Line, and the Maersk Line, with fifty to one hundred ships each, match or surpass the largest U.S. companies in size. But, like most foreign-flag firms, they operate ships on many routes throughout the world. Thus each foreign firm, even the very largest, is only a small contributor to the total fleet trading at American Pacific ports.

In contrast, the larger American-flag firms, especially those with headquarters in Pacific ports, are not only collectively but individually very important in American Pacific trade, despite their relatively

Table 1: *Number of Companies, Ships, and Sailings, Pacific Coast Trade by Country of Registry, 1965.*

Country	Number of companies[a]	Total ships registered[b]	Ships in U.S. Pacific trade	Estimated sailings per year[c]
Total U.S.	31	487	218	1,225
Firms with Pacific Coast headquarters[d]	9	106	106	725
Other U.S. firms heavily engaged in Pacific Coast trade[e]	5	107	62	375
All other U.S. firms	17	274	50	125
Japan	33	529	173	410
Norway	28	406	99	220
Great Britain	27	383	54	130
Germany	14	239	46	115
Denmark	7	129	35	90
Sweden	7	109	30	70
Philippines	8	55	21	75
Netherlands	5	99	19	35
All other foreign[f]	42	358	90	205
Total foreign	171	2,307	567	1,350
Grand Total	202	2,794	785	2,575

[a] Only those companies with some ships calling at U.S. Pacific Coast ports during the year.

[b] Total fleets registered to companies identified in (a).

[c] A departure from the Pacific Coast of the U.S. for ports other than those on the Pacific Coast was counted as one sailing. A ship calling at three or four U.S. Pacific ports was counted only once.

[d] Alaska Steamship Company, American President Lines (including its subsidiary American Mail Line), Crown Zellerbach Corporation, Permanente Steamship Corporation, Matson Navigation Company (including its subsidiary The Oceanic Steamship Company), Pacific Far East Line, States Steamship Company, West Coast Steamship Company, Weyerhaeuser Line.

[e] Calmar Steamship Corporation, McLean Industries (consists largely of a ship-operating subsidiary — Sea-Land Corporation), States Marine-Isthmian Agency, United Fruit Company, Waterman Steamship Corporation.

[f] Italy, India, Liberia, Taiwan, Greece, France, Panama, Colombia, Yugoslavia, Finland, Switzerland, Israel, Mexico, Lebanon, Ecuador, and others.

SOURCES: The Pacific Shipper, weekly issues for 1965; *Lloyd's Register of Shipping*, Vol. I (*Register of Ships, 1965–66*), and Vol. III (*Register Book, 1965–66, Owners*) (London, 1965).

small size. The American-flag companies sail fewer and shorter routes than the foreign lines in the trade. Alaska Steamship, for example, carries goods only to and from Alaska. Matson's principal routes are between Hawaii and the U.S. mainland. Calmar Steamship is engaged exclusively in trade between and along the U.S. coasts. Other companies operate only between U.S. Pacific ports and Australasia, Southeast Asia, or the Far East. Each ship of these firms sails routes as little as one sixth and seldom more than one half as long as the typical foreign-flag route. Further, the nine American-flag companies with Pacific Coast headquarters devote their entire fleets to Pacific trade, and several Atlantic and Gulf Coast firms allocate a large fraction of their ships to trading at West Coast ports. Thus the leading American-flag firms not only exceed the ship commitment of most foreign lines but account for far more sailings and tonnage handled at U.S. Pacific ports. Matson Navigation Company, for example, accounts for nearly 10 percent of the annual vessel departures at Pacific ports, which is almost four times as many as the largest of the foreign firms. As a group, the American-flag firms have 30 percent more ships in the trade but account for three times as many sailings as next-ranking Japan.

Within the American group the companies with their main offices in Pacific ports are most influential. Ships of the West Coast companies make up half of the American-flag ships in the trade, and they account for about 60 percent of the sailings. Further, the West Coast companies have their entire fleets committed to the Pacific trade. Only four U.S. firms with headquarters elsewhere are even heavily engaged: McLean, States Marine-Isthmian, Calmar, and United Fruit devote 30 to 70 percent of their ships to carrying cargo to or from Pacific ports. Not surprisingly, the large American-flag ship operators, especially the western companies, have been the leaders in stimulating improved Pacific Coast port facilities, investment in terminals, and more efficient cargo-handling methods; they have also been the most aggressive in dealing with the union.

Seven companies dominate the American-flag segment of the industry, five of them with main offices in Pacific ports. American President Lines, engaged in foreign commerce, has the most ships in the trade. Matson leads in dry-cargo tonnage handled. Pacific Far East and States Steamship are rather small by world standards, but they have modern and, in recent years, profitable fleets. Together, these four companies, all headquartered in San Francisco, operate more than one third of the ships and account for almost half of the American-flag sailings in the trade. Alaska Steamship, a Seattle-based subsidiary of the California Packing Corporation, accounts for another 10 percent of American-flag sailings. McLean, the leader in intercoastal trade, and States Marine-Isthmian, a nonsubsidized operator of an aging fleet, round out the list.

Many of the smaller American ship operators are subsidiaries or divisions of corporations whose chief activity is manufacturing or tropical agriculture. The parent corporation of Permanente Steamship, for example, is a cement manufacturer. Crown Zellerbach is a paper and newsprint manufacturer. The Weyerhaeuser Company is a lumber producer and wood products manufacturer. Calmar Steamship is a subsidiary of the Bethlehem Steel Corporation, and United Fruit is in the banana business, with extensive holdings in Latin America. The Matson Navigation Company, before 1965, almost qualified for this category. Three fourths of its ownership prior to antitrust consent decree was held by four of the five companies that own nearly all Hawaii's sugar and pineapple plantations and processing plants. The ship operation, however, was as important as nearly all their other activities put together.

Another important distinction among American firms involves government subsidies. Most of the ships of companies operating with subsidies carry goods in foreign trade. The companies receive subsidies only for those ships operated in trade with other countries, along specified routes and in conformance with detailed requirements of the U.S. Maritime Administration. The operating differential subsidy reimburses the ship operator for the difference between his costs, or, for some items, average U.S. costs, and the weighted average costs of foreign competitors on the same routes. The chief items for which differentials are calculated include wages and subsistence of officers and crews, vessel maintenance, repairs, and insurance.[3]

Although some improvements in efficiency, or lower costs, could increase a subsidy-ship operator's profits, much of the market pressure for increased efficiency is lost. Where his own costs enter the calculations, a ship operator would not change his profits at all by

3. See U.S. Department of Commerce, Federal Maritime Board and Maritime Administration, Manual of General Procedures for Determining Operating Differential Subsidy Rates (Washington, 1957).

greater efficiency. In other situations lower costs would improve profits — assuming no change in cargo-moving rates — but the subsidy program explicitly provides for recapture of half the profits in excess of 10 percent of "capital necessarily employed" in the business. Nonsubsidized competitors and other critics impute to subsidized ship operators the belief that, despite higher profits in the short run, improved efficiency and lower costs would lead to a weakening of the subsidy program. On the other hand, the imputation continues, higher costs are unlikely to hurt the subsidized operator's profits; no matter what happens to costs, Congress will take steps to keep a representative number of companies in the trade. In fairness, the proper test is performance. Although some of the subsidized operators appear to be indeed lethargic and indifferent to costs, several of the West Coast subsidy lines have pressed aggressively for more efficiency and appear to be not at all hampered by their protected status.

Of the fifteen companies in the country drawing operating differential subsidies in mid-1964, five were West Coast companies. These five — American President and its subsidiary American Mail, Matson through its subsidiary Oceanic, Pacific Far East, and States Steamship — operate 61 of the 318 ships included in the subsidy program (see Table 2). Grace Lines, Moore-McCormack, American Export Isbrandtsen, and U.S. Lines, all headquartered in New York, together operate another 29 ships under subsidy in the Pacific Coast trade.

Most of the ships operated by West Coast nonsubsidy firms are used in domestic commerce, as are many of the other ships owned by U.S. firms that participate in the Pacific trade. Domestic commerce has been reserved, for 175 years, to ships built in the United States and owned and operated by American citizens. The domestic trade companies are thus protected from foreign competition, but, unlike firms in foreign trade, they are not eligible for subsidies. Some 130 nonsubsidized ships are doing at least part of their carrying in the Pacific Coast trade.

In general, Pacific Coast ocean shipping, including foreign trade and foreign lines, is a competitive industry. To be sure, there are areas of exceptions; the subsidy program distorts resource allocation, while rate-making in the industry rather resembles public utility regulation. Nonetheless, there are, for foreign firms in foreign trade and American firms in all branches of the industry, no barriers to entry.

Table 2: Principal U.S. Companies in Pacific Coast
Ocean Trade, 1964.[a]

Company	Subsi-dized ships	Total ships in Pacific Coast trade[a]
Firms with main offices in Pacific ports		
Alaska Steamship Company	0	15
American President Lines[b]	33	34
Matson Navigation Company[c]	5	23
Pacific Far East Line	10	13
States Steamship Company	13	13
Weyerhaeuser Line	0	6
Three other companies	0	6
Firms with main offices in Atlantic and Gulf ports		
Calmar Steamship Corporation	0	5
McLean Industries[d]	0	7
States Marine-Isthmian Agency	0	31
United Fruit Company	0	7
Four subsidized companies	162	29
Twelve other companies	0	31

[a] Only those American companies with regular routes, or long experience involving the Pacific ports are listed. The number of ships in the Pacific trade is estimated from the *Pacific Shipper* and similar sources. To the total of American ships in the trade should be added a variable number of vessels of other U.S. companies and ships operated for the Military Sea Transport Service.

[b] Includes American Mail Line, a subsidiary.

[c] Includes The Oceanic Steamship Company, a subsidiary.

[d] Includes its ship-operating subsidiary, Sea-Land Corporation.

SOURCES: *Pacific Shipper*; various issues; *Lloyd's Register of Shipping*; Benn, *Shipping World*; and U.S. Congress, Joint Economic Committee, *Subsidy and Subsidy-Effect Programs of the U.S. Government*, 89th Cong., 1st sess. (Washington, 1965), p. 51.

The product is homogeneous — that is, services sold by one firm are very nearly indistinguishable from those sold by others. A relatively large number of firms are in the industry, and profits, at least for the U.S. firms, are not large.

The direct employers of longshoremen are the stevedoring contractors.[4] Most of the stevedoring companies are small firms providing technical knowledge and supervision of cargo loading and

4. In the common usage of Pacific ports, a "stevedore" is the firm contracting with a ship operator or his agent to load or unload a ship. The "longshoreman" is the laborer employed by the stevedore to do the work.

unloading, and, in most cases, only a small amount of machinery — forklifts and the like. Some of the cargo-handling services are performed by relatively large terminal operators or special-facility operators. These companies provide all the handling, sorting, storing, and moving of cargo between the ship and the rail or truck carriers. Although these firms often use substantially more machinery than the typical smaller stevedore, they nonetheless usually lease, rather than own, the buildings, land, and heavy capital goods.

The number of firms offering cargo-handling services varies with port size. Small ports typically have only one or two stevedoring or terminal companies. The larger ports may have from five to fifteen privately owned firms engaged in loading and unloading ocean cargoes or providing various dockside services. About a dozen such firms, or branches of firms, operate in the Los Angeles–Long Beach area, about twenty in the San Francisco Bay Area and northern California, and slightly more than two dozen in the Pacific Northwest. A small number of the companies do business in more than one port.

Some of the large ship-operating companies provide terminal and stevedoring services. The Matson Terminals Company performs all these services for its parent corporation, the Matson Navigation Company, and operates as a stevedoring contractor for other ship-operating companies. Consolidated Marine, a joint venture of American President Lines and Pacific Far East Line, provides terminal services and stevedoring in the Los Angeles–Long Beach harbor area for its parent companies. Most of the stevedoring and terminal firms, however, are independent companies serving the smaller American-flag lines and all the foreign ship-operating companies.

Stevedoring contractors sell labor services and little else to ship operators or their agents. Contractual relations between stevedores and ship-operating companies rather resemble those between contractors and their customers in building construction, building maintenance, and other business situations in which labor service is the largest or only commodity exchanged. In principle, competitive bids are submitted by the stevedores to ship operators or agents. In their bids the stevedores quote rates for various commodities by conventional physical units. The commodity rate reflects the stevedore's productivity experience, the wage rates and penalties prevailing at the time for difficult or obnoxious cargo, and a standard added proportion to cover overhead, insurance, and profit.[5] In practice the bids vary little, and the business relationship between a given stevedore and ship operator or agent may continue for a long time without interruption. Direct hourly labor costs, including fringe benefits, are uniform for the entire Pacific Coast and are specified in the labor agreement between the PMA and ILWU. Before 1961, work rules, manning requirements, hours, wage guarantees, penalty rates, and similar contractual or conventional "established practices" were uniform in a port and enforced by union vigilance. In more recent years many of these matters are still prescribed by the Coast contract, arbitration awards, or negotiated rules.

The hiring hall rules also foster uniform productivity among stevedores. Gangs or individual longshoremen are dispatched on a "first-in, first-out" basis to each job. The job — loading or discharging a single ship — lasts no more than several days, and the men report back to the hall for redispatch, often to a different stevedore. Although longshoremen often prefer one or another employer or part of the port, they are not permitted to establish a permanent employment relationship with an employer. Over a reasonable length of time, the men usually work everywhere, and for everyone, in the port. Occupational specialization exists, but it is limited to "shovel gangs," dock gangs, and certain highly mechanized operations. Thus a given employer has a continuously changing work force, and his productivity eventually tends to equal the port average. Other practices also suggest that stevedores, in effect, work on a cost-plus basis. In the event that they err in bids, or the union makes unforeseen demands, the ship operator pays the bill; the stevedores do not suffer.

The docks where stevedores oversee, and longshoremen work, are publicly owned in nearly every Pacific port. Piers, quays, transit sheds, warehouses, and other facilities at the water's edge are constructed, owned, and managed by public agencies.[6] The most com-

5. In 1955 the PMA calculated the "stevedore's override" at 30 percent of straight-time hours of longshoremen's wage costs, and 10 percent of overtime hours. See U.S. Congress, House of Representatives, Committee on Merchant Marine and Fisheries, Study of Harbor Conditions in Los Angeles and Long Beach, Hearings (October 19–21, 1955), 84th Cong., 1st sess. (Washington, 1955), pp. 101–102.
6. A brief description of Pacific Coast ports, their facilities, services, and legal form of ownership is available in U.S. Department of Commerce, Maritime Administration, United States Seaports, Alaska, Pacific Coast and Hawaii: Port Series, Part I (Washington, 1961), pp. 12–17. In addition most of the port

mon legal form is the independent state commission, in which ownership of the assets is vested in the state, but management is delegated to the commission. The San Francisco Port Authority, the Port of Seattle, and similar bodies in eleven other Pacific ports are such autonomous state agencies, charged with management of the physical assets of their ports and enabled to issue bonds for capital improvements. In several major ports — Oakland, Los Angeles, Long Beach — and a number of minor ones, the harbor and port facilities were developed and owned by the municipality. The legal form of organization varies: Oakland has an independent commission; Los Angeles, a department of the municipal government; Long Beach, a municipal public corporation. Another form of public ownership is the district, created by the state and embracing a city, part of a city, or all or part of one or several counties. The district — not the state — owns, manages, and adds to the port facilities. Stockton, Astoria, and the Port of Portland are examples of this variety of publicly owned ports. Portland also has a municipal agency, the Commission of Public Docks of the City of Portland, performing administrative, navigation, traffic promotion, and terminal services.

The publicly owned port agencies lease most or all of their facilities to private terminal or ship-operating companies and perform various services. Port planning and development, traffic promotion, and navigation services are provided by almost all the port administrations. The port authorities in Seattle, Portland, and many smaller ports in Washington, Oregon, and California also provide terminal services. Finally, in one port, Richmond, the city leases its facilities wholly to a private operator and has no function other than ultimate ownership and collecting fees. In one other, Alameda, all of the facilities are privately owned and operated.

The Pacific Maritime Association was founded in 1949 as the successor to various waterfront employers' and ship operators' associations. It includes all of the large firms and most of the smaller firms engaged in ship operations, terminal or other shoreside facility operations, stevedoring companies, and agents for foreign lines calling at U.S. Pacific ports. Stevedoring contractors and terminal operators together are a slight majority of the firms making up the Pacific Maritime Association — about 60 of PMA's 118 members in 1964.

authorities publish annual reports, occasional special studies, and so on, describing their facilities, services, and operations.

The PMA negotiates and administers collective bargaining agreements with the ILWU and with several unions representing ships' officers and crews. It provides the facilities and staff to maintain personnel records, including payroll, vacation, and other fringe benefits for longshoremen. It also operates central pay offices in each port and participates, with the unions, in supervising the dispatch halls, administering the pension, welfare, and other funds, and in registering the work force. In brief the Association has a great deal to do with the employment relationship on the docks and ships of the Pacific Coast.

THE UNION

Dock workers in the Pacific Coast ports are members of the International Longshoremen's and Warehousemen's Union. The smallest formal unit of organization is the local, defined along geographical and occupational lines. Typically, each Pacific port has a local for longshoremen, another for shipclerks, another for immediate supervisors (the "walking bosses"), and another for warehousemen, and so on. The California, Oregon, and Washington locals of the principal dockwork occupations constitute a major department of the union, formally organized into the longshore division. The division is governed by the equivalent of an executive board, the three-member Coast Labor Relations Committee, and annual convention — the Longshore, Shipclerk, and Walking Boss Caucus. The Caucus is a representative body composed of about one hundred delegates from thirty locals; it meets at least once each year to establish policy, formulate collective bargaining demands, elect officers, and so on. About one fourth of the union's 65,000 members are in the locals of the Pacific Coast longshore division. The rest of the ILWU membership consists of dock workers in British Columbia, Alaska, and Hawaii, warehousemen, mostly in northern California, and the fieldworkers and other employees of the Hawaiian sugar and pineapple plantations and processing plants.

HISTORICAL BACKGROUND

Attempts at unionization of dock workers along the Pacific Coast began as early as 1853, within just a few years of the first American settlement of the region, and recurred decade after decade.[7] Unions of longshoremen in Pacific ports affiliated themselves with the Knights of Labor in 1887, but very nearly vanished along with the rest of the Knights within a few years. A resurgence of union activity in the 1890s culminated in the merger of the Pacific Coast longshore unions with the countrywide International Longshoremen's Association in 1898. In 1909 the coastwide Longshoremen's Union of the Pacific was granted autonomy within the ILA. The early unions were generally unsuccessful. Big strikes were lost in 1901 and 1916, and the unions almost eliminated. Wartime recovery led to nothing as the locals broke up again under the pressure of lost strikes and strong employer opposition in the years 1919 through 1922. The strike of the San Francisco Riggers and Stevedores in 1919, demanding, among other things, larger gangs and decreased sling loads, was broken by the employers' formation of a company union in which membership was compulsory. Similar tactics eliminated unionism in the other ports up and down the coast. From 1922 to 1934 no union was recognized by the employers; although independent unions continued to exist, they had no voice in determining wages or working conditions on the docks.

The great depression, a more favorable political climate, and the National Industrial Recovery Act of 1933 stimulated activity on the docks of Pacific ports. Union organization and reorganization moved forward rapidly in many of the ports during 1933. Pacific Coast locals of the International Longshoremen's Association met in February 1934 and decided to seek recognition, a coastwide agreement, union participation in the hiring halls, and improvements in wages and working conditions. Negotiations failed, and the longshoremen struck most Pacific ports in early May.[8] The seamen followed on

7. For the early history of unionism on the Pacific waterfronts, see Ira B. Cross, A History of the Labor Movement in California (Berkeley, 1935), and Robert C. Francis, "A History of Labor on the San Francisco Waterfront" (doctoral dissertation, University of California, Berkeley, 1934). For more recent periods, see Betty V. H. Schneider and Abraham Siegel, Industrial Relations in the Pacific Coast Longshore Industry (Berkeley, 1956) and International Longshoremen's and Warehousemen's Union, The ILWU Story (2nd ed. San Francisco: 1963). An excellent study of collective bargaining and its results in the maritime industry, including longshoring, has been written by Harold Levinson in his Determining Forces in Collective Wage Bargaining (New York, 1966), pp. 133–214.

8. A great deal has been published about the 1934 strike. In addition to the general references noted in the preceding footnote a detailed account from the employers' point of view appears in Paul Eliel, The Waterfront and the General Strike (San Francisco, 1934), and the union view in Mike Quin, The Big Strike (Olema, Cal., 1949). A good account of the immediate poststrike period and

strike later in the month. The employers attempted to continue operations, and in a number of confrontations between strikebreakers, pickets, and police, several strikers were killed and hundreds injured. The most serious incident took place in San Francisco on July 5, 1934. Two strikers were killed by police and many others injured, and the date became the "Bloody Thursday" still observed as a holiday on the Pacific Coast docks. Harry Bridges, who had by this time emerged as a leader of the strikers, immediately called for a general strike in the area to support the longshoremen. Within ten days, most unions on both sides of San Francisco Bay had joined the strike. On July 19 representatives of the employers agreed to submit the issues in dispute to arbitration, and the general strike was called off. The longshoremen were persuaded to agree to arbitration and ended their strike on July 31, 1934.

The arbitration board, after more than two months of hearings and deliberations, granted most of the union's demands. The decision established a uniform coastwide contact, a jointly run hiring hall with a union appointed dispatcher, and the thirty-hour week.[9]

Within a few days of the arbitration award, handed down on October 12, 1934, the characteristic nature and a dominant theme in waterfront labor relations for the next fifteen years had appeared. Four "quickie" strikes, or "job actions," took place. All were to protest speedup or dangerous working conditions associated with heavy sling loads or undermanned gangs. The brief stoppage directed against a single ship or company to protest a specific work practice became the union's principal weapon against the employers. Hundreds of job actions took place during the next few years. The rate diminished during the war but picked up again in the immediate postwar years. Sling loads, manning, methods of work, and jurisdiction were the chief issues disputed between the union and employers during the early years. Of the 115 arbitration cases in the union files during the years 1935–1940, 75 involved these matters.[10] In negotiations in 1937, 1939–1941, and 1944–1945, work rules and manning in one or another form were prominent issues. These matters

subsequent union-employer relations appears in Richard Alan Liebes, "Longshore Labor Relations on the Pacific Coast, 1934–1942" (doctoral dissertation, University of California, Berkeley, 1942), pp. 62 ff.
9. "Proceedings before the National Longshoremen's Board," San Francisco, August 8–24, 1934 (San Francisco, typescript).
10. From examination of the awards filed at the union's offices in San Francisco. Liebes relies on the arbitrations as a principal source for his work; the arbitration cases through 1941 are listed in Liebes, appendix E, pp. 369–383.

continued to be the grounds for work stoppages, grievances and arbitration, and strong employer complaint through the entire period to 1960.

The present structure of labor relations in Pacific Coast longshoring had been created by 1937. The Pacific American Shipowners Association was formed in 1936 to represent the ship-operating firms in negotiations and agreements with the offshore and dockside workers' unions. Stevedores and terminal operators replaced their several port organizations with the Waterfront Employers Association of the Pacific Coast in June 1937. The Pacific Coast District of the ILA broke away from the parent body and joined the newly organized Congress of Industrial Organizations in 1937. The seceding District reorganized itself into the present organization — the International Longshoremen's and Warehousemen's Union — and became, in name as well as fact, completely independent of the East and Gulf coasts longshoremen. The present system of regional joint labor relations committees, corresponding to the major port areas, and a Joint Coast Labor Relations Committee had already come into existence. The committees are composed of an equal number of representatives from the union and from the employer group. The regional or port joint committees resolve disputes of local interest, and the Joint Coast Committee deals with problems of significance for the whole industry. By 1937 the union ran the hiring halls, under rules negotiated with the employers, and was well on its way to job control.

In the next ten years labor relations on the docks consisted essentially of employer counterattacks and union consolidation. In the 1939–1941 negotiations the employers sought to regain control over work methods. They refused demands for a wage increase on the grounds that efficiency had declined seriously since the union first was recognized. To buttress their position the employers commissioned the first substantial attempt to measure changes in longshoring productivity. The techniques were crude — highly aggregated tonnages were used — but the results suggested that productivity had declined from 1934 to 1940 by about 38 percent in San Francisco and Los Angeles, and by 20 to 30 percent in the Northwest ports. The data indicated that almost all of the drop in efficiency had taken place by 1936.[11] The union hotly denied that any drop in efficiency

11. For San Francisco, for example, cargo was handled at an average of 1.58 tons per shipwork man-hour in 1934, 1.05 tons per man-hour in 1936, and

had occurred and dismissed the productivity study results as the product of hopelessly defective methodology. The 1940 wage dispute was submitted to arbitration. The arbitrator agreed that the union and worker practices impaired efficiency, but he also upheld the union's contention that the productivity study was inadequate as evidence. The employers' attack changed nothing. Wage increases were granted, and no change in work rules or methods were made. The efficiency controversy continued into 1941 but vanished temporarily with the approach of the American entry into the war.

In 1941 Harry Bridges announced his union's willingness to improve dockside efficiency. The sharp expansion of the war — notably the German invasion of the U.S.S.R. and U.S. rearmament and material support to the Allies — produced a marked shift in attitudes in most left-wing organizations and groups in the country. Waterfront employment mounted, and stoppages decreased. However, work rules and productivity revived as an issue in 1944, and this led to the second major study on longshore efficiency. As in 1939, employers opposed a union proposal for a wage increase on the grounds that productivity had decreased. Data gathered by the Army were offered in evidence at a National War Labor Board hearing in early 1945. The same information was later assembled in a comparative productivity study of U.S. ports by the War Shipping Administration. As in the studies used in the 1939–1941 negotiations, the productivity measures were highly aggregated, using overall tonnages or general cargo, broadly defined. Unlike the earlier studies, however, the 1944–1946 inquiry indicated relatively little change in productivity over the three years in most of the ports. Tons handled per man-hour differed from port to port, and the rates for San Francisco and Los Angeles, for example, were below those in New Orleans, but about the same as those in New York.[12] The Board found the productivity data inconclusive and ordered a wage increase on other grounds.

Relations between the union and the employers continued to be poor in the immediate postwar period. The last three months of 1945

0.97 tons per man-hour in 1942. The decline from 1936 to 1942 in Los Angeles was a bit steeper, but the timing and results otherwise were about the same as in San Francisco. Productivity did not decrease in the Northwest ports after 1936. For an interesting discussion and summary of the data for this period, see James Chester Armstrong, "A Critical Analysis of Cargo Handling Cost in the Steamship Industry" (master's thesis, University of California, Berkeley, 1947). The data cited are from Armstrong's chart 30, p. 136.
12. Ibid., pp. 204–211.

and nearly all of 1946 were filled with negotiations, strike threats, Wage Stabilization Board hearings, awards, reopenings, and then new negotiations for the next year's contract. The 1946 settlement was reached only after a fifty-two-day strike. The chief issue was a wage increase to keep up with the postwar inflation.

Years of ill will finally led to a complete breakdown in the relationship between the parties in 1948. The Waterfront Employers Association once again challenged union operation of the hiring hall. Although near a settlement on that issue — it was agreed to suspend the employer challenge until the courts had decided the legality of the hiring hall under the newly passed Taft-Hartley Act — unity with the offshore unions led the ILWU to join the strike called in early September.

Officials of the Waterfront Employers Association changed their demands after the strike began. They insisted that the union leaders sign non-Communist affidavits, again relying on a provision in the Taft-Hartley Act. The demand quickly developed into a flat refusal to bargain with any of the union's current leaders. The Army threatened to use troops to move its goods across the docks. The World Federation of Trade Unions resolved to boycott Army-loaded cargoes. The ILWU then offered to work the Army goods at rates tendered in the earlier contract negotiations or with the understanding that wage increases be made retroactive. The arrangements were to be handled through the Mutual Stevedoring Company, a new and independent contractor formed with the union's approval. The Waterfront Employers Association remained adamant, insisting that it would have nothing to do with a Communist-led union. The impasse was total.

The ILWU had been alleged to be Communist-dominated almost from its beginning. Harry Bridges, the union's president, was the subject of a number of deportation hearings, the first in 1936, in which the government sought to prove that he was a member of the Communist Party and deportable as an undesirable alien.[13] While the

13. The most publicized hearing took place in 1938. Although trial examiner James M. Landis ruled, in 1939, that the allegation was not proved, the case continued through the courts until 1945, when the U.S. Supreme Court nullified the deportation order. Bridges filed for and was granted U.S. citizenship in 1945. There is a large amount of published material on the "everlasting Bridges case." A summary of all the hearings and court appearances is included in The ILWU Story, pp. 68–73. The 1938 hearing and its immediate

1948 waterfront negotiations and strike were in progress, the Justice Department was assembling a new court action against Bridges and two other officers of the union.[14] The charges included several counts of fraud and conspiracy, alleging that Bridges had falsely denied Communist affiliations in his citizenship proceedings. At this time, in addition, the AFL and CIO were preparing to withdraw from the World Federation of Trade Unions, which included representatives from the Soviet Union and the Eastern European countries. Bridges was then president of a WFTU affiliate, the Maritime Federation of the World, and relations between the ILWU and its parent federation, the CIO, were becoming increasingly strained.

In late November 1948, representatives of the ship-operating firms, led by officials of Matson and American President Lines, met with union leaders. None of the staff of the Waterfront Employers Association participated. The new group and the union reached agreement after sixteen days of negotiations, and the strike ended in early December. The agreement changed relatively little; the hiring hall was still run by a dispatcher named by the union. Work rules and methods were not changed. Nonetheless, the agreement was a new beginning. The parties agreed to institute a new grievance procedure, and in exchange the union gave its pledge not to strike. Although bargaining continued to be at arm's length, relations between the parties steadily grew better in the subsequent years.

The final changes bringing about the present waterfront collective bargaining institutions took place in 1949 and 1950. In the spring of 1949 the Pacific American Shipowners Association and the Waterfront Employers Association merged to create the Pacific Maritime Association. The new association of employers continues to the present time, substantially unchanged. The union was strained by the continuing repercussions of the Communist issue. The CIO withdrew from the World Federation of Trade Unions in 1949. At about the same time the ILWU Convention overwhelmingly supported the

aftermath is described in detail in Estolv E. Ward, Harry Bridges on Trial (New York, 1940). Impressions and his role as Bridges' attorney in the later court appearances are included in Vincent Hallinan, A Lion in Court (New York, 1963), pp. 227–277. A brief review of the whole Communist issue from the "anti" point of view appears in Max M. Kampelman, The Communist Party vs. the CIO: A Study in Power Politics (New York, 1957), especially pp. 199–215.

14. J. R. Robertson and Henry Schmidt. See The ILWU Story, pp. 70–71.

union's leadership and voted about 564 to 59 in favor of remaining with the WFTU.[15] The CIO leadership soon began its program, including hearings, that led to the expulsion from the federation of a number of unions on the grounds that they were dominated by Communists. In 1950, after several days of hearings, the ILWU was expelled. The expulsion stirred the membership, and pressure was increased by the continuing litigation, the Korean War, and the Coast Guard's screening of security risks from the waterfront. Later in the year the leadership changed its stand. Bridges resigned his office in the Maritime Federation of the World, and the ILWU withdrew from the WFTU.

There have been no major strikes since the ninety-five-day stoppage in 1948. The contract was renegotiated in 1951, to run for a two-year period. Changes dealt with wages, amendments to the pension fund, and minor amendments to the hiring hall procedures. In 1953 a wage increase was negotiated, and the rest of the 1951 contract was extended for another two years, but with provision for reopening on some matters in 1954. The next year minor changes were made in wages and skill differentials, welfare contributions, and penalty rates, and the contract was again extended, to run to mid-1956. In these negotiations agreement was reached without overt strife and before the expiration of the previous contract.

The union and employers were not completely without problems during this period. From 1949 through 1955 Harry Bridges was involved in litigation and subject to imprisonment, revocation of citizenship and deportation; in 1955 the courts ruled, apparently with finality, that the federal government had no grounds for action. The ILWU was engaged in a series of jurisdictional disputes with the Sailors' Union of the Pacific from 1950 to 1955, and one or another employer suffered a bit as a ship was struck. In one bitter case, the ship operator withdrew from the PMA and threatened to recognize and hire ILA longshoremen.[16] For the most part, however, labor relations on the Pacific Coast docks were peaceful.

15. The fractional votes were rounded; ILWU, Proceedings of the 8th Biennial Convention (San Francisco, April 1949), p. 229.
16. The Isthmian Line; this is discussed in considerable detail in Schneider and Siegel, pp. 81–83.

II | THE ACQUISITION OF JOB CONTROL

Selig Perlman, in his widely influential *Theory of the Labor Movement*, argued that job control is closely linked to conservative "business unionism." It is the outcome of an "organic labor mentality" and an integral part of labor's "home-grown philosophy." Perlman contended that the work rules — control over entry to the industry, work sharing, control or limitations on the production process, and so on — were manifestations of the "fundamental scarcity consciousness" of the manual worker.[1] On the other hand, socialism and similar ideologies were mystical, ruthless, alien, and opposed to the native views and interests of the worker.[2]

The ILWU fits Perlman's thesis poorly. The union has been led throughout its existence by men whose goals were revolutionary — to achieve power on behalf of, and to improve the lot of, the entire working class. Under this leadership the ILWU sought and won a degree of job control exceeding that of even the International Typographical Union, Perlman's archetype of job consciousness. If Perlman's analytical scheme is accepted, the most reasonable conclusion is that the ILWU leaders were unusually apt in sensing and adapting to the members' inherent needs and wishes, despite their own values and views. An alternative view is that Perlman was wrong; job control is not a function or evidence of specific ideology, and it derives from motives other than the manual worker's timidity and

1. *"Thus the International Typographical Union of the United States and Canada, which, through an early start and an excellent strategic position in the industry, has been able to work out the most far-reaching system of 'job control' yet devised by any union, gives us an insight into the characteristic group psychology of the wage earner today. . . . Central . . . is the vigorous claim of common 'ownership' of the totality of the economic opportunity open to the membership (which is considered scarce and limited and therefore needing to be controlled)."* Selig Perlman, Theory of the Labor Movement, *pp. 271–272.*
2. Ibid., *chap. 8.*

insecurity.[3] The circumstances and development of the ILWU strongly support the latter view.

The ILWU is unusual also in that it developed its rules and practices in the modern era, and in a very brief span of time. The union is only about thirty years old, and its rules were in force within the first two to five years of its existence. In contrast, the rules and practices of the printing trades or the railroad brotherhoods were elaborated gradually, often over decades, and have their roots in circumstances of eighty to one hundred years ago. The principal building trades unions — carpenters, plumbers, bricklayers, painters, lathers and plasterers — also were strongly unionized and had developed their job-control characteristics five to eight decades ago.[4] The leading studies of job control, both analytical and descriptive, have relied extensively on the experiences and practices of the older unions.[5] The ILWU experience suggests that some modifications of the prevailing views are necessary.

It is useful to distinguish two aspects of job control — work-force control, and control over the production process. The former in-

3. *Suspicion of Perlman's theory is not new. Lloyd Ulman challenged Perlman's views of worker psychology, the motives for job control, and his use of the evidence; see Lloyd Ulman,* The Rise of the National Trade Union *(Cambridge, Mass., 1955), chap. 18. Gulick and Bers attacked Perlman's logical inconsistencies, especially his use of the role of the intellectual and social reform ideologies; see Charles A. Gulick and Melvin K. Bers, "Insight and Illusion in Perlman's Theory of the Labor Movement,"* Industrial and Labor Relations Review, *VI (1953), 510–531.*

4. *The pioneer study of the printers is George E. Barnett, "The Printers,"* American Economic Association Quarterly, *third series, X (1909), 433–819; excerpts are reprinted in Paul A. Weinstein, ed.,* Featherbedding and Technological Change *(Boston, 1965), pp. 34–42. A more recent work dealing almost wholly with the printers is Arthur R. Porter,* Job Property Rights *(New York, 1954). The rules of the printing pressmen are noted in various passages in Elizabeth Faulkner Baker,* Printers and Technology *(New York, 1957), especially pp. 215–281; the job-control practices of the lithographers are part of the study by Fred C. Munson,* Labor Relations in the Lithographic Industry *(Cambridge, Mass., 1963). The railroad unions and their rules are explored in Jacob J. Kaufman,* Collective Bargaining in the Railroad Industry *(New York, 1954), and in Reed C. Richardson,* The Locomotive Engineer, 1863–1963 *(Ann Arbor, 1963). The best study of work practices in the construction unions is William G. Haber and Harold M. Levinson,* Labor Relations and Productivity in the Building Trades *(Ann Arbor, 1956).*

5. *See, for example, Ulman,* Rise of the National Union, *chaps. 11, 17. A classic study is Sumner H. Slichter,* Union Policies and Industrial Management *(Washington, 1941), chaps. 2, 3, 6, 7. This work was updated as Sumner H. Slichter, James J. Healy, and E. Robert Livernash,* The Impact of Collective Bargaining on Management *(Washington, 1960); chaps. 11 and 12 deal with work rules and policies.*

cludes regulation of entry of workers to the industry, control over the size of the work force, and designation of persons to be employed. The latter includes control over output, methods, and pace of work. The two aspects of job control are often found together, but not invariably so. The building trades and maritime unions exercise some control over both aspects. The printing trades, railroad unions, and musicians have attempted, with varying success, to exercise control over the production process, especially with makework rules and manning requirements. Direct control over the work force is much less evident in their practices.

CONTROL OF THE WORK FORCE

In the Pacific Coast longshore industry the drive for regulating entry to the occupation and control of the employment process itself was rooted both in the grievances of the workers and the institutional requirements of the union. These motives led the ILWU to demand, at the very outset, recognition as the representative of the entire industry work force and decasualization under union auspices. The need for decasualization, and the opportunities it afforded the union, are the keys to work-force control.

In its natural state, longshoring is an outstanding example of a casual labor market. There are usually many employers, all relatively small; a stevedoring contractor handles cargo loading and discharging for one to, at most, a few ship-operating lines. Ship arrivals and departures are infrequent for any one line, and irregular for many. A single stevedoring firm may be working several ships, or none at all, on any given day. In addition the total port volume is erratic; peak days or weeks may involve three or four times the ships or tonnage of the low periods. The consequence is a widely variable daily demand for labor; the variability is substantial for a port and enormous for a single employer.

Competition among employers is keen, both in the product market where they sell their services and in the labor market. The stevedore's customer, the ship operator, demands not only low prices but also quick service. Each hour the ship is in port represents hundreds of dollars in capital costs, crew's wages, and similar expenses. To win or hold his client, the stevedore must furnish, in full measure, the labor necessary to do the job. On the other hand, the ship operator has no use for longshoremen when his ship sails, and the stevedore, if he has no other work available, cannot afford to keep the longshoremen on his payroll. The consequence is a typically brief employment relationship. The job lasts a few days at most, or even only a few hours.

The supply side of the labor market is usually glut. The work is essentially unskilled. The extremely high turnover — perhaps 50 percent per day — is evidence of the large amount of daily hiring. Large numbers of unemployed or casually employed persons capable of doing the work are attracted by the reasonable probability of a job, however brief. Occasional success in actually getting a job strengthens the attachment to the industry of even the grossly underemployed. The employers collectively are interested in maintaining a labor force at least sufficient to meet peak period demand, but this interest usually requires little more than hiring the fringe worker just often enough to keep him coming to the docks.

Ease of entry and employers' interest result in a labor force appreciably larger than even peak demand, and perhaps double the average demand. In New York, shortly before the beginning of decasualization in 1954, about one third of the longshoremen during a given year worked 100 hours or less; another third worked 100 to 1199 hours. Thus, only about one third of the longshoremen even approached full-time employment. The number of longshoremen employed during the year, about 40,000, was approximately double the required full-time equivalent.[6] An authority from an earlier period, F. P. Foisie, manager of the Waterfront Employers Association of Seattle, noted: "In so far as generalization is ever worth anything, where we begin to know conditions before and after decasualization, both abroad and in this country, usually there is said to be double the number of men in a decasualized port than the port can support well."[7]

In San Francisco just before unionization, the longshore labor market was completely untouched by decasualization schemes that had been attempted in other large Pacific Coast ports. The longshoremen gathered at 6:00 to 6:30 each morning near the Ferry Building on the waterfront.[8] Gang bosses gathered in one place, other steady

6. See Vernon H. Jensen, Hiring of Dock Workers (Cambridge, Mass., 1964), pp. 82–85; Charles P. Larrowe makes the same point in Shape-Up and Hiring Hall (Berkeley, 1955), pp. 49–54.
7. National Longshoremen's Board, Proceedings, 1934, pp. 886–887.
8. This description is from ibid., testimony of longshoremen. The Ferry Building is near the center of the waterfront in San Francisco, and the point of depar-

men in their own accustomed places, and the rest of the men in undifferentiated groups. Stevedore general foremen filled their needs for men by picking the gang bosses, who were instructed about time and place to report for work, number of men required, and so on. First to be selected were preferred gangs, who offered their services as much as possible for the same employer and, in exchange, were given the maximum employment opportunity by the firm. Assuming sufficient need, the employer next picked from the available gangs, represented by their bosses, those who had worked for him with some regularity in the past. The gang bosses in turn gathered their sixteen or so men, replacing absentees and adding men, if needed, from the group of casuals. The casuals also provided additional men or gangs when needed by a stevedore foreman or boss. Some of the men not offered work at the early shape-up "prospected" jobs by appearing at the busier piers later in the morning. From time to time, casual laborers, or "swampers," were hired from the groups of men at the pier.

The Pacific Coast longshore labor market yielded results, and produced worker grievances, similar to those associated with casual labor markets everywhere. Hours worked and earnings were extremely variable from one week to the next, and the average tended to be low. The typical longshoreman worked as little as one hour or as many as twenty or more consecutive hours on a single job, and then devoted hours or days of unpaid time to seeking and waiting for the next job. In the depression the symptoms were aggravated; perhaps three fourths of the potential working time was idle time.[9] The distribution of work time was extremely unequal and led to allegations of favoritism and nepotism.

The "brass check" payment system was an added source of worker grievance. Small metal tags were issued, as identification and evidence of work performed, to each man hired by a stevedoring contractor. Some gangs were required to discount the checks to the boss or at certain taverns. The discount, or kickback of 5 percent or so of each man's earnings was a necessary condition of employment.[10]

There is little doubt that the casual labor market does lead to re-

ture of longshoremen ordered to work ships in the East Bay harbors and docks.

9. See, for example, the testimony of F. P. Foisie, ibid., pp. 939–941.

10. Ibid., pp. 60, 144–146, 225–226, 265–266.

sults that are objectionable and engender grievances from the worker's point of view. But the nature of the market, not the innate psychology of the workers, is the underlying source of distress. The chief characteristics of a casual market are the extraordinarily brief employment relationship — itself a function of technical conditions and small size of the firm relative to the product market — and the absence of barriers to entry to the work force. These necessarily lead to chronic underemployment, substantial unpaid time required to find and hold employment, low average earnings, a markedly skewed earnings distribution, and so on.[11] Not surprisingly, unions in casual labor crafts or industries have sought to change the casual-market results. Union control over entry to the work force, establishment of a hiring hall and hiring rules to reduce unpaid job-seeking time and inequalities in work opportunity, and similar devices have grown up in these industries. More important, only in these industries has this spectacular form of work-force control been sought or established.[12] If job control derives from worker psychology, then these industries, and only these, must have workers with peculiar attributes. A much more reasonable explanation is that these industries have ordinary workers but peculiar labor markets.

The establishment of hiring halls in each port area, with union control of participation in their operation, was the principal objective of the ILWU in the 1934 strike. Just before the walkout the employers were prepared to concede recognition of the union on a port-by-port basis, and they offered to establish hiring halls to be operated by the employers, but subject to union challenge through the grievance

11. *These results assume, reasonably for the United States, less than full employment in the economy. The low average earnings mean earnings at or below the competitive market solution. The casual market holds workers at their individual reserve prices, reflected in their earnings over time, and the result is analogous to monopsony discrimination. The competitive market would clear at the wage necessary to attract the needed last few increments of labor service, presumably along a rising supply curve; that wage would be the average wage and be the same for all workers. The casual market and monopsony discrimination, by wide earnings variation in the former and wage rate differences in the latter, transfer the labor-market equivalent of consumers' surplus to the employers. The resulting earnings level in the casual market, therefore, is below the competitive market level.*
12. *The hiring hall and union-established limits to entry to the work force are found principally in the building and maritime trades in the United States. See Slichter, et al., Impact on Collective Bargaining, chap. 3; the authors' most detailed illustration of the hiring hall deals with the ILWU, Local 10 (p. 32).*

procedure.[13] The union insisted that it be granted direct participation in the hiring halls and that the bargaining unit be coastwide. Employer-run halls were emphatically rejected. The union and its members were familiar with employer-operated decasualization. Seattle had had an employer-run central hiring hall from 1921 to the early 1930s; Portland had two halls for nearly a decade before 1934, and Tacoma, a smaller but nonetheless important port, had an ILA hall from 1919 to 1934.[14] The workers and union spokesmen charged the employers' halls with favoritism, blacklisting for union activities, unequal distribution of work opportunity, and low average earnings. In other words, the employers' plans did not eliminate most of the worker grievances concerning the workings of the market, and, even worse, they had been used successfully to weaken and then to break the union.

The board hearing the case in 1934 was impressed by the union's arguments. The arbitration award settling the strike provided for registration of longshoremen and created hiring halls in the major ports. Joint port labor relations committees, on which union and employer representatives had an equal voice, were charged with registration of longshoremen in their areas and supervision of the local hiring hall. Dispatchers were selected by the union to manage the hiring hall, sending men and gangs to fill employer requests.[15] The various joint port labor relations committees provided the facilities and established the rules governing the operation of the hiring hall and dispatching.[16]

Registration generally was not a serious problem. The initial award created the broad outline to be followed. Men who had worked the docks for at least one of the three years preceding the 1934 strike were eligible for registration, and all longshoremen who were members of a gang, or were on any registration or extra list in the five months before the strike, were required to be registered. In subsequent interpretation the arbitrator required that all men qualified by the one-year attachment to the industry should be registered in the

13. *National Longshoremen's Board,* Proceedings, *pp. 20–23, 39–40, 129–131. The union's position is outlined on pp. 19–20 and 24–27.*
14. *Ibid., pp. 137–138, 161, 526–530, 880–882, 923–927. See also Liebes, "Longshore Labor Relations," p. 176.*
15. *Each local of the union elected the dispatchers for its hall.*
16. *A good description of an ILWU hiring hall and its operation is given by Larrowe, pp. 139–153.*

absence of any reasonable grounds for exclusion.[17] Neither anti-union nor anti-employer attitudes were deemed to be reasonable grounds for denying registration.[18] However, preference in registration for union members was conceded by the employers in the negotiations of 1937.

Although registration and the ability to challenge applicants and to close the lists were important, union controls of hiring hall operations were far more important in establishing union hegemony in size, composition, flexibility, and allegiance of the longshore work force. For the first few years, employers accepted the hiring hall with relatively little concern. In most ports the employer could request specific men or gangs to be sent. In some, men or even whole gangs could be permanently assigned to an employer, reporting to the dock, not the hiring hall, for work every day. For the extra men or casual gangs needed, the dispatching rules provided for rotation of jobs, in order to equalize earnings and job opportunities, and appeared to be reasonable. There were some problems concerning fair treatment of nonunion men. When the union failed to dispatch them, the employers tried hiring from the docks. Although the arbitrators condemned

17. *M. C. Sloss award of March 7, 1935; Harry Hazel award of April 15, 1935.*
   The arbitration cases and awards frequently cited in this book are taken from typescript copies of the awards from 1935 to 1965 in the union files. The method of identification adopted includes only the arbitrator's name and the date of the award; the hearing date and city have not been included chiefly because the simple form already uniquely identifies the case, and brevity of citation was desirable. The awards are not long, generally no more than a few pages, thus page numbers are not necessary.
   Some preliminary comments are in order about the use of arbitration in the industry and the awards in this study. The four area arbitrators decided cases only for their own areas; they, and industry spokesmen, frequently pointed out that the area decisions were neither precedent for other areas nor for similar cases in the same area. The decisions of area arbitrators could be overturned by the Joint Coast Labor Relations Committee or by the Coast Arbitrator. In other words, joint agreements and Coast arbitration awards were the authoritative supplements to the contracts. In this study, however, the awards by area arbitrators were heavily used, rather than Joint Coast Committee minutes, because they are superior sources of description of actual practices. Further, area arbitration awards illustrate, even though they are not authoritative, general statements of required or permitted procedures.
   Where arbitration awards are cited to support authoritative statements of practice, they are invariably Coast arbitration decisions. The principal Coast Arbitrators have been M. C. Sloss, Wayne Morse, A. M. Kidd, Clark Kerr, and Sam Kagel. On occasion, other men served on an ad hoc basis, chiefly before 1945.
18. *A. M. Kidd award of December 29, 1943.*

the employer failure to use the hiring hall, they also required the union to apply the rules impartially, without discrimination, to all properly registered men.[19] In the 1936 contract negotiations, employer representatives included in their demands a neutral or outside dispatcher to replace the union's man in the hall, but their commitment to this point was not strong. When the contract was signed after the strike, they not only accepted the hiring hall the way it had been run but also granted preference in employment to union men. For the first half-dozen years of the relationship between the parties, the employers were more concerned with the existence of the union, with the hundreds of work stoppages, and with declining productivity, than with the hiring hall.

In granting preference of employment to members of the union in 1937, the employers gave up more than they had planned. Believing that they had conceded no more than first choice in registration, employers sought to continue the nondiscriminatory dispatching of nonunion men. Employer representatives in 1938 pressed their grievances over the union's conduct of the hiring hall to arbitration. Wayne Morse defined "employment" and ruled on the dispute:

Registered longshoremen, or permit longshoremen, waiting in the hiring hall to be dispatched to a job assignment, are not employed prior to their being dispatched. Until the time of their dispatchment their work status is simply that of longshoremen who are eligible for employment under the terms of the Agreement. . . . His employment starts when the contractual relationship between himself and the employer is created by the dispatchment order.

[Preference of employment] means only that so long as union members are available for specific job assignments they shall be given preference, and that other registered longshoremen or permit men not members of the I.L.W.U. shall be entitled to their share of the work, following the application of the preference of employment clause.[20]

When employment was thus defined as the casual job of a few hours or a few days, not attachment to the industry, the employment prospects of the nonunion man became bleak indeed.

Employer attempts to weaken the union's grip on the hiring hall by one or another device failed. Hiring directly from the docks was

19. *Watkins award of March 11, 1935; part of Wayne Morse award of September 17, 1938, and others.*
20. *Morse award of September 17, 1938.*

stopped by union protest and arbitration decisions.[21] When the employers sought to put their representatives in the hiring hall to receive and consolidate employer requests for men, they were found guilty of violating the contract.[22] The hall was to be run only by the union-selected dispatcher. Employers could participate in setting the rules by which the hall was run, and they could press their complaints through the grievance procedure. They could neither bypass the hall nor interfere with its day-to-day operations.

The relatively mild circumvention of the hiring hall involved in the employer practice of retaining longshoremen as more or less permanent employees next came under attack. San Francisco waterfront employers had used preferred gangs for years, and the custom was included in the port's dispatching rules in February, 1935. Any employer with sufficient cargo-handling business to furnish reasonably steady work, provided the men agreed, could have one or more gangs permanently assigned to him. Extra gangs were requested as needed from the hiring hall. The employers believed that the preferred gangs were more efficient; through experience the gang members became familiar with the practices, and more skillful in handling the particular commodities, of the employer. The preferred gang members benefited from the regular hours, steady work, and the more desirable jobs — casuals or extra men did the heaviest or dirtiest work.

In early 1939 the union convention passed a resolution requesting the San Francisco local to eliminate the preferred gangs. The union pointed out that the continued existence of preferred gangs was a threat to the hiring hall and to improved conditions in other ports. A major justification for the hiring hall was to provide equalization of work opportunities, but the preferred gang members had more than their fair share. Jealousy, petty annoyance on the part of longshoremen not privileged to be preferred, and weakened allegiance to the union of those working for the same employer week after week were among the results of the system. Perhaps most disturbing to the union officials was the frustration of attempts to introduce the San Francisco working conditions in other Pacific Coast ports. Employers elsewhere responded to demands for concessions to match

21. *Watkins award of March 11, 1935.*
22. *Morse award of September 17, 1938.*

San Francisco with the offer to exchange improved conditions for the right to use preferred gangs.

On May 1, 1939, the San Francisco local resolved, by vote, that all gangs in the port should be casual.[23] There were ninety-six preferred gangs and ninety-one casual gangs in San Francisco at this point. Within a few days a number of the gangs declared their desire to return to the hiring hall. The employers charged the union with coercion and took their complaint to the arbitrator. Morse ruled against the employers. He believed the union's claim that it had used only appeals to solidarity and similar noncoercive persuasion. By the end of the month no preferred gangs existed at San Francisco, or any other Pacific port. Renewed employer allegations of coercion were dismissed by Morse; he accepted the union showing that independent votes among the members of the gangs had been heavily in favor of going casual.[24]

By late 1940 the transfer of nearly every aspect of hiring, and very likely the allegiance of the worker, from employer to union was nearly complete. Employers could hire only through the hiring hall; they could not request specific gangs or men, nor could they reject gangs or men properly dispatched to them. They could not even request that certain gangs or men *not* be dispatched, on grounds, for example, that behavior, effort, or competence was less than satisfactory.[25] In effect, within five years after union recognition the longshore employer had the right only to request that men be sent to him. He had to put to work the men, and only those men, sent by the hiring hall. Although employers continued the struggle to regain their former dominance in hiring for another half-dozen years, the union's control was never weakened.

The shift from the employers to the union of much of the responsibility for maintaining an adequate supply of labor soon created a serious union dilemma. Decasualization required that the number of men in the industry be fixed at a level high enough to meet em-

---

23. "Casual" is used with two meanings. Some longshoremen, neither registered nor granted a permit to work, were dispatched to jobs on a temporary basis when there were no registered men available; these men are referred to on the docks as "casual" workers. In the context of the preferred gangs, "casual" means no more than that the gangs or men return to the hiring hall after a job and take their place to be again sent out in rotation. With the disappearance of preferred gangs, this meaning usually is not relevant.
24. Proceedings and awards by Morse, May 26 and August 14, 1939.
25. Morse award of November 7, 1940.

ployer needs for labor, but low enough to provide approximately full
employment for the workers. The two objectives were not easy to
reconcile. Fluctuations in cargo volume — seasonal, cyclical and
otherwise — led to peak labor-force requirements appreciably above
slack period requirements. As noted earlier, a principal article in the
union's set of values was equalization of work opportunity, embodied
in practice by giving priority in the hiring hall to the men and gangs
with the fewest hours worked. But if equalization were applied to
the entire work force needed at peak demand, the substantial unemployment of the typical week, month, or year would be shared by all
longshoremen, and average hours and earnings would be low. On
the other hand, closing registration and union membership rolls at a
work-force size small enough to provide nearly full employment for
all the members implied the use of substantial numbers of casual laborers who were not members of the union. This appears to be clearly
inconsistent with the tenets of progressive, social-reform unionism.
The union met the dilemma by establishing, gradually over time,
two classes of registration, with only one entailing full union membership.

From 1937 on, admission to the permanent waterfront work
force was a matter for mutual agreement between the employers and
the union. Both sides were to agree not only to the number of men to
be added but also to the specific persons. Disputes were settled by arbitration. The agreement, as interpreted, required the union-elected
dispatcher in the hiring hall to send to employers only registered
men, unless the port joint labor relations committees specifically approved exceptions.[26] In practice, most of the committees early gave
the dispatchers the right to put to work casual workers to cope with
occasional manpower shortages. The recruitment of casuals was done
by the hiring hall and the union. Dispatchers in most of the ports
found it easier to meet peak demand for labor by identifying and
issuing permits to those casual laborers who were available and reported for work with some regularity. When the registration lists
were opened to admit new men, the casuals who had been working
regularly — the permit men — had an advantage. The union advocated, and the arbitrators accepted, experience in the industry as an
important criterion in selecting men for registration. Thus, control

26. *Morse award of September 17, 1938.*

over employment of casuals gave the union substantial influence, beyond its equal partnership, over admission of individuals to the permanent work force.

The union's role in the employment of casuals could be used to circumvent the joint registration process, at least when used sparingly. Employers objected from time to time to the practice of dispatching nonregistered men on a regular basis. Several of these grievances went to arbitration. In one case a number of men to whom the employers had successfully denied registration had actually worked full time for six or seven years.[27]

The union's control was threatened during the several years immediately following World War II. Bitter and rising employer opposition to the hiring hall and its rules culminated in the 1948 strike and subsequent collapse of the employers' association. In the strike settlement the new employer leadership agreed to continue the operation of the hiring halls without change. However, during the negotiations and strike, and later, unfair labor practice charges were brought against the union and employers. The Taft-Hartley Act of 1947 included among the unfair labor practices forbidden to unions any discrimination, or causing an employer to discriminate, against nonunion workers in hiring and conditions of employment. The principal suits involved the long-standing contractual provision giving employment preference to union members and allegations, by experienced casuals, of discriminatory denial of registration. The issue was resolved by closing the registration lists and, in 1951, changing the contract to give preference in employment to registered men, without mentioning union membership or its lack.

Despite the challenges posed by some employers and aggrieved longshoremen, the peak demand, full-employment dilemma actually eased, temporarily, during the several years immediately following 1945. The vast increase in shipping and in demand for longshoremen of the World War II period led to substantial expansion of the registered work force. At the end of the war, however, cargo volume and demand for labor dropped much below their wartime levels in most ports. The use of casuals atrophied, the number of permit men de-

27. Kidd award of December 29, 1943. Viewing their employment record, the arbitrator observed that the earnings record of the men seeking registered status compared favorably with those of fully registered men, despite the union's contention that they had worked only as casuals.

clined, and even the registered work force shared the unemployment through shorter workweeks. The Korean War, however, revived the problem; new men had to be added. It was clear that opening the registration lists could be painful; the San Francisco registered work force especially had endured several years of short hours and earnings up to 1950. But denying registration to men who were to work with any regularity could be costly. The unfair labor practice complainants sought compensation for lost earnings as well as full-time employment, registration, or reinstatement.[28] The consequence was the creation of limited registration status.

In the Northwest the employers and union established, at the beginning of the Korean War, a "temporary labor pool" of men registered and dispatched separately from the experienced, fully registered men.[29] The "poolmen" were used as a supplementary work force and could be put to work each day only after the available, fully registered men had been employed. In southern California, also adding men in 1950, the new men with limited registration rights were called "B" men; the fully registered were "A" men. When San Francisco opened its lists later in the decade, several hundred men were given limited registration status on a "B" list. By 1958 the terminology and the status had become standard in most of the Pacific ports.

Fully registered men, on the "A" list, were the regular union members. They participated in the work opportunity equalization of the dispatch hall and had full political rights in the union. Limited-registered men, the "B" list, were eligible for work only when all the "A" men seeking work were employed. They were required to abide by tougher availability-for-work standards than the "A" men, had more limited claims to jobs, and so on. The "B" men were covered by the welfare benefits of the union, but they were not union members; they were not able to vote for union officers, and the like. The "B" men did the dirtier or heavier jobs, and worked the less desirable hours. They had less job security, more erratic earnings, and little participation in determining their wages or working conditions.

28. A good account of both the union and employer views on the perils of registering new men in the early 1950s appears in U.S. Congress, Study of Harbor Conditions, pp. 323–330, 344–346, 382–383.
29. Larrowe describes the establishment and workings of the pool in Shape-Up and Hiring Hall, pp. 151–153, and 171–173.

Clearly, they could become disgruntled from time to time. On the other hand, "B" men were part of the industry, and they could reasonably expect admission to fully registered status when work-force renewal or expansion were required. Their position was analogous to apprenticeship or probation.

The employer's right to suspend or discharge men for incompetence or for disciplinary infractions was closely bound to his right to reject or specify men or gangs in hiring hall orders. From the first days the union claimed the sole right to impose discipline, and it refused to negotiate or submit to arbitration either specific cases or a general schedule of penalties. Early employer attempts to impose suspension unilaterally were defeated by the persistent refusal of the hiring hall to fill orders to replace gangs already properly dispatched, by job actions and by early arbitrators' rulings.[30] Discipline and penalties were so seriously disputed that the arbitration machinery broke down completely in 1935 and 1936. The employers demanded contract provisions on discipline in the 1936 negotiations; in the resulting agreement, in early 1937, they conceded to the union the right to try offenders and impose penalties. The joint port labor relations committees were to assume jurisdiction if the union failed to take action in good faith.

By this agreement the employers gave up their control over discipline. A series of stoppages occurred in 1938 and 1939 in which the longshoremen refused to cross picket lines demonstrating against shipping scrap iron to Japan. The employers protested the union failure to stop the disputes or to penalize the participants in the illegal demonstrations. The most serious dispute, a series of stoppages in Los Angeles Harbor in 1939, culminated in the castigation of the union's policy and actions as indefensible by the area arbitrator. For the first time in the relation between the parties, he imposed penalties — in this case, one-week suspensions — on a number of men.[31] The union retaliated by distributing the penalized men among a large number of gangs and dispatching them to work. Employer attempts to discharge the "penalty men" led to stopping of work by the whole gang of which they were a part. Discharge of the gangs was countered by

30. The Sloss award of October 5, 1935, ruling that the employer had no right to deny employment to gangs properly dispatched, actually dealt with grievances rising from employer attempts to suspend longshoremen involved in "hot cargo" strikes.
31. Irvin Stalmaster award of July 17, 1939.

refusal of the hiring hall to dispatch replacement gangs. The port-wide tie-up was submitted to the Coast Arbitrator for resolution.

Wayne Morse reviewed the disciplinary procedure: (1) in cases of misconduct, the union is obligated to impose discipline; (2) any employer may charge an offense including illegal work stoppage, and the union is obliged to discipline the offender if he is found guilty; (3) the union is required to report its action to the local joint labor relations committee within ten days of receipt of the complaint; (4) if the union fails to impose discipline, or imposes inadequate penalties, the employer may take up the matter in labor relations committee; (5) if the committee, one half of its votes being union officials, fails to satisfy the employer grievance, appeal may be made to the arbitrator. But Morse then found that the arbitrator had no power to impose penalties except for drunkenness and pilfering.[32] The union thus had gained the right to impose discipline almost completely free from challenge. No further discipline cases were submitted to the arbitrators until 1947, and very few before 1960.[33]

Worker grievances were important in establishing the hiring hall, but even at the outset the union's needs to preserve and enhance its power were motivating elements. The pursuit of power ought not to have invidious or derogatory connotations, assuming that the union is conceded the right to exist and to function. The essence of unionism is power. In every view of the institution and its role, from the most conservative to the vanguard of the revolution, the union must have power to survive and to pursue its goals. Without economic power the business union is helpless to do more than acquiesce to market and employer pressures. The politically oriented union requires economic or political power to survive and win improvements or to change society through political action. Without some minimum power the union would vanish or become a fraternal society of little consequence.

These institutional needs were clearly predominant in the transformation of a plan for equitable decasualization into a system of al-

32. *Morse award of September 11, 1939.*
33. *The dozen or so discipline cases that reached arbitrators in the years between 1947 and 1958 almost invariably involved an employer charge of inadequate union punishment, countered by a union allegation of wrongful discharge and claim for pay.*

most total work-force control by the ILWU. Every union dealing with a competitive industry perceives very quickly that unionization of the entire industry work force is a necessary condition to any significant improvement in wages and working conditions. When dealing with only a fraction of such an industry, the imposition of changes in wages or any benefit associated with higher labor costs quickly results in diversion of demand to the lower priced, nonunionized firms, or bankruptcy in the unionized firms, resulting from their inability to cover increased costs with higher prices. (This assumes that the most efficient production techniques are available to all firms and that the efficiency of labor is not a function of the wage rate or working conditions. Both are reasonable assumptions for competitive industries in the United States, and especially for the longshore industry.)

In longshoring, union organization and imposition of higher labor costs in only one port would immediately result in diversion of shipping to nonunion ports and, fairly quickly, a weakening if not obliteration of the union. The amount of the diversion and its relation to the increase in costs are functions of the substitutability of the services of the various ports. Adjacent large ports are almost perfect substitutes for each other — for example, San Francisco and Oakland, Los Angeles and Long Beach, and even Seattle and Tacoma. Los Angeles and San Francisco are more distant substitutes, but are substitutes nonetheless. Economic circumstances, then, compelled the ILWU to seek coastwide uniformity in wages and working conditions.

Further, every union in a casual labor market quickly notes the relation between labor supply and the wage rate or earnings level — the larger the labor supply, given long-term industry demand and the wage rate, the lower the average earnings. The casual market, with very high job turnover as a result of widely varying day-to-day labor demand and the short-term employment relationship, works to share rapidly the work opportunity, or its absence, among all or a large proportion of the work force and union membership. Unemployment in a casual-market union is perceived as fewer hours of work each week or other time period by almost all of the members. In a factory union, unemployment of the membership — layoffs by the firm or industry — must be large to affect even a minority of union members. The nature of the market thus compels the union to relate control over the work force, including limits to entry, to higher average earnings and, ultimately, to higher wages. The development of the ILWU-controlled hiring hall and its rules and limits on employer freedom to hire and discharge workers are the specific implementation of the casual-market union's need for work-force control.

The coercive pressures in competitive industries, and their effects on unions and union policies, have been noted by many authors, from the Webbs to Slichter, Healy, and Livernash.[34] However, these authors neglect to show that only the casual market compels a high degree of union job control. Further, they fail to note, or to explain, that unions in imperfectly competitive markets need not behave as do unions in competitive markets.[35] Indeed, they will not. Unions dealing with very large firms neither seek nor exercise control over entry to the work force or, in the case of union-shop contract provisions, entry into the union itself. Although they are interested, these unions are not forced to organize all of the industry work force. Within rather broad limits, the survival of the firm and its market share are not jeopardized by cost increases imposed on it alone by the union. The firm earns profits above the competitive level before and after the union-sought changes, hence its existence is not in doubt. Market shares are determined by collusion, selling costs, or other product-market considerations, and are further protected by barriers to entry to the industry. Under these circumstances a union whose member-

---

34. *Sidney and Beatrice Webb,* Industrial Democracy *(London, 1897), especially part 3, chap. 2.* Slichter, in Union Policies, *describes the failure of union policies of obstruction to, and competition with, technical change largely in terms of competitive market pressures (chaps. 7 and 8). In* Impact of Collective Bargaining, *(pp. 36, 336) Slichter, Healy, and Livernash approximate my discussion above in noting that industries with intermittent employment also often have hiring halls and that restrictive work practices depend on the union's control of the market. "Control of the market means that the union is able to impose the make-work rule on all competitors alike, thereby putting no employer at a disadvantage."*

35. *This criticism also extends to the analytical model of the union developed by John Dunlop, in* Theory of Wage Determination under Trade Unions *(New York, 1944). Dunlop's model is admirably suited to the union in a casual-market industry or craft. These unions do have a "membership function" wholly or largely within their control; they are interested and able to estimate demand for the output of the industry. They control, or know a good deal about, the production function and, as a result, are well aware of the nature of the demand for labor — their average wage-income function. Many of these unions act as if they were indeed maximizing wage income for their membership. This approach is vastly less applicable to a union dealing with one or a few very large firms.*

ship includes 50 percent of the industry work force, or even as little as perhaps 20 percent, may not only survive but actually bring about wages and other improvements for its members above the results that would have been obtained in the absence of the union. These unions express little interest in control over production processes. Their interest in the product market is usually slight and easily deflected by the employer's adamant insistence on his management prerogatives in product price decisions, and so on.

In summary, some unions, but not all, find themselves in circumstances that make work-force control a necessary condition for survival or meaningful existence. These circumstances are wholly apart from any specific attributes of the work force [36] and from ideologies or broad social or economic goals of the union. The ILWU found itself in an economic environment that required it to obtain job control. The ideology of its leaders in no way hindered the pursuit of job control; indeed, it may have sharpened their appreciation of the union's need to acquire power, including economic power.

WORK RULES AND PRACTICES

It was noted earlier that work-force control and control over the production processes, the latter usually manifested in work rules and practices, are often found together. There are several reasons for this. First, in competitive markets, work-force control is necessary for any cost-increasing work rules and practices; without uniformity in the industry, competitive pressures would destroy the firms granting work-rules concessions. In other words, many work rules are logical extensions of work-force control in that the competitive-market allocation of demand to firms responds not to the wage rate directly but to the labor cost per unit of output. Work rules are often an attempt to bring about labor cost uniformity throughout the industry. Second, casual-market industries require some measure of work-force control in order to define clearly the group to benefit from work rules and other working condition improvements. Finally, work rules and practices are unusually relevant to casual labor markets. The brief

36. *Psychological attributes were denied earlier. In addition, it is clear that casual-market unions include workers of extremely diverse skills and associated characteristics: low-skill groups include building trades laborers, marine cooks, ordinary seamen and longshoremen; and high-skill groups include structural iron workers, electricians, and ships' officers in the maritime industry. These persons have in common only their employee status and a casual labor market.*

employment relationship leads to broad participation in the benefits of work rules — the easier work, in terms of effort, is shared by a large proportion of the membership as they move from one job to another, and the employment-maintaining effect of the rules enhances the job prospects of all members.

Unions often describe their work rules as protective. They protect the health and safety, employment opportunities, and other intangibles of value to the members. Health and safety are most prominent among the publicized motives; they may be viewed as humane limitations on the production process. Production functions describe economic activity, but what is often overlooked is that they do so in a context of rules, usages, or customs. Many of the actions of unions are attempts to define or limit the production function by clarifying or changing existing rules or usages. At the minimum, unions seek to exclude production possibilities that endanger the lives or health of their members or some broader group of workers. The method selected to achieve these ends is often legal enactment, but collective bargaining may be used as well.[37] Health and safety measures become codes of industrial safety and similar statutes when won by legal enactment; they become work rules when won by collective bargaining. The themes of health and safety recur repeatedly in the development of work rules in Pacific Coast longshoring.

Employers, and most economists, are more accustomed to describing work rules as restrictive; indeed, many are. The rules may be restrictive at the outset by being designed to require redundant labor, retain obsolete work methods, and so on. On the other hand, they may become restrictive by their immutability in a world of changing techniques, inventions, discoveries, dynamic market shifts, and other environmental transformations. The most reasonable definition of a restrictive work rule or practice is that it is an institutional arrangement requiring the employer to hire more labor than he would have hired, in the absence of compulsion, at a given wage rate.[38] The rules are, by definition, "inefficient" in that other than least cost combinations of inputs are required. It does not follow,

---

37. *In the United States the social and political environment favored collective bargaining rather than legal enactment as the method to achieve most union objectives. Ulman gives a good analysis and explanation in* Rise of the National Union, *pp. 594–604.*

38 *This definition is implicit in Slichter,* Union Policies, *explicit in Ulman, p. 439 ff., and in the writing of other economists on featherbedding and restrictive work practices.*

however, that the allocation of resources as a result of the work rule is worse than would have been the case without the rule. If the pre-rule allocation was nonoptimal as a result, for example, of the presence of monopoly or monopsony elements, the rule no more than substitutes one nonoptimal solution for another.

NATURE OF THE LONGSHORE TASK.[39]

Longshore work consists of loading and discharging cargo to and from ships. Typical break-bulk goods [40] destined for outbound ocean shipment arrive in the port area by land transport. The goods usually are received by a terminal operator some time — days or weeks — before actual loading. They are taken from the truck or railcar, sorted if necessary, and then assembled and stored in lots for further shipment in a warehouse or transit shed. In the normal pre-1960 circumstances on the Pacific Coast the goods were stacked directly on the warehouse or pier floor. The cargo-handling work up to this point is usually performed by truck drivers, helpers, casual laborers, and warehousemen. When no further movement within the warehouse, shed, or storage area is necessary, the goods are in the "last place of rest" before the beginning of the actual ship loading.

Longshore work begins at the last place of rest. Dock gangs stack the outbound goods on pallets,[41] building the loads to be hoisted aboard the ship. The loads are moved from the last place of rest

39. This section is based largely on the author's observation of ships being loaded or discharged at berths in San Francisco and Oakland. Personal observation has been supplemented by descriptions by dock workers, both oral and written in arbitration cases, caucus proceedings, and the like. Good descriptions published elsewhere appear in National Research Council, Maritime Cargo Transportation Conference, Cargo Ship Loading (Washington, 1957), and National Research Council, Maritime Cargo Transportation Conference, San Francisco Port Study (Washington, 1964), Vol. I, parts 2 and 3.

40. Break-bulk goods are packaged in cartons, boxes, bags, barrels, drums, bales, and loose pieces. They include goods capable of being loaded with more than one unit to the draft and of being manhandled into stowage position.

41. The pallets or skids are raised rectangular wood platforms of varying sizes — most often about four to six feet on a side — and may be moved easily by forklift. Forklifts and pallets came into widespread use on the Pacific Coast during the late 1930s and World War II. Pallets were preceded on the docks by lift boards, or sling boards. Lift boards were much longer than they were wide, one or two feet by six or seven feet, and were introduced as early as the mid-1920s. Sling boards were simple planks used with rope slings to be attached to the hook on the ship's gear. They had been used in the United States since before World War I. See Charles B. Barnes, The Longshoremen (New York, 1915), pp. 34–40.

by a forklift truck, across the apron (the open area between the ware-house or transit shed wall and the waterside edge of the pier or quay), to the side of the ship. The lift truck deposits the load on the apron within reach of the ship's hoisting equipment. Frontmen, or slingmen, attach the load to the ship's gear to be lifted aboard. Pal-letizing and driving the lift truck or jitney are dockwork. On the Pa-cific Coast, attaching the load to the ship's gear is the beginning of shipwork.

The ship to be loaded has five, seven or, on large ships, even more hatches. Each hatch is about twelve feet square or more and opens to several levels of the hold below. The interior decks have openings directly beneath the exterior deck hatches; that part of the hold in the hatch opening is the "square of the hatch." The distance from the square to the bulkhead or the most distant corner of the wing is perhaps forty feet. Each hatch is served by deck-mounted me-chanical hoisting equipment — the ship's gear. The typical ship's gear, for the past thirty or forty years, consists of masts and booms built along one side of a hatch, with two adjacent winches at the cen-ter near the hatch opening. The hook, or hook gear, is fastened to two cables. Each cable runs from the hook through blocks at the head and heel of a guyed boom to a winch. The head of one boom is directly over the desired hookup position on the apron; the head of the other is over the square or on the offshore side of the hatch. The winch driver faces the open hatch and is able to see most of the hold area within the square of the hatch. A hatch tender signals the winch driver when the latter's view of the load in the hold or on the apron is obstructed. The gang boss may also signal; he is often on the deck. Hatches may be double-rigged — that is, two sets of gear may be used to work the same hatch. Ships vary to some extent in their gear: in place of masts, booms, winches, and a maze of cables, a rotating crane mounted at a corner of the hatch may be used.

The draft, attached to the hook or hook gear by the frontmen, is lifted by the cable attached to the winch nearest the pier. The draft travels between the boom heads by taking up cable on one winch, paying it out on the other. The load is lowered to the hold by the offshore winch. If the operation uses a bridle [42] rather than sling and

---

42. *A bridle consists of two steel plates, shaped in a right angle, about four inches wide on each of its two sides and as long as the pallet side — about four to six feet. The plate is attached by a cable from each end to the ship's*

hook, the loaded pallet often is placed — by the lift driver on the apron, and by the winch driver in the hold — on planks about one inch thick to enable the plates to be attached and removed easily. The frontmen fit the angle plates to opposite edges of the pallet; the weight of the load holds them in place. Other devices that may be attached to the ship's gear include an oversized pallet, hung by cables between each corner and the hook. The lift driver places one or more loaded smaller pallets on the oversized one for each draft. Other special hook gear includes hooks for drums of liquids, steel frames for automobiles, and tubs or scows for frozen fish and similar goods.

In the hold the draft may be placed directly on the deck on one side or in a corner of the square. The hold gang takes the goods, case by case or bag by bag, carries them into the wing and stacks, piles, or otherwise stows the packages. Rollers set in steel frames may be used to move the goods from the square to the wing by gravity. Alternatively, the draft may be placed on a dolly, or "four-wheeler," which is then pushed, by man power, to the part of the hold where the goods are to be stowed. Finally, a lift truck, powered by gasoline or electric motor, may be used to move and stow the goods. Longshoremen or carpenters perform lining, lashing, bracing, blocking, and other work necessary to protect the cargo and prevent shifting when the ship is at sea.

Cargo discharging is essentially the loading process reversed. The hold gang breaks out the cargo and builds the loads. The ship's gear lifts the drafts to the apron; frontmen disengage the gear and dockmen move the goods to the first place of rest on the dock. Longshore workers depalletize, sort, and stack the goods, if necessary.

A substantial amount of the tonnage, but a small fraction of longshore labor, is involved in "special operations." Bulk handling of grain, ore, coke, sugar, potash, salt, and similar goods is capital intensive. Each operation tends to be specialized to the commodity; the bulk methods used with the various goods have little in common other than that they all require rather complex and extensive shoreside facilities. The operations use relatively little labor, and most of it is skilled or specialized. In 1960, bulk-handling facilities loaded or dis-

gear. The bridle resembles two triangles attached at their apexes; the steel angle plate is the base of each triangle, and the wire cables are the sides. The bridle remains attached to the gear throughout the cargo-handling period, unlike rope or cable slings which are attached to the hook and lifted off with each draft.

charged about 40 percent of total Pacific Coast tonnage but used only about 5 percent of the longshore labor. Another group of commodities calls for handling that is intermediate between bulk handling and conventional break-bulk methods. The commodities require much more labor than the former, but more extensive onshore facilities or mobile equipment than the latter. These goods — copra, bananas, iron and steel scrap, newsprint, and lumber — accounted for about 15 percent of total tonnage handled and longshore labor used in 1960. Goods handled by bulk facilities and other special operations are often used to illustrate dramatically the progress of mechanization in cargo handling.[43] Nonetheless, a bit more than three fourths of longshore labor has been used, in recent years, in conventional break-bulk work and consists largely of unskilled manual labor.

The preceding description of the longshoring task is deliberately vague on a number of important points. The number of men on the dock, on the deck, in the hold, or for the hatch or ship as a whole, is not specified. The need for palletization, number of forklifts or jitneys at each hatch, size of draft, frequency of drafts or speed of hoisting aboard and placing goods in the hold, the number of drafts in the hold at one time and number of men to work each draft, and similar details were omitted. The demarcation was not clearly drawn between longshoremen's work and sailors' or carpenters' work on the ship, and between longshore tasks and those more appropriate to warehousemen or casual laborers on the dock. These points are the substance of the second aspect of job control — control over the production process, or work rules and practices.

CONTROL OVER THE PRODUCTION PROCESS

In Pacific Coast longshoring, gear priority is the individual worker's right to a job to which he has been properly dispatched and put to work. For example, a Los Angeles port rule in effect in 1953 required:

7. One jitney or combination jitney driver shall be assigned to a gear if needed *and shall be entitled to all jitney or fork lift work at that gear*, provided however, that a jitney driver may be replaced by a fork lift or com-

43. In Louis Goldblatt and Otto Hagel, Men and Machines (San Francisco, 1963), are excellent photographs of longshore work and methods. The most impressive pictures are those of special operations. The photographs illustrate the extent and nature of mechanization of the special operations at the beginning of the 1961–1966 mechanization and modernization agreement.

bination driver at the termination of a day or night shift if and when such equipment is needed.[44]

Individual specialists and, even more important, ship gangs had priority at the gear to which they were first assigned upon arrival from the hiring hall. Their priority gave them the right to all work performed in connection with the gear or hatch. They could be reassigned by the employer, under appropriate circumstances, or even dismissed; but if more work at that gear were necessary, the original specialist or gang had to be recalled to do it. The rules permitted relief of the day shift by the night shift without violation of priority, but if work remained to be done the next day, the original gang had the right to it. If a second gang or specialists were assigned to help work a hatch, they could be dismissed when no longer needed, but if the employer again sought added men at the hatch, the same second gang or men had priority. Priority rights ceased only when the ship sailed.

An Oregon dispute provides a good illustration of gear priority rights. An employer ordered nine forklift drivers to work a ship. Only four hatches were to be worked, and the employer assigned the drivers in the order in which they arrived at the job. The first four drivers were put to work, and had priority, at each of the four hatches. The aggrieved employee was the fifth driver to arrive, who was assigned as a second driver to a hatch. Work slackened in the afternoon, and the employer dismissed all but the first four to arrive. One of the retained drivers was ordered to work at the grievant's hatch as a second driver. The grievant claimed priority and alleged wrongful dismissal. The arbitrator pointed out that the rules permitted the employer to move drivers from one hatch to another, but only when workers were not displaced. He ruled that the aggrieved employee had been so displaced and improperly discharged.[45] The penalties for violating priority were stiff: the men or gangs wrongfully replaced were paid for work opportunities lost, which varied from a few hours for one man to as much as several shifts for whole gangs. Of course, the men who actually did the work were also paid the full rates.

44. Quoted in the David Ziskind arbitration award of March 1, 1953. Emphasis supplied.
45. E. P. Murray award of November 29, 1955.

Gear priority resembles seniority in the industrial union in some respects, but differs in others. Both gear priority and seniority give the individual a claim to a specific job. Both are devices to protect the individual against favoritism or arbitrary dismissal and derive from workers' complaints on those grounds. In both situations the employer retains the right to dismiss employees for incompetence, disciplinary infractions, or other good cause. In both, the breadth or narrowness of the definition of the job and the relevant employing unit are crucial in their effects on employer flexibility in worker reassignment. Gear priority differs from seniority in that, at least in part, it was sought in order to promote equalization of work opportunities. An important motive in the establishment of the hiring hall had been the desire to reduce the marked inequality of earnings of the work force. Dispatching rules giving first call to men and gangs at the bottom of the hours and earnings list, and the elimination of preferred gangs, were major steps toward equalization. But the employers could defeat the hall and violate its chief rule and ethical basis by continuously dismissing gangs and ordering new ones until they had, in effect, hired the men who would have been hired in the absence of the hall. The creation of the individual job right sharply reduced the danger.

Unlike seniority, the development of gear priority on the docks became associated with requirements that sharply limited employer flexibility. Gear priority, like seniority in narrowly defined seniority units, of itself very likely would have only slight adverse effects on efficiency or costs. The requirement that one competent man be used, rather than another, is not inherently burdensome. But the concurrent development of a narrow definition of the employment unit, job specialization, and minimum guarantees is more likely to interfere with efficiency. The employment unit within which men could be transferred to work was defined to include only ships being worked by one stevedoring contractor at one dock.[46] In effect, men could be transferred to another hatch of the same ship or only to one or two other ships, assuming, of course, that no one had gear priority at

46. The limits to employer flexibility then in existence were the subject of considerable discussion during the 1958 and 1959 contract negotiations. The Minutes of the Union Negotiating Committee and Joint Negotiating Committee, May 15–June 11, 1958, and May 18–22, 1959, define many of the points. The Roderick arbitration award of March 24, 1959, illustrates the narrow job definition just before its elimination in negotiations later that year.

those hatches or ships.[47] In addition, within the system of gear priority, individuals and gangs sought the right to their individual tasks, however slightly specialized. Not surprisingly, skilled workers — winch and lift drivers, for example — were almost unchallenged in their right to work only in their specialty. Other workers tried to follow. Frontmen objected to assignment to work aboard the ship, dockmen refused to work in the hold, and so on. Although employers resisted this step to almost total rigidity in directing the work, and arbitrators upheld them, the locals won many concessions on individual task claims. General cargo gangs were not ordered to shovel work, special cargo gangs could not be turned to work general cargo, "palletizing gangs will not depalletize, and vice versa," and more.[48]

Finally, the minimum work or pay guarantee of four hours to every man properly dispatched completed the constraints to job assignment flexibility. If work needed to be done, however little, the employer often was barred from transferring men already at work for him by gear priority requirements and narrow job definition. He was compelled to order a skilled worker or gang of the appropriate specialty. The newly hired men were guaranteed four hours' work or pay, or even more if the employer had the misfortune of needing small amounts of work widely spaced by time in which no work at all could be done; gear priority then required the original men to be retained for longer periods of time, or to be recalled with renewed four-hour guarantees. To illustrate, one southern California employer protested the need to hire a lift-truck driver for only ten minutes of work, some in the morning and some in the afternoon, because the eight hours' pay appeared excessive. The union sympathized, but successfully insisted that the rules be followed.[49]

Analytically, the combined effect of gear priority, relatively inflexible shifting provisions, and minimum guarantees is to require a

47. A dock in Pacific Coast usage is a pier or quay with usually two to perhaps six berths. The probability is not great that one employer would be working more than two ships at the same dock.
48. In his award of December 9, 1940, for example, Wayne Morse ruled that any gang member could be assigned to any job at his hatch. But in the Clark Kerr award of June 21, 1947, for example, the arbitrator upheld the right of a shovel gang to refuse to work general cargo. The Ziskind award of October 9, 1959, supported the refusal of dockmen to work as high pilers. The quote is from ILWU, "Coast Labor Relations Committee Report" to the Longshore, Shipclerk and Walking Boss Caucus, October 15, 1957 (San Francisco), p. 14.
49. Ziskind award of March 1, 1953.

minimum absolute amount of labor input for any output above zero. The rules could require inefficiently large amounts of labor, and lead to lower productivity, given the wage, the price of capital, and so on, if the employer is unable to provide enough work to fill out the guarantee. Actually, however, the adverse effects of the rules are likely to be slight; the shippers and longshore employers would escape most of the inefficiency by concentrating cargo handling in fewer ports and at fewer piers in order to reduce the number of shipments involving very small amounts of cargo loading or discharging — i.e., less than the minimum efficient amount, given the rules. This conclusion is consistent with the intent of the rules — to regularize, not maximize, employment.

At the same time that the union was developing its control over the size, composition, and job assignment of the work force, its efforts to control manning, methods, and pace of work were also proceeding. In the first few days after the 1934 award establishing the conditions of the first working relationship between the employers and the union, grievances were brought to the labor relations committees. Within six days employer representatives were protesting the numerous job actions to force reductions in the size of the sling load and to slow the pace of work. In rebuttal union representatives argued that the main issues in the big strike itself had been heavy loads and general speedup of work. Both sides agreed to maintain existing practices in work methods until port work rules had been adopted. Despite this agreement, disputes over sling loads continued.

The size of the sling load is an important variable in cargo-handling productivity and pace of work. Employers and longshoremen knew in the mid-1930s, and later engineering studies confirmed, that productivity — tons stowed or unloaded per man- or gang-hour — varies directly with sling-load size, given the hold-gang size. Larger loads are associated with larger fractions of time on the job devoted to the actual handling of goods, or faster work pace. There are limits, of course, but the range is wide. According to National Research Council studies, with efficient winch operation and a hold gang of eight, ten, or twelve men held constant for load-size variation, and assuming that no other work practices are limiting efficiency, the tonnage handled per hour varies proportionately with sling-load size up to about 3,000 pounds, and for even heavier loads with dense goods.[50]

50. *See* Cargo Ship Loading, *pp. 27–28.*

The first union protest on sling loads was taken up in the San Francisco Joint Labor Relations Committee on October 29, 1934, only seventeen days after the recognition award. The union had stopped work briefly to protest the size of loads of cases of coconuts. Fifteen 140-pound cases had been handled before union recognition, but the standard was reduced to twelve cases soon after the strike had ended. When the employer again required the longshore gangs to handle fifteen cases in each draft, they stopped work. Contract language notwithstanding, the local union officials insisted — as they continued to do for the next thirty years — that in matters of health and safety the union standard was to govern if the work was to go on. The union lost this case; the arbitrator ruled that the sling load was neither harmful to health nor unsafe. He also pointed out that the union erred in not working as the employer directed, pending settlement of the dispute.[51]

The longshore gangs and local business agents, influenced in part by the loss of nearly all the early cases, preferred not to rely on the arbitrator. As noted in *The Waterfront Worker*, a newspaper written by an informal leadership group and distributed on the docks: "We know full well in whose favor this impartial chairman would vote — the shipowners, of course." The favored tactic was the job action, and the objective was control over the pace and method of work. *The Waterfront Worker* observed:

Struggle along the docks has succeeded very largely in keeping off scabs and cutting down on the speedup and the way in which this award works out depends largely on the militancy of the longshoremen in keeping up this struggle. . . .

No more do the docks of San Francisco hear the booming echo of some bosses' voice, the winches do not groan with their heavy loads as before, although it would do no harm to make the loads still smaller. . . .

The gang and dock steward system which we have inaugurated is most satisfactory in keeping job control, and must become a permanent thing. . . . .

Aggressive militancy and the will to push forward will bring us to our goal. Our goal, as we know, is FULL JOB CONTROL, the right to say where and how we shall work.[52]

51. Sloss, proceedings and award of January 4, 1935. See also Liebes, pp. 74–80.
52. The Waterfront Worker, October 22, 1934. The Waterfront Worker *expressed the views of the left ideological faction of the union.*

In the 1934–1936 perod alone, only five of thirty arbitration cases dealt with sling loads, but, according to the employers, there were ninety work stoppages over the same issue.[53]

The first steps of record among the employers to move toward uniform sling loads took place early in 1935. By April of that year the San Francisco waterfront employers' group had drawn up a schedule of recommended reasonable maximum loads and circulated it among the various firms. Employers continued to insist, however, that methods of work, including sling loads, were matters for management to decide and not for bargaining.[54]

Sling-load disputes continued, partly because the union refused to accept the employer claim to sole control, and partly because employers themselves regarded the proposed uniform loads as advisory only. For example, the San Francisco employers' schedule of 1935 recommended as reasonable and fair for most goods load limits of about 2,100 pounds; for cement and other goods in bags or sacks of about 100 pounds each, the suggested limit was nineteen bags to the load, and so on. Yet, nearly a year after the first circulation of the schedule, employers in Los Angeles Harbor were requiring heavier loads. In one dispute the employer ordered drafts of twenty-one large sacks of potash, each sack weighing 150 pounds; twenty-four smaller, 125-pound sacks of potash; and thirty sacks of cement. The loads totaled 3,150, 3,000, and 2,850 pounds, respectively. The longshoremen handled these loads for three days. On the fourth day, ordered to a ship recently berthed, they refused to continue to work the heavy loads. The union insisted on a general load limit of about 2,100 pounds, or fourteen large sacks of potash, seventeen of the smaller sacks, and twenty-two sacks of cement. The arbitrator agreed with the union's contention that the large loads were hazardous. He found cause for the union allegation of speedup and condemned the practice, ruling in favor of the union.[55]

The union continued to press for smaller sling loads and coastwide uniform maxima, generally of about 1,800 to 1,900 pounds. Pressure by the job action — the "quickie" strike — was maintained. In one case in the Northwest, the union sought forty, rather than forty-eight cases of salmon to the load; in another, they pressed for

53. Liebes, p. 95.
54. San Francisco Joint Labor Relations Committee, Minutes, April 9, 1935.
55. Paul A. Dodd award of May 26, 1936.

twenty-four sacks of sugar instead of the employer-ordered thirty.[56] By early 1936 the smaller load was standard in San Francisco, but not in the other ports. The work stoppage was not the only device available to bring about smaller loads. The employers alleged, and some union people agreed, that moving a bit slower on the job was an effective way to achieve results. *The Waterfront Worker* pointed out:

If the shipowners want big loads, why can't we give it to them? — but — we can take our time. They are out to break our union, there is no question about that and it would be wrong policy at this time to strike, so stay on the job, boys, and slow down — take it easy.[57]

The union also turned to negotiations to try to win uniform sling loads. In early 1936 it countered the employers' schedule of reasonable maximum loads with one of its own. The employers rejected it.

The sling-load impasse was broken in 1937. In earlier arbitrations the union attributed much of the uncertainty in sling-load disputes to the lack of negotiated work rules. Arbitrators agreed. In early 1937, after a three-month strike over a new contract, the employers conceded the issue. As one of the numerous points in the settlement the parties established a joint committee to look into and recommend sling-load limits. Both parties accepted the schedule of limits, by commodity and package, recommended by the committee. The schedule was first incorporated into the contract in July 1937, and was continued unchanged until 1960. Perhaps even more important, the union won employer agreement that working conditions and safety could require even smaller loads. Disputes over sling loads continued, but from mid-1937 the loads were no longer subject to unilateral management determination. In early 1939 the Coast Arbitrator, preparatory to settling a number of load disputes, ruled:

It is the opinion of the arbitrator that the size of sling loads of commodities not listed in Section 11 (h) [of the 1937 contract, renewed in 1938] are subject to the jurisdiction of local Labor Relations Committees . . . and that the same criteria — health, safety, and reasonable loading and discharging rates in light of the working conditions of a given operation — must be taken into account in settling any dispute which may arise within the industry over the size of sling loads.[58]

56. From the Hazel award of July 20, 1936.
57. Waterfront Worker, December 10, 1934.
58. Morse award of April 3, 1939.

Most problems in the administration of the sling-load agreement have concerned questions of fact, determination of safe loads both for goods not explicitly listed in the schedule and in instances in which the union sought limits smaller than those of the schedule, and similar differences of interpretation. For example, in one typical case the arbitrator decided that, in fact, the thirty-foot lengths of steel pipe in dispute were about eight and one-half inches in diameter, not just eight inches, and therefore the maximum load was three pieces, not four. In another typical case the arbitrator ruled that four drums of liquids were a safe load, against union objections that three were the maximum tolerable. On the other hand, the union was held correct in alleging that two bundles of steel rods, total weight 2,280 pounds, were an unsafe load; only one bundle of 1,140 pounds was permitted. An employer attempt to justify twelve sacks of coffee to the load on the grounds that mechanical power was used to move the goods on the dock was struck down. The men still worked the cargo by hand in the hold, and the schedule limit of nine sacks had been unambiguous for decades.[59]

The issue of the standard gang is almost inseparable from sling-load limits. The union alleged that operations had been speeded up in the years just before the 1934 strike; the resulting fatigue was not only unpleasant but actually dangerous to the workers.[60] Union spokesmen pointed out that the pace of work had been increased not only by moving larger loads with the same number of men but also by using unchanged load size with fewer workers. In addition to controlling the size of the load, the union sought to require that a standard minimum gang be used in all conventional break-bulk operations.

Before unionization, gang size varied a great deal not only from port to port and from one employer to another but also from time to time at a given task, dock, or employer. Gang size was not spelled out in the earliest written agreements; the contract specified only that local rules or existing practices be followed. In San Francisco the standard minimum gang adopted in 1935 consisted of the

---

59. *Ziskind award of September 3, 1953; Sam Kagel award of June 27, 1951; Ziskind award of October 4, 1955; and Kagel award of April 23, 1956.*
60. *The hearing of the National Longshoremen's Board was filled with testimony from union witnesses describing the increased pace of operations, increased accident rate, and so on.* Proceedings, pp. 174–218, 235–257, 318–335, 341–365, *and more.*

following: one gang boss appointed by the union, two deckmen, six holdmen (eight men on loading operations), six dockmen, and one jitney driver. In other ports the standard gang was defined as the ship gang; it excluded the dockmen, but included two frontmen, or slingmen. Standard ship gangs in the various ports ranged from ten to thirteen men from the mid-1930s until 1960.

Most important, with respect to speedup and coastwide uniformity, was the hold gang. The union could and did tolerate differences between ports in the use of gang bosses and the long gang or the short gang; [61] dock gangs also were of variable sizes from port to port and even within some ports. However, the minimum basic hold gang of eight men on loading and six men on discharging was considered invariable and important. The hold gang was the largest single group within the longshore gang. The pressure of speedup was more likely to be felt there: closed, irregular, and often cramped work space made any kind of mechanization difficult. The eight- and six-man hold gang was the prevailing practice by 1935 and was maintained through the subsequent years. In 1957 the union leadership reminded the longshore delegates: "It is true, in general, except for the radical shifts to bulk operation, that we have retained and added to our basic manning scales in the hold." [62]

Although sling-load and manning requirements greatly narrow the range within which the average tonnage handled by a gang or man may vary, informal direct control over the pace of work narrows the remaining range and may depress the average further. A number of practices have been of some importance in controlling output in Pacific Coast longshoring. The ship's gear may be capable of delivering sixty to one hundred drafts per hour, but the quickness with which the men attach or disengage the gear from the load and the requirement that loads be carefully spotted have an important effect on the number of drafts. [63]

---

61. *The long gang included the full complement of dockmen; the short gang excluded them. By 1947, however, all ports were using short gangs as the minimum standard; San Francisco lost the long gang by action of the National War Labor Board during World War II.*
62. *ILWU, "Coast Committee Report," October 15, 1957, p. 11.*
63. *The hook cycle — time to lift the attached load from the apron to the hold and return, exclusive of hook-on and removal time — with typical ship's gear is about thirty-six to forty-eight seconds. The National Research Council Study* Cargo Ship Loading *included chiefly East Coast and Gulf Coast ports. Pacific ports were not studied directly, but were mentioned with data from*

Pacific Coast longshoremen were aware that they could slow the pace of work by their own actions in failing to meet the hook and other means. Some locals of the ILWU imposed slowdowns or resisted speedup by requiring, for example, that no more than two drafts could be handled at one time by an eight-man hold gang, four men and one draft to each side of the hatch. Although two drafts were often standard procedure, many goods can be worked by two men to the draft; with six or eight men in the hold, three or four drafts can be worked at one time. Both the post-1960 experience and the pre-1960 "four on-four off" practices confirm the slowdown. Very soon after the 1960 agreement was negotiated, many employers, especially in southern California, began to use three or four drafts. When challenged through the grievance procedure, the method was judged to be neither unsafe nor onerous.[64] The "four on-four off" practices were local customs generally involving working only about half of the time. In one variant, half the hold gang would be working while the other half rested. With only four men on the job, and four off, only two men actually worked each draft, one pair on each side of the hold.

The "four on-four off" practices originated in the hold gang. In acceptable standard procedure, a hold gang, eight men when loading break-bulk general cargo, is split into two teams, each working its side of the hatch. The four men on one side disengage the hook from a load lowered to the hold and stow the cargo. The hook, meantime, returns to the dock for another load and lowers it to the hold where it is met, disengaged, and stowed by the four men on the other side. In most cases all the men in the gang are actively stowing goods at the same time only in a brief overlap period; when the first team finishes stowing and rests while waiting for its next load, the second team is still working its more recently arrived goods. Although the hold gang works only about 60 percent of the time, this practice has not been condemned. Conventional break-bulk handling of the goods involves hard physical labor, and the brief but frequent respite

other investigations. The authors found wide variation in number of drafts per hour among ports — from about seventeen to more than forty — and attributed a large part of the reduction in speed to careful landing of the load in the hold to minimize the distance the goods had to be moved to be stowed. Failure of the hold gang to meet the hook was important, but less so than pinpoint landing of the draft.

64. *See, for example, the Germain Bulcke awards of January 28, 1963, March 8, 1963, and March 26, 1963, and others.*

of the normal loading or discharging cycle prevents excessive fatigue. In fact existing research indicates that the marginal productivity of work time beyond about 60 to 70 percent of total time in the hold is negative; that is, the total tonnage that a gang is able to handle actually starts to decline.[65]

In some ports, however, the men began to reinterpret their customary right to about half of the time off to mean that only half the men would work at any one time. In practice this resulted in two men from each team working while the other two rested. With no more than the usual slight overlap as one side finished stowing while the other was just beginning, the hold gang worked only about 25 to 30 percent of its time in the hold.

Another practice slowing the pace of work was refusal, in some locals, to allow more than one jitney or forklift to serve the gear at a hatch. When distances between dockside place of rest and the ship are great, the practice substantially limits output.[66] Employers' allegations of slowdown in the early period of unionization were quoted by Sumner Slichter:

Winch drivers time hoists and if they get ahead of their set schedule, they stop the winches; if they get behind, there is no effort to make up the loss.

Jitney drivers time their trips, going to the extent of fastening their watches in sight to be sure they do not take a load ahead of schedule. No one will relieve jitney drivers and jitneys will not haul loads out of "turn." All work stops if the jitney driver is off for any reason.

Hatchtender deliberately delays signals.

On commodities requiring extensive sorting, hold men purposely mix marks in building loads to slow down the dock work.

With different conditions prevailing in different hatches, gang stewards slow operations to rate of slowest hatch.

Hold men fail to leave wings to "meet the hook" promptly.[67]

Two principal motives impelled the union to attempt to control the pace of work. Safety was important, and concern with safety reflected almost wholly the interest of the workers. The union and its representatives relied extensively on the safety issue in seeking sling-load limits, manning requirements, and similar rules in negotiations,

65. Cargo Ship Loading, *pp. 30–32.*
66. *Described in the Kagel award of November 3, 1952.*
67. Union Policies, *p. 174.*

publicity, and arguments before arbitrators. Large sling loads could spill or collapse more easily. Emphasis on speed in operations often was associated with neglect of safety precautions: hurried winch drivers spilled partly detached loads or set them down on unwary longshoremen. Harassed ship gang members fell in the hatches, or were injured by the toppling of poorly stowed goods, and so on.[68] A variant of the safety argument asserted that the life-span of the worker was shortened by overwork and excessive fatigue. In the 1934 hearings the union argued that Pacific Coast longshoremen in fact had shorter life expectancies than workers in most industrial occupations. Union spokesmen contended that the hazardous conditions associated with increased pace of work were responsible.[69]

There is little doubt that safety was a legitimate grievance. In the years after union recognition scores of decisions of joint port labor relations committees and arbitrators upheld union contentions of unsafe procedures in specific instances. The allegation on life expectancy probably had some validity, but it cannot be given major importance. Even assuming a demonstrably shorter life-span for longshoremen, the causal effects of working conditions are difficult to separate from income, education, cultural environment, and similar variables bearing on health and the availability, quality, and utilization of medical care. On the other hand, there is little doubt that in many cases safety was merely the ostensible reason for slowing down the work; the workers were in fact most interested in easier jobs.

A second motive to control the production process is the "effort wage." If the nominal wage level is unchanged, the requirement to work harder, faster, or for a larger proportion of the time on the job decreases the wage relative to the effort required. The employee is worse off than before, and, in a perfectly competitive economy, the employer would be compelled to increase the nominal wage in order to retain employees. Seen from the supply side of the labor market, effort or pace of work is one of the parameters involved in choice of occupation and employer. In the traditional analysis of wage determination, the typical exposition allocates labor by demonstrating that the rational worker chooses the job with the highest wage, if the

68. *The relation between large loads, smaller crews, increased work pace, and accidents was vividly drawn in testimony in the 1934* Proceedings, *pp. 174–176, 235–247, 311, 315, 321–323, 328–329, 337, 338–339, and elsewhere.*
69. *Ibid., pp. 373–386, testimony of H. P. Melnikow, counsel for the union.*

available jobs are otherwise identical. The argument could just as well show that, holding the wage constant and given the other parameters, the rational worker chooses the job with the least effort. The analyses plausibly assume that the worker desires both income and leisure, that he is willing to exchange leisure for income if the price is right, and he prefers more to less of both.[70] Physical effort is probably an important consideration in unskilled or semiskilled tasks, including longshoring. In large part, the acquisition of control over the pace of work was an attempt to maintain, or later, to increase the effort wage.

Most of the pressure came from the workers themselves; disputes over sling loads were associated with dozens of illegal local strikes, and many of the informal work practices were retained at the local level despite opposition from both the employers and the top leadership of the union.

Nonetheless, protection of the effort wage is also an institutional need of the union, at least at earlier stages of development. In a competitive industry with the nominal wage rate held constant, market pressures are deflected from the factor price to efficiency of the physical input. In order to survive or grow, firms must reduce costs. Cost reduction often includes attempts to elicit greater effort from the workers.[71] Effort-wage pressure is as potentially dangerous to the union as is money-wage undercutting; in both, market demand is diverted to the lowest-cost firms, and the union and its conditions in the organized sector are seriously threatened. The danger would continue until the union had organized the entire industry and had acquired sufficient job control to protect wages and production standards.

The result of the combined effects of load limits, break-bulk minimum manning, and direct informal control over the pace of work was to require that output vary proportionately with labor in-

---

70. *Effort is easily treated by the neoclassical indifference map and utility maximization approach. In a rather different context, Lloyd Ulman explicitly incorporated effort in his formal analysis of incentive pay. Ulman,* Rise of the National Union, *appendix 3, pp. 624–627.*

71. *The classic description of competitive market pressures and their impact on the employee is Sidney and Beatrice Webb,* Industrial Democracy, *"The Higgling of the Market," pp. 654–702. The Webbs discussed the results largely in terms of wages, but the adaptation to effort notions is not difficult.*

put. An employer could double or triple his output only by doubling or tripling the man-hours used. If wages were so high relative to capital costs that reducing labor input and increasing capital would lead to lower average costs, then the rules, by inhibiting capital-for-labor substitution, were unambiguously restrictive at all output levels. The extent to which the rules imposed inefficient proportions of labor and capital, or led to reduced productivity as a result of nonoptimal employment of labor, cannot be predicted without additional information about the technological conditions of production and about the demand for the output of the industry. At this point it is sufficient to note that the rules could require inefficiency; they appeared, by description, to do so, and the employers and many members and officials of the union believed that they did in fact do so.

Multiple handling is a dramatic example of a restrictive practice. Unlike basic manning or load limits, multiple handling was sought to maintain employment and, in part, involved opposition to technical change. Standard dockwork procedure was described by a Los Angeles employer representative:

the present practice in this harbor area is to require that any outbound cargo prepalletized before arrival at the dock by persons other than longshoremen must be removed from the pallet boards by teamsters, placed on the dock and then reloaded on stevedore pallet boards by longshoremen. The same situation obtains in reverse on the discharge of palletized cargo from the ship.[72]

The heart of multiple handling is jurisdiction on the docks. Direct transfer was not much of a problem; when the cargo was to be moved to the ship directly from an adjacent barge, railcar, or truck, longshoremen quickly won the right to handle the goods in the barge or shoreside vehicle. Indirect movement, involving temporary storage of the goods before further movement to the ship or land carrier, was a different matter. Jurisdiction was disputed in railcar loading and discharging, but it did not immediately lead to multiple handling. The issue was contested most seriously in Los Angeles. Southern California employers had used prepalletizing more extensively than stevedores elsewhere on the Pacific Coast, partly as a result of the physical facilities of the port and partly in order to reduce

72. From statement of Lee G. Paul, counsel for Southern Division of the Pacific Maritime Association and for the Master Contracting Stevedores Association of Southern California, in Study of Harbor Conditions, p. 153.

the otherwise large amount of weekend work time by longshore-men. The union sought jurisdiction and attempted to require either that the railcars be loaded and unloaded by longshoremen or that pallets or sling boards not be used to store the goods. All arbitrators agreed that such work was not included in the contract definition of longshore work. In an early award, the impartial chairman ruled:

I cannot accept the claim of the I.L.A. that the entire series of steps, begin-ning with the unloading of the cars, is longshore work. . . . On the other hand, I cannot accept the claim of the employers that the "last place of rest" is at ship's side or ship's tackle. In the illustration given above, i.e., the movement of lumber piled on sling boards from the cars to a point at which it is piled on the dock, and from which it is thereafter removed to ship's side, the last place of rest is the point at which the sling loads are thus piled on the dock.[73]

Disputes continued, but in 1936, employers in Los Angeles con-ceded the work to the union. Pallets were used, and longshoremen did the work, from May 1936 to the present. There were many sub-sequent challenges to this aspect of longshore jurisdiction, compli-cated for a time by the union's uncertainty as to whether it wanted the work for its warehouse or longshore division. Nonetheless, the arbitrators repeatedly held that the union had acquired the work for its longshoremen by an implied contract.[74]

Cargo carried to and from the dock in trucks, other than for di-rect transfer to the ship, was a much more serious problem. Prior to 1934, truck drivers and helpers could and often did unload their goods on the docks directly to sling boards or pallets. Immediately upon unionization, longshoremen pressed for jurisdiction over all building of sling loads. They required that either the trucks be loaded or unloaded by longshoremen, if the goods were to be palletized directly, or that the goods handled by truck drivers and their helpers be placed on the "skin of the dock." The International Brotherhood of Teamsters, on behalf of truck drivers and laborers, refused to al-low longshoremen to unload the vehicles. The only mutually satis-factory solution was to allow both claimants to handle the goods. Truck drivers and Teamster laborers unloaded to, or loaded from,

---

73. *Sloss award of February 28, 1935. See also Dodd award of May 26, 1936, Albert A. Rosenshine award of April 15, 1938, and others.*
74. *Rosenshine award of April 15, 1938; Morse awards of September 21, 1938, February 10, 1939, and September 15, 1939.*

the dock floor, and longshoremen then moved the goods to and from pallets or sling boards. Employers acceded to this method of demarcation in 1934 and 1935, and it became a local existing practice in almost every Pacific port, not to be changed except by negotiation.

The multiple-handling rules are restrictive in that many goods are or easily could be palletized by the original shipper to facilitate truck loading. The palletized goods are loaded and discharged from the truck by forklift. In the absence of a skin-of-the-dock requirement, the goods could be stored and later moved to the ship's gear and to the hold while still on the original shipper's pallet. However, the multiple-handling rules required an additional Teamsters' handling — depalletizing to the dock floor — and at least one extra longshore handling — repalletizing for movement to the ship or storage area.

Attempts were made to extend the requirement that goods touch the dock floor. For example, longshoremen tried to claim both palletizing and depalletizing the same goods. In one Portland dispute, longshoremen were discharging coffee on pallets owned by a stevedoring contractor. The bags were removed from the pallets to the skin of the dock by longshoremen, and Teamsters rebuilt the pallet loads to be lifted to the trucks. The longshoremen claimed the right to repalletizing on the grounds that the truck drivers and their helpers were using stevedoring company, not coffee company, pallets. The arbitrator disliked stretching the rules, but he decided that the shipment "in this particular incident be permitted . . . with the understanding that in the future, stevedore companies will not loan their longshore lift boards for a similar operation where workers other than from the ILWU would handle cargo on or off those boards on a dock."[75] In another case the longshoremen required that the goods touch the floor of the dock even when unloaded from trucks by longshoremen. Although the arbitrator ruled against the practice, the work was in fact performed for several months in accordance with the local union officials' interpretation of the work rules and contract.[76]

Ship-to-ship movement of goods posed problems. In general the union sought to require that the goods come to rest on the skin of

75. *Murray award of May 22, 1953.*
76. *Morse award of June 7, 1939.*

the dock despite the fact that the whole operation was performed by longshoremen. To illustrate, goods are moved from their storage position in the hold of a ship to the square of the hatch by longshoremen. Drafts are built on pallets in the hold by longshoremen. The draft is lifted from the hold to the apron of the dock and disengaged from the ship's gear, again by longshoremen. Employer attempts to move the loaded pallet to the side of another ship to be loaded aboard and stowed were met with the demand that the goods be taken from the pallet, piled on the dock or warehouse floor, then repalletized — all by longshoremen — for further movement. The parties and the arbitrators agreed that the distinguishing characteristic of ship-to-ship goods transfer was continuity of movement. The union could not require unloading and reloading the pallet when the goods movement was continuous and between adjacent or nearby ships.[77] However, goods whose movement was interrupted by storage or for other reasons must be depalletized, then later repalletized for loading to the second ship. A Seattle dispute is typical:

The cargo is loaded on a liftboard in the hold of the vessel. The liftboard is discharged to the dock, loaded aboard trucks by a longshore liftbull, trucked to another dock, taken from the truck by a longshore liftbull, placed on the dock, put in the hold of the second ship and finally the board is unloaded there.

The union demanded that the goods be discharged to the skin of dock. The employer asserted that the movement was continuous and, as a result, the extra dockwork was not required by the rules. The arbitrator clarified the rule:

It is ruled, therefore, that if the cargo from one ship is destined to go directly, and does go directly, to the hold of the second ship, this contested method should be allowed. If, however, the cargo from one ship is loaded upon liftboards and trucked to another dock and left on the boards on that dock for subsequent loading, this method should not be allowed. Nor should it be allowed if the liftboards do any more than merely pause anywhere in transit.[78]

The skin-of-the-dock rules involved unnecessary work even at the time they were imposed. Safety was invoked as a motive; specifically, the workers could be sure the goods would not spill or the load

77. See, for example, the Rosenshine award of July 26, 1938.
78. Roderick award of April 16, 1956.

collapse only by the requirement that all sling loads be built by long-shoremen. However, the chief objective was to maintain or expand employment and the prime movers were the rank and file. Unemployment was high during the first half-dozen years of the union's life and in the immediate post-World War II years. The casual labor market spread the loss of work widely throughout the longshore labor force; rank and file longshoremen were justifiably concerned with employment. Once established, the rules were maintained largely because their abandonment appeared to be associated with a large loss of employment opportunity.[79] As in the case of sling-load limits and direct informal control over work methods, multiple-handling rules were acquired and strengthened by resort to scores of "job actions."

Multiple-handling rules often were accompanied by requirements similar to the controls on manning and pace of work regulating shipwork. Dockwork gang size was specified for many goods in most ports; for example, four men were the minimum for break-bulk cargo in Los Angeles. Informal output controls were also applied. Los Angeles employers complained:

In addition . . . the employers have objected to the following practices encouraged by the union. . . . (a) Palletizers insisting on working at a predetermined rate, such as 2 cars of borax, 3 cars of cottonseed meal or 3 cars of cotton per day. (b) Refusal to start loading cargo onto stevedore pallet boards in situations where such cargo is brought to the dock by truck until all the truck's cargo has been placed upon the skin of the dock.[80]

Multiple handling requires a significantly larger input of labor for each ton of cargo. The added labor is not an absolute quantity, but varies with output. As was true with load limits and inflexible hold-gang manning, multiple-handling requirements bar technical change when strictly applied. Unitized loads and various containers were forestalled, especially in Los Angeles and Portland, by requiring the former to be broken and the latter to be emptied on the dock and refilled by longshoremen. An interesting variant, involving easier work but nonetheless a bar to technical change, developed in Portland. As usual, the union demanded that unitized loads be bro-

---

79. *The delegates to the longshore caucuses from 1956 through 1960 repeatedly emphasized employment in their arguments against giving up the rules. See below, pp. 82–100.*
80. Study of Harbor Conditions, *p. 153.*

ken down and rebuilt on the docks. The arbitrator agreed that the union was justified in its demands, "But rather than tearing the crates apart and reloading the cargo, it was stated by the arbitrator that they could be loaded as they were if the employers would pay for the time it would have taken to rebuild the loads, which the committee agreed would be four hours for four men." [81]

Multiple-handling requirements, however, were not always strictly applied; they varied from port to port, and they did change over time. The requirements were most extensive and inflexible in Los Angeles, and nearly as stringent in Portland. In these two ports a substantial amount of unnecessary work was required, and prepalletization, unit loads, and small containers were almost completely barred. (In Portland and nearly all the other Northwest ports, bulk goods and logs are a large proportion of the tonnage handled and provide most of the longshore employment. Thus, although Portland did indeed require multiple handling for break-bulk goods, those goods were relatively unimportant to the total.) The rules were rather stringently applied to much of the break-bulk goods in Seattle as well, but containers were permitted by agreement in 1953. By the end of the decade a large proportion of Seattle's nonbulk tonnage — the Alaska trade — was unitized or in containers and thus escaped multiple handling.

On the other hand, the union in the San Francisco area had given up much of its dockwork manning and multiple-handling practices during World War II; on the eve of the 1960 agreement the San Francisco requirements were the least restrictive of the major ports. Unit loads generally were permitted. Employer attempts to shift to prepalletized cargo — eliminating at several points the piece-by-piece handling of cartons, bags, or other packages — were met not by prohibition but by compromise. Some fraction of the loads, alleged to be improperly or unsafely built, would be repalletized, and all loads in excess of the stipulated sling-load limits would be "skimmed" — some of the cartons or other packages removed from the load to reduce it to the contract schedule limit. The result was to require more labor than would have been used without the rules, but less than was necessary with the flat insistence that only longshoremen may palletize cargo to be loaded on the ships.

81. *Murray award of March 12, 1956.*

Manning scales on many special operations, usually involving bulk handling of various goods, often were used to illustrate longshore featherbedding. In the 1955 Congressional hearings dealing with the southern California ports, an industry spokesman described the situation with respect to loading iron and steel scrap:

It is my understanding that in that kind of an operation only two men are required on the ship in connection with the hatch where the scrap is being dumped. Those two men are employed, if I understand the operation correctly, in guiding the container carrying the scrap to the chute. Nevertheless, the employers are obliged in that operation to employ 4 additional longshoremen, and I think on occasion 6, who literally have nothing to do but stand by while the operation is going on.[82]

The four or six holdmen required for each hatch in fact had very little work to do. The six, or twelve, or even more redundant men on the ship (depending on the number of hatches being worked, the commodity, and the port) played cards, napped, went for a beer, or simply stayed out of the way for most of their shift. At most, they uncovered and covered the hatches, helped position and move the chute if one was used, and cleared jams in the chute if any occurred. Work time might be as little as a few minutes to no more than a few hours in an eight- or nine-hour shift.

In different circumstances, a critic of the union and its part in the 1960 agreement — largely on the grounds that he believed the younger men to be insufficiently protected against harder work and unemployment — described the first containerized operation on the Pacific Coast: "On the day that I watched the loading of the *Hawaiian Citizen*, during the waning hours of the old contract, several of the "witnesses" (the redundant men in the longshore gangs) were snoozing and chatting just aft of the number two hatch."[83]

Other bulk or special operations — involving iron ore, nonferrous ores, grain of various kinds, animal feeds, and other similar goods handled with mechanized, capital-intensive techniques — were similarly overmanned.

Special operations have in common the fact that the goods may be loaded or discharged with more or less labor intensity as methods

82. Study of Harbor Conditions, *p. 164.*
83. *Harvey Swados, A Radical's America (Boston, 1962), p. 50. Swados, however, is sympathetic. He adds: "Since I do not have to meet a payroll, I am so far from feeling that there is anything shocking about this I incline to the belief that maybe we would all live longer if there were more of it."*

and the amount of capital applied vary. Iron and steel scrap, for example, may be loaded by shoveling the pieces from a truck to tubs or scows. The tubs are lifted aboard ship and lowered to the hold by the ship's gear, and the scrap dumped in the hold and trimmed by shovel gangs. The method clearly resembles conventional break-bulk handling, and reasonably could require twelve to sixteen or more men.[84] Alternatively, the scrap may be lifted by shoreside cranes directly from a truck or railcar and dropped, using a chute, to the hold. Trimming is reduced if not eliminated by the equipment; any remaining trimming necessary may be done by a bulldozer or a few shovelers.

Manning could be any number from three or four to the conventional break-bulk gang of sixteen or so men for each hatch. The union could have insisted, for example, that the sixteen-man gang associated with the most labor-intensive combination of labor and capital be used under all circumstances. In fact, however, the union usually permitted reductions in manning and pace-of-work requirements to accompany the increased capital input, but not so much as to reach the technological least-cost combination. In the Los Angeles area, continuing with the iron and steel scrap illustration, the local rules required ten men to each hatch for gantry crane and magnet operations. For years some of the employers sought reductions to the apparent least-cost combination of four men, but others were prepared to compromise at six.[85]

Similar manning scales were applied in nearly every port where and when substantial capital was used in a cargo-handling operation. Ore, newsprint, grain, packaged lumber, and other goods handled in large quantities were worked with negotiated manning and methods ranging from only slight alteration of the conventional break-bulk standards to half or even a third of the conventional manning, and an average output far above the conventional method rates.[86] In

---

84. *The Murray award of June 27, 1956, describes this procedure in connection with a dock-manning dispute in Portland. The situation in Los Angeles is described in ILWU,* Proceedings of the Longshore, Shipclerk and Walking Boss Caucus, *April 1956, pp. 357–358.*

85. *See, for example,* Study of Harbor Conditions, *p. 164 ff.*

86. *Special operations manning is described, or was determined, in numerous arbitration cases, labor relations committee meetings, and so on. Reasonably recent illustrations include the Kagel awards of March 7, 1955, July 29, 1955, January 16, 1956, Ziskind award of April 17, 1959, and Roderick award of February 4, 1959.*

most cases, the manning scale included a significant proportion of "witnesses."

Manning on special operations and much of multiple handling and related practices do not fit well in the analyses of previously described rules. They clearly do not require fixed labor inputs. Although the rules do require more than the technically efficient labor inputs, given factor prices, and are restrictive by definition, they are no longer fixed-proportions rules. They are most appropriately treated as a third kind of rule — the negotiated production function — which attempts to retain part, but only part, of the employment that otherwise would be lost upon adoption of new methods or the shift to more capital.

Analytically, this variety of rule requires inefficient factor proportions — capital and labor — at all output levels and all factor prices. It does, however, permit capital-for-labor substitution. An important consequence, and distinguishing characteristic, of the negotiated production function rule is that its elimination may result, for a given output level, in reductions in employment and costs and increases in productivity, with no increase in investment. The lifting of the constraint leads to the elimination of the redundant labor inputs, and no change or only slight changes in the input of capital. That is, the result is analogous to a change in technology such that all inputs are more efficient than they were before the change.

The negotiated production function is the most important analytical view of the effects of work rules in longshoring. Not only does it describe realistically the approach of the union and employers when the rules were imposed or modified, but the consequences of rule abandonment, discussed in subsequent chapters, are consistent only with this analytical interpretation.

A minor element in job control, but important in cargo-handling costs, are the union-won changes in hours of work and hours paid. The hiring hall played a central role here as it did in many other changes in the employment relationship. The six-hour day was written into the first award establishing relations between employers and the union. The union quickly, and unilaterally, converted that provision from a device to increase leisure or to mitigate unemployment to one providing larger incomes to longshoremen. Employers found, in 1935, that they could not hire second-shift gangs to report at the end of the day shift's first six hours. In contract renewal negotiations in 1936 the employers asked for two six-hour shifts, both at straight-time pay, or one eight-hour shift at straight time, all other working time to be paid at overtime rates. But after the strike they agreed, in effect, to a nine-hour standard day shift; six hours were paid at straight-time rates, three hours at overtime. This arrangement continued unchanged until 1958.

Before and during the union drive for recognition, longshoremen complained of substantial amounts of unpaid time required by some jobs, such as time spent traveling to remote docks. The union demanded and eventually won payment for travel time and expenses of travel between the hiring hall and docks more than several miles away. In San Francisco the work rules adopted in January 1935 provided for expense and pay for time traveled when longshoremen were dispatched to vessels in stream or outside the city of San Francisco. By June 1935 the Portland work rules provided an extra payment to compensate for time and expenses for workers dispatched to work in Vancouver. Seattle rules allowed travel-time pay and expenses in May 1935. Los Angeles lagged, but the union won travel-time and expense pay by 1939.[87]

Employers tried to reduce paid dead time involved in traveling by demanding the establishment of branch hiring halls in some ports. The original award created hiring halls in each of the four major Pacific ports and left to further negotiations the issue of halls in smaller parts. Halls were established eventually in the small ports far from the large cities, but the union never agreed to branch halls in or near the large ports. At one time southern California employers pressed to arbitration their demand for a branch hall in Long Beach, whose docks are within eight miles of the Los Angeles harbor area. The Coast Arbitrator denied their claim, pointing out that the hiring hall was an important institution, and the branch hall would divide the port workers and perhaps be a source of job inequities.[88]

One other element of the work environment deserves mention. Selig Perlman was impressed by the union membership of foremen in the printing trades, and he regarded this as added evidence of a high degree of job control by the union. The ILWU also includes the foremen within its ranks. The gang bosses are the lowest level

87. *Stalmaster award of June 19, 1959.*
88. *Morse award of June 17, 1940.*

supervisors and are members of the longshoremen's locals; indeed, they are often the most influential subgroup within the local. Walking bosses supervise cargo handling for a whole ship, or a large part of it. Unlike gang bosses, walking bosses are permanent employees of a stevedoring company. However, they are members of the ILWU, but in locals separate from the longshoremen. In most ports men promoted to walking boss must be, at time of promotion, members in good standing of the longshoremen's local at the port.

SUMMARY

The Pacific Coast longshoremen and their union acquired an extremely high degree of job control. Further, nearly all the important elements were won during the first half-dozen years of the union's existence. The principal tactics adopted by the union were economic — several coastwide strikes of long duration and hundreds of smaller, local job actions. The motivation for seeking most of the rules and practices was in large part the dissatisfaction of the workers themselves. Chronic underemployment, extremely irregular hours and earnings, market and employer pressure for greater effort relative to earnings, and other grievances disposed the rank-and-file longshoremen to become members of the union, and then to force substantial changes in the work environment. The casual nature of the labor market and the structure of the competitive product market required the union to seek a large measure of job control in order to survive and function as an effective institution. Limits to entry to the occupation and control over the effort wage were especially necessary institutional goals.

Interestingly, among longshoremen in the United States the strong and unabashed drive for full job control came from the leftists, not the conservative "business" unionists. Longshoremen on all the seacoasts of the country were unionized and reestablished collective bargaining at about the same time. The ILWU was led, at least in part, by men with left-wing views, whereas the ILA continued to be dominated by conservatives. The Pacific Coast union sought and won job control very quickly. The Eastern union did neither; the New York harbor area, for example, was not decasualized until 1954 — twenty years after the Pacific Coast — and even then only under government pressure and government auspices.

There is little doubt that leaders and members of the union extended jurisdictional claims and clung to many work practices that were constraints on cargo-handling efficiency because they appeared to maintain employment at higher levels. In the depression, with millions of men out of work, the featherbedding of multiple handling and opposition to man-displacing changes in cargo-handling techniques appeared to be reasonable. The members' interest in maintaining employment is direct and obvious. The leaders' interest, recognizing their ideological inclinations, is less obvious. Perhaps they saw the restrictive rules, as did Harvey Swados, as "an employer contribution to the struggle against rising mass unemployment," and "a defensible principle . . . for a radical union which sees it as a holding action."[89] Once adopted, the rules and practices tended to remain as a result of the fear of many of the officials and workers that rule elimination would sharply reduce employment and earnings opportunities.

A widely accepted view of the origin of the restrictive nature of work rules is that the union wins rules that are reasonable at the time they are first established. The steady progress of technical change gradually, or perhaps even quickly, renders them restrictive. For example, Slichter, Healy, and Livernash assert:

Make-work rules do not usually begin as attempts by unions to force employers to hire an excessive number of workers. There may have been agreement between union and management as to the desirable size of crews, or management may have made the decision unilaterally. Then if technological changes reduce the number of workers needed, it is natural for the union to resist the employer's effort to dispense with the unneeded employees. The result is a make-work policy. . . . Technological change and the struggle of the men to keep their jobs bring into existence a make-work policy.[90]

This view generally does not apply to Pacific Coast longshoring. Many of the practices were restrictive at the outset. Employers often used larger sling loads in 1934 and 1935 than those specified in the 1937 agreement. Multiple-handling rules clearly involved multiple handling at the time they were adopted. Break-bulk standard manning was not inherently restrictive, but coupled with load limits and informal work-pace controls — the latter a deliberate slowing down

89. *Swados, p. 54.*
90. *Impact of Collective Bargaining, pp. 317–318.*

of the speed of work — they became an element of restriction, and at a very early date. A substantial number of the manning scales on special operations, including those instances in which the union granted concessions, were restrictive at the moment the rules were established or modified. Both parties accepted the solutions as compromises.

Finally, the early and persistent employer complaints of decreased average productivity as a result of union policies and work practices are credible. Despite some of its denials in negotiations and for public consumption, the union intended, with many of the rules, to slow the pace of work or to require more men than would have been used without them. The prevention of excessive fatigue, adherence to safety standards, preservation of jurisdiction and work opportunities, establishment of uniform practices and labor costs, all were legitimate and believable motives. However, there is no natural barrier or clear boundary between praiseworthy protective rules and objectionable restrictive ones. The evidence strongly suggests that at least some of the rules slipped from the first category to the second.

III | THE MECHANIZATION AND MODERNIZATION AGREEMENT

The employers' last outright attack on union job control led to their defeat and drastic reorganization (as the Pacific Maritime Association) in 1948. In the years that followed, Pacific Coast employers never again tried confrontation and conflict to win back the managerial authority on the docks that they had given up bit by bit in the years before.

The first few years after 1948 were good ones for the maritime industry. The Korean War stimulated Pacific Coast shipping substantially. All branches of the trade benefited, not just the trans-Pacific routes. Within three years, by 1951, coastwise trade tonnage had tripled. Intercoastal and foreign trade, considerably larger than coastwise in 1948, nonetheless increased by more than 50 percent in the same period. Trade with offshore U.S. territories increased as well, but less sharply. Employment in the maritime trades was high, and nearly all fears of a serious postwar depression had vanished. The 1951 agreement between the employers' association and the longshore union was negotiated peacefully; settlement was reached before the date of expiration of the preceding contract. Changes were chiefly in wages and fringe benefits; day-to-day relations on the docks were unaffected. There were relatively few job actions or other minor disputes during this period.

IMPETUS TO CHANGE

The shipping boom, especially for American-flag ship operators, soon ended. Dry-cargo tonnage in foreign trade dropped by 25 percent from 1952 to 1953. It continued at a low level through the next year, then it began to rise, but only slowly. Domestic trade barely held steady during the immediate post-Korean War period. In 1955, Pacific ports handled about the same overall volume as four years earlier. The American-flag operators suffered not only from the general drop in trade but also from severe foreign competition as the

Norwegians, Japanese, and others replaced their wartime shipping losses. The number of ships covered by labor agreements negotiated by the Pacific Maritime Association dropped from about 400 in 1951 to 175 in 1955.

As a result of the cost squeeze, American ship operators took renewed interest in longshoring efficiency. The PMA research department undertook its first (but waterfront employers' third) major productivity study. More important, in October 1952, the PMA launched the first of a long series of "conformance and performance" programs. The ship operators, through the PMA, exhorted each other and the stevedores to improve efficiency and reduce costs by requiring longshoremen to observe the collective agreement and work rules. They were challenging not the method and manning regulations, however restrictive, that had already been accepted in negotiations, but practices added by the men in some of the union locals. Early quits, late starts, prolonged coffee breaks, failure to use the grievance procedure resulting in illegal work stoppages, and the various "four on–four off" abuses were among the ship operators' complaints.[1]

Although the "four on–four off" practices originally were devices to lengthen the brief rest periods associated with the hook cycle in cargo handling, variations began to develop. Some of the men in a hold gang took their time off in larger blocks. Instead of working every other load coming to their side, and resting in between, the men alternated half-hour periods or longer. As the rest periods grew longer, many of the men began to leave the hold, and then even the ship, during their time off.

The four on–four off practices were most widespread in the Los Angeles-Long Beach harbors. One study of cargo-handling efficiency noted the very low proportion of time worked by the hold gangs in the Los Angeles harbor and described a variation of four on–four off in their accounting for the low figure.[2] One set of Congressional hearings dealt almost exclusively with idle-time practices of the Los Angeles longshoremen, including the four on–four off

1. *Interviews with union and industry officials. See also* Pacific Maritime Association, *Annual Report, 1953, 1954, and U.S. Congress,* Study of Harbor Conditions, *pp. 12, 154–158, 162–193.*
2. *National Research Council, Maritime Cargo Transportation Conference,* Cargo Ship Loading, *pp. 30–32. The authors also stated, incorrectly, that the Los Angeles–Long Beach area was the only U.S. port where this practice existed.*

variants.[3] Finally, the men themselves referred to the prevalence of the practices in southern California, often pointing out the notoriety the ports were gaining. For example, one Los Angeles delegate to the 1957 Longshoremen's Caucus referred to "people running off the job or sitting in the beer joint and bragging to some guy who possibly got laid off two days ago that 'I am making $4.00 an hour sitting here drinking beer.' And it is done every day." [4]

The practices of the holdmen were not unknown in other Pacific ports. In Coos Bay a hold gang was discharged by the employer because only two men were working each side while the other four men just sat and watched.[5] A caucus delegate from northern California noted: "in San Francisco . . . we have situations that even the Local officers cannot cope with, such as gang structure. We know it is 8-2-2 and 1 on a loading job, but we also know that 8-2-2 and 1 is on paper and not found in the ship's hold. Because there are 4 men in the ship's hold and 4 men in the coffee shed." [6] According to a Stockton union official, the situation could get even worse than in Los Angeles, where two men typically worked each side of the hold: "In our port, too, we have had four on and four off. . . . And we have had even the gangs split up and we had as many as just two men working, one on each side. And that wasn't good either, because the employer was right there looking down our back. Our bulk operation was the same thing. Two men would be down there for hours while the rest of the six men would be playing cards." [7]

The most irritating — to employers — extension of the four on–four off practices involved alternating half shifts. The team or man that worked the first half shift went home after the second half team or man had arrived to take over. Both teams claimed, and were paid for full shifts. This variant was most common on the night shifts, but it also included men other than the hold gangs. The same Stockton delegate quoted above noted: "We have had winch drivers

3. Study of Harbor Conditions.
4. ILWU Proceedings of the Longshore, Shipclerk and Walking Boss Caucus, April, 1957, pp. 98–99.
5. E. P. Murray award of December 18, 1952. The arbitrator found that the men had properly been discharged. He observed that he had been a practical longshoreman and that it was almost always possible for all eight holdmen to to work at the same time.
6. ILWU, Caucus Proceedings, April, 1958, p. 234. (The numbers in the quote refer to eight holdmen, two winch drivers, two slingmen and one gang boss.)
7. ILWU, Caucus Proceedings, March, 1956, pp. 457–58.

go home in the middle of the shift. One man will be driving her all night." [8]

None of the four on–four off practices were "legal" in the sense of being embodied in the contract or negotiated port working rules. The practices had grown and flourished under lax supervision, especially on the night shifts, or toleration by stevedores, who were themselves under pressure to let the ship sail.

The 1952 conformance and performance program failed, as did the 1953, 1954, and 1955 programs. The various PMA publications of the period repeat the refrain. In 1953, "The conformance and performance program, initiated in the Los Angeles-Long Beach area . . . did not produce as promising results as anticipated." And in 1954, "PMA had initiated a program of contract compliance which centered on . . . elimination of 'late starts and early quits' and the so-called 'four men on and four men off' practice." And in 1955, "the conformance program was reactivated in the Long Beach-Los Angeles area in July, with concerted effort directed towards the elimination of the so-called 'four-on and four-off' practice." [9]

Employer self-interest was responsible, in large part, for the frustration of the various programs. Not all ship operators were equally concerned. Rather than risk delaying their ships, they instructed their stevedores to accede to local union pressure and to work the ships. On their own behalf the stevedores were less than enthusiastic. The late J. Paul St. Sure, President of the PMA from early 1952 to 1966, testified to a Congressional committee:

We found almost immediately [after starting the 1952 effort] that, particularly among the stevedoring group up and down the coast, they said, "Well, PMA members aren't our only clients. We serve foreign lines, we serve eastern lines, and we are going to find it very difficult to maintain a firm position for the enforcement of the contract for our PMA clients and at the same time have our eastern clients and our foreign clients tell us that they want the ships to sail."

The West Coast ship operators accepted the stevedores' position that enforcement under the 1952–1954 conditions was impossible. The union would not accept one set of work rules on some ships but more stringent ones on others. If four on–four off practices were tolerated

8. Ibid.
9. PMA, Annual Report, *1953, 1954, and 1955.*

by any ship operators or stevedores in a harbor, they had to be accepted by all. In 1954 the PMA instituted a plan to reimburse ship-operating companies in the event of a ship's delay brought on by enforcing the contract with respect to illegal work stoppages, elimination of the four on–four off practices, and early quits and late starts. The PMA passed a bylaw providing for a special assessment if necessary to raise the funds to support the program. The scheme failed. As of late 1955, St. Sure noted:

No single claim for reimbursement has been made. I can say that in reverse: Nobody seems to have taken the risk involved in connection with an enforcement program which would involve a loss. At least, there have been no claims made for losses in this connection.[10]

The growing malaise of the shipping industry in the years following the Korean War concerned more than the ship owners. In 1954 the mayor of Los Angeles appointed a committee to investigate complaints by businessmen and others about the city-owned harbor. These complaints alleged that some ship operators were bypassing the port, others were threatening to impose surcharges, and that cargo was being diverted because harbor conditions were so poor. The committee report detailed a long list of union malpractices, reproduced some of the complaints received, and noted the relatively higher costs of loading and unloading cargo at Los Angeles–Long Beach than elsewhere.[11] This was not the end of the matter. The U.S. House of Representatives Committee on Merchant Marine and Fisheries held an extensive series of hearings during 1954–1956, which dealt in large part with Pacific Coast longshore practices and conditions.[12]

The October 1955, hearings, led by Chairman Herbert C. Bonner of North Carolina, looked into the complaints of business and municipal officials in the Los Angeles–Long Beach harbor area. The

---

10. Study of Harbor Conditions, pp. 395, 398.
11. Reproduced in ibid., pp. 9–15.
12. In addition to the Study of Harbor Conditions, see U.S. Congress, House of Representatives, Committee on Merchant Marine and Fisheries, West Coast Maritime Industries Survey, Hearings, October 1–14, 1954, 83rd Cong., 2nd sess. (Washington, 1954); Labor Management Problems of the American Merchant Marine, Hearings, June 20–July 20, 1955, 84th Cong., 1st sess. (Washington, 1955); and Labor-Management Problems of the American Merchant Marine, Hearings, March 12, 1956, 84th Cong., 2nd sess. (Washington, 1956).

committee gathered evidence on the relative efficiency of cargo handling in the Los Angeles–Long Beach harbor and looked for the causes of the complaints. Despite a good bit of data, the evidence on productivity was not conclusive. At best, it appeared to indicate that the tonnages handled per man-hour in Los Angeles were lower than in other ports by perhaps 20 percent. However, accepting rather lower productivity and higher costs in the port as facts, the committee sought explanations. Employer statements led to a large amount of testimony on gang shortages, work stoppages, and a number of practices outside the contract involving idle time — early quits, prolonged washup time, extended coffee breaks, and the various four on–four off practices.[13]

Although the employers' complaints were principally of various contract violations, the members of the committee noticed and questioned practices sanctioned by the contract that appeared to hamper efficiency. On multiple handling, the committee counsel emphasized the waste:

Mr. CASEY. Now, am I correct in saying that the employers feel this palletizing operation is completely unjustified from the economic or any other standpoint?

Mr. PAUL. [attorney for the southern California waterfront employers] That is their feeling.

Later in the hearings, he took up the matter with the president of the union's Local 13, George Love:

Mr. CASEY. I know it [multiple-handling] has been the practice. I am talking about the justification for the practice.

Mr. LOVE. Well, I said that there is no justification from a practical view point and standpoint of taking it off the board and putting it on the skin of the dock and then taking it and putting it on another board. We agree it is not practical.

Mr. CASEY: So can we agree that that is one practice that can be corrected?

Mr. LOVE. That's right.

A member of the committee was adversely impressed by sling-load limits and handling practices in the hold; after questioning the Local's president, he commented,

13. Study of Harbor Conditions, *pp. 71–80, 98–102, 152, 229–283.*

I just make this observation as a layman, and admittedly not knowing the problems of either the industry or the longshoremen; but it would seem to me that certainly that was not an efficient operation.[14]

Finally, outsiders — the Maritime Cargo Transportation Conference of the National Research Council — began in 1953 an extensive program of research dealing with longshore productivity and various techniques to improve efficiency and to reduce costs. The studies were instigated by high costs in cargo handling, and the research was intended to inform and provide data for policy to the industry and government.[15]

The union was clearly under pressure. In the interests of maintaining viable collective bargaining the top officers could only agree to try to stop the practices violating the agreement; employer representatives repeatedly countered union demands in negotiations with insistence that the contract be observed. New concessions would not be exchanged for empty promises. By 1955 the ILWU officers had apparently succeeded in convincing the local leadership; in the Bonner Committee hearings, testimony indicated that the idle-time practices had been anathematized, at least for that time, by the leadership. The committee counsel prodded the president of Local 13:

Mr. CASEY. However, if the practice of 4 on and 4 off should be practiced and a foreman or a stevedore should take action, disciplinary action, and knock the men off and send them back, he would be reasonably sure of the support of the union?

Mr. LOVE. Right now he is getting total and allout support.[16]

The Congressional investigations added to the pressure. The threat of harassment, if not restrictive legislation, was real. In the October 1955 hearings the committee justified its interest in longshore practices by noting that although longshore costs are not directly subsidized, the provisions for recapture of part of the ship operator's profits does give the government a financial stake in im-

14. Ibid., pp. 170, 288–289; Representative Elford A. Cederberg of Michigan, p. 227.
15. The first important study was The SS Warrior: An Analysis of an Export Transportation System from Shipper to Consignee (Washington, 1954). Meetings were held, papers presented, and a second major study, Cargo Ship Loading, was conducted during 1955–1957.
16. Study of Harbor Conditions in Los Angeles, p. 223. See also pp. 183–184.

proving efficiency in all segments of ocean cargo movement. In addition, the possibility of a public agency or regulatory commission was raised. Finally, Paul St. Sure, President of the PMA, asked the committee to consider seriously the establishment of a federal commission to deal with problems of maritime labor relations.[17]

Government intervention threatened not only the unilateral local practices violating the contract but also the negotiated work rules. Many of the members of the committee had no doubt about the need for changes in practices. Representative Thomas L. Ashley noted the "countless allegations as to inefficient operation on the part of longshoremen" and added:

I am wondering if any such studies [greater efficiency, technological change] are being made within the Longshoremen's Union. I am wondering just how much interest has been shown in positively attacking the problem which faces the waterfront, namely, the lack of production to the extent that it does exist in this port.

Moreover, in their cross-examination of the union's president, Harry Bridges, the committee drew an interesting admission, and promise:

Mr. BRIDGES. Let's put it this way: We know what they [the employers] want. The two operations, the unnecessary operations and so-called limit [multiple-handling and sling load limits]. Let's say we agree. And again I want to warn you. George Love agreeing here and me agreeing is one thing. Getting the people down there to do the work is another thing. You understand that.

Mr. ASHLEY. We appreciate that.

Mr. BRIDGES. But you have got our promise and the employers have got our promise that we will go down there and persuade and push and do our best. That's all we can promise. As an operation we think that is an uneconomical one and unnecessary and just means harder work for the fellows instead of easier work.[18]

MAKING THE AGREEMENT [19]

The first serious steps toward removing work rules and advocating mechanization came in 1956. Within five months of the October hearings, and almost concurrently with yet another hearing in

---

17. Ibid., pp. 409–410.
18. Ibid., pp. 301, 306, 359.
19. A good summary of the background of the 1960 negotiations and the agreement from the union point of view is Lincoln Fairley, "The ILWU-PMA Mechanization and Modernization Agreement," Labor Law Journal, XII (1961),

March 1956, the matter was brought before the Longshore Caucus of the union. The Coast Labor Relations Committee, in effect the top leadership of the longshore division of the union,[20] presented its report. The report referred to the conformance and compliance discussions between the committee and the PMA in 1954 and 1955 and reviewed the results of the hearings before the Bonner Committee:

It seems clear now that the general cooperative attitude displayed by the longshore locals in respect to contract compliance and the willingness of the rank and file members to make necessary adjustments in certain work practices were primarily responsible for convincing Congressman Bonner that the East Coast type bi-state legislation was not needed or workable on the West Coast. . . .

However, we doubt that the Coast negotiating committee will be able to consummate the next longshore contract without participating in a complete examination of all the problems that surround mechanization, both past and future, in the industry.[21]

Although the caucus was not primarily concerned with mechanization, conformance problems, or work rules, a good bit of discussion on the topics did occur. Significantly, Harry Bridges spoke at length on the problems and foreshadowed in large part the more famous report to the caucus in late 1957. Speaking to a resolution introduced by a Pacific Northwest local to retain the minimum gang on all operations, Bridges conceded that he was going to be "awfully unpopular." He noted that laborsaving devices were at the heart of the matter:

I would say that we have resisted the impact of labor-saving machinery, mechanization, automation, whatever you want to call it, possibly with greater success than any other organization. It has been a combination of

pp. 664–680. A good account from the employer's side is Pres Lancaster, "The ILWU-PMA Mechanization and Modernization Agreement," in Jerome W. Blood, ed., The Personnel Job in a Changing World (New York, 1964).

20. The Coast Labor Relations Committee consisted of the ILWU president, Harry Bridges, one elected member representing the Pacific Northwest, and one elected member representing southern California. The Coast Committee, together with three representatives of the PMA, constitute the Joint Coast Labor Relations Committee. The Joint Committee meets frequently on call by either party to adjust disputes of coastwide significance concerning contract interpretation or violation. In addition to Bridges, the Coast Committee members in 1956 were Howard Bodine, a member until his death in 1966, and L. B. Thomas, who resigned in 1962 to become one of the four area arbitrators in the industry.

21. ILWU, Caucus Proceedings, March, 1956, pp. 194–195, 202–203.

ways and means of doing things and it has involved strikes, slow-downs and what-not. However, we have reached the point possibly, and some of the demands that you are putting in (take this resolution, for example) and some other proposals for changes reflect the feeling that you have reached the point, where the battle against the machine for us has become a losing one. And we can continue to fight a losing battle, and we will lose in more ways than one, and finally after we have thrown away a lot of energy and a lot of bargaining power we will put on a showdown, last-stand fight, and we will lose that one, too.

Harking back to earlier struggles against innovations and loss of jurisdiction — lift boards, cranes, packaged loads, disputes with the sailors and teamsters — Bridges argued that continued fighting would only weaken the union. He urged flexibility, that the union consider what it could gain by abandoning resistance. A new approach might involve permitting the employer to determine manning and to use any machinery or new devices. Then, in phrases he was to use often in subsequent caucuses, Bridges continued:

Starting with that, we can put on, then, some restrictions, after we follow the premise. And here is where we start to bargain and demand our share or cut or what-have-you. And the kind of cut or share we should demand should be a share for the people who are left on the job, not the kind of a demand to retain people on the job. We don't go without any restrictions, of course: some safeguards. And it is a damn difficult problem to face up to, but we have to start swinging over to where we have to protect the interests of the people who are going to be left and to put less and less in it at the expense of the people who will have to remain on the job, trying to keep on the job those who are, you might say, dispensable under the new order of things.[22]

Bridges' approach was not well received by the delegates. Although most of the speakers on the topic favored mechanization because it made the work easier, they definitely rejected the idea of giving up men on the job. Opposition was not impassioned, but the speakers against Bridges' views came from many ports — Stockton, the Oregon Coast, and Portland as well as Los Angeles. A stronger reaction than the usual was the position of a Los Angeles delegate,

We have relinquished enough men. . . . It cost us plenty right in the San Pedro area, like on the crane operation, the bulk operation. There are the banana conveyors down there, there is the copra conveyor, there are pack-

22. Ibid., pp. 425, 427, 437.

aged loads of lumber. Christ! We have given them enough. Let's stop it. We don't have to give them any more.[23]

The caucus approved the resolution to attempt to maintain standard gangs and voted down a motion to appropriate funds to establish a committee to explore the mechanization issue.

Reaffirming the objective of shorter hours was the one positive action relevant to the broader issue taken by the caucus in 1956. The Coast Committee explicitly tied the shorter work shift to mechanization. Their report noted that the shorter workday perhaps could be won only by concessions on mechanization. L. B. Thomas advocated shorter hours as a means to absorb some of the men displaced by adoption of a mechanization program. The caucus rejected a motion to try for seven-hour shifts, but adopted the Coast Committee's recommendation to seek an eight-hour shift.[24]

The two-year coastwide agreement was due to expire in June 1956. The parties met in May and quickly settled a number of minor issues. They held the shorter shift issue open for June talks and put over until September final negotiations on wages. The wage talks were postponed, then prolonged, in an effort by the union to win a common contract expiration date and wage parity with the ILA longshoremen. The desire for the common action was stronger on the part of the ILWU than the ILA, and the attempts at the common contract expiration date gradually were given up. Wage parity had been, and continued to be, approximately maintained.[25] In general the 1956 agreement followed the pattern of contracts in the immediately preceding years, which were basically extensions of the 1951 contract with changes in the wage scale and some rather minor revisions of penalty cargo rates and vacation benefits. The parties agreed, however, to a significant exception: negotiations were to begin on hours and workshifts with a full exploration of work practices and questions of mechanization and manpower.[26]

The union attempt to win the eight-hour shift failed. In June the employers rejected the demand on the grounds that the union had been unable to live up to its promises on conformance and per-

---

23. Ibid., pp. 46 ff, pp. 463–464.
24. Ibid., pp. 203, 654.
25. Wage movements and the attempted rapprochement between the two unions during this period is discussed in detail in Harold M. Levinson, Determining Forces in Collective Wage Bargaining, pp. 193–198.
26. Memorandum of Understanding, May 25, 1956.

formance. The employers agreed, however, to keep the matter open for discussions later in the year, contingent upon better performance by the union in eliminating contract violations. The employers also wanted to tie multiple handling and "restrictive and make-work rules above those already mentioned" to the eight-hour day. In September the employers categorically rejected the demand. Paul St. Sure noted that "We are not getting conformance," and turned down further negotiations for the year on the issue.[27]

In the April 1957 Caucus the union leadership linked the frustration of progress in winning improvements in conditions to the failure of some of the members to comply with the existing agreements. The Coast Committee pointed out the failure to conform in its report, and Harry Bridges spoke bitterly about the possible consequences.

Now it is about time that we got this down below. . . . 'Look, if you want four on, four off, put it in the contract. . . .' If you are going to keep those things, you are going to strike for them. . . . Four consecutive negotiations we have guaranteed in writing to cut it out, and we have guaranteed it in writing as a condition of extending the contract, getting pensions, welfare and wage increases . . . . When this contract ends it is not going to be renewed unless these things are straightened out. So the whole coast is going to get a whirl at it. The whole Coast! And if we want the things, they are going to be written in the contract. Four on and four off. . . .

We had another little action too that I want to remind you of. A congressional committee, with a lot of power, got rolling and they had a monstrosity of a law in there against the maritime labor movement. That was the Bonner Committee. . . .

They took a tour around the harbor. They looked at a lot of things. Four on, four off. . . .

The key behind the whole thing was that Bonner was going to pass a law saying that no government funds could be spent for this kind of stuff. That wouldn't have been any battle between the Union and the Employers. We were head on into a battle with the Government on a bum issue, an issue you couldn't win.[28]

---

27. Minutes of the Joint Negotiating Committee, *June 6, 1956, p. 5; June 7, 1956, pp. 1, 2; September 11, 1956, p. 2.* Verbatim records of negotiations are not kept. Each party does summarize the negotiations for its own use. All references to negotiations in this study are to the union's records.
28. ILWU, Caucus Proceedings, April, 1957, pp. 82–83, 84–85. The relatively few speakers to Bridges' topic supported him.

Mechanization and the eight-hour day were again put before the delegates. The Coast Committee recommendation to press for the eight-hour day passed with very little debate. Mechanization — including jurisdiction and work rules as well as new methods — was discussed at some length. In general, the delegates from Los Angeles and Stockton, occasionally supported by one or another Portland man, were in favor of a strong stand to retain existing rules and even to try to regain work lost by the prepalletization of loads in warehouses away from the docks. Delegates from the lumber ports and San Francisco tended to support a program of exchanging current restrictions for benefits. A motion was adopted to refer the matter to the Coast Committee for investigation. The caucus voted to reconvene later in the year to consider more fully the matter of mechanization and related issues.

Negotiations in 1957 settled little. Technically the two-year contract signed in 1956 was open in 1957 only to negotiate wages. However, the parties devoted most of their time to other matters. The union's demand for the eight-hour day was again turned down. The PMA representatives again pointed out the lack of contract compliance, but St. Sure conceded, "We'll admit that we have been inept in any enforcement program." [29] The parties also deadlocked on wages and submitted both the eight-hour day and wage issues to arbitration. [30]

The most interesting feature of the 1957 meetings was the preliminary negotiations on the mechanization and modernization-program. In a series of "off the record" talks, [31] the negotiating committees explored abandoning some work rules and exchanged ideas and information. The union side made it clear that it was willing to give up work practices hampering mechanization in exchange for guarantees of jurisdiction over the new methods and machines and guarantees for maintaining the current work force. The union spokesmen warned that giving up restrictions would cost money to the employers. The employers showed interest, but the failure of their

29. Minutes of the Joint Negotiating Committee, May 16, 1957, p. 3.
30. Professor of Law, Sam Kagel, University of California School of Law, Berkeley, has been the Coast Arbitrator for the industry since 1948. His June, 1957, award denied the union the eight-hour shift but granted wage increases.
31. The parties referred to these sessions as "off the record." However, the union did keep summary notes of the meetings, perhaps a bit less adequately than for the regular sessions, and has permitted me their use.

conformance programs made them reluctant to concede benefits for a work-rules relaxation that might prove illusory. The then-existing rules were already less restrictive than actual practices in some ports, and the employers sought guarantees that their financial sacrifice would actually bring about more efficient performance on the docks. The informal talks were frank, amicable, and fruitful.[32] They ended when the parties decided to change the subject and to resume negotiations on wages and hours.

In October, 1957, the caucus took up the widely publicized Coast Committee report on mechanization and modernization.[33] The report was dispassionate, rather scholarly in tone. It described recent developments and estimated likely changes in the near future in cargo-handling techniques. The report noted that bulk handling had been instituted recently in some ports for several commodities. Although these methods were tremendously laborsaving, not much additional displacement of longshoremen from this source was expected; few goods with the appropriate physical characteristics were handled in sufficient volume at Pacific ports. More serious inroads were likely from the various kinds of unit loads — strapped bundles, cribs, vans, and other devices. The shipment of lumber, much of the trade to Alaska, and military goods were increasingly moving in one or another form of unit load. According to the authors of the paper: "There is nothing, except our unwillingness to handle them, which prevents a very considerable increase in unit loads, made up by the shipper." [34]

The report then took up the principal restrictive work rules. It pointed out that inflexibility in manning requirements did exist and that the inflexibility could lead to employer demands to do away with the standard ship gang. However, a more serious problem was multiple handling. A significant reduction of longshore work was

32. *In his June, 1957, arbitration award Professor Kagel commented: "The record in this case is conclusive that the P.M.A. and the I.L.W.U. have evolved a relationship which is marked by candidness and forthrightness in their dealings. The evidence is clear that there is an abundance of good faith and mutual respect. Most important is the fact that the parties have isolated the problems that require immediate and constant attention. 'Conformance and performance,' mechanization, new methods, manpower and others."*

33. *ILWU, "Coast Labor Relations Committee Report," October 15, 1957. The Coast Committee report was reproduced and has been widely circulated and discussed in articles by Fairley, Kossoris, Lancaster, and others, cited elsewhere in this study.*

34. *Ibid., p. 9.*

likely to result from its elimination — as much as 11 percent. The report estimated that about one third of the dockwork hours were involved in multiple handling and dockwork represented about one third of all longshore work. Some ports would be harder hit than others; possible jurisdictional conflict with the Teamsters complicated the matter. Finally, rules or informal practices permitting extreme specialization and rigidity in job assignment — palletizing gangs will not do depalletizing, and so on — very likely would accelerate employer-directed changes to new methods to eliminate dock work. The report reviewed the current policy of resistance to change.

Locals try to avoid using the grievance machinery for fear that decisions will go against us. What takes place then is job action and the economic threat of tying up or delaying a ship in order to try to keep the usual number of men on the job or to force more men on the job along with the introduction of machinery.

The method worked, but:

As to how long it will continue to work in the future and what it may cost in the way of overall improvements in the wages, hours and working conditions to keep it working is a matter that warrants serious consideration by the caucus.

The basic issue was whether to continue resistance, or to turn to a different policy "in order to buy specific benefits in return." The report recommended that the leaders of the union and the Coast Committee be authorized to pursue unofficial negotiations with the employers.[35]

The caucus discussed the report for nearly two days. Opposition was stronger than in earlier caucuses. A delegate from Portland objected to attempts to hurry the report through. Two speakers from the southern California local voiced some distrust of the leadership. It appeared to them as if the top leaders wanted to negotiate the important matter on their own. The heaviest opposition came from Local 13 of Los Angeles–Long Beach harbor. The main arguments were that the members had a lot to lose by giving up the rules, and that resistance was indeed a feasible program. One leader of Local 13 pointed out,

I come from a port that has perhaps the most to lose, if you please, if we go into a full mechanization program and we eliminate double handling

35. *Ibid., pp. 18, 11.*

or triple handling or quadruple handling. . . . In San Pedro everybody [*sic*] hits the skin of the dock both ways, on discharge and on load-out. The dock work in Los Angeles–Long Beach Harbor represents from 30 to 40 per cent of the work of the port. That is why I say that perhaps we have the most to lose of any Local on the Coast.

Another delegate from Local 13, speaking particularly to loss of work associated with unit and prepalletized loads, argued,

But there are certain amounts of that work that are going to have to be done somewhere along the line, and the more that we can keep on the docks the more guarantees and rights for our people.[36]

Supporters of the Coast Committee report rather outnumbered opponents. Probably the strongest supporters were the delegates from Local 10, San Francisco, but delegates from the smaller locals in the Pacific Northwest and from Portland and Seattle also spoke in favor of the new approach to mechanization and modernization. They argued that machinery made the work easier, and on that account was favored by the rank and file. The relevant issue was not whether to try to stop progress, but how to reap the benefits. Typical of this view was the statement of a delegate from Local 10:

So what we have to consider here is getting our just share of the extra profits that the shipowners have been able to provide for themselves through mechanization of the operation; and the only genuine advance that we can make is by cutting down the number of hours we have to put on the job and make a living.[37]

Opposition softened as debate neared the end of the second day, and the Coast Committee's report and recommendation for informal talks were adopted by voice vote.

The first solid evidence that the parties genuinely intended to solve the problem of obsolete work rules came in 1958. In the preceding year the employers had begun to study and to discuss among themselves the probable benefits from changes in work methods and manning. The Pacific Maritime Association undertook preliminary collection and analysis of data with which they hoped to assess productivity changes. In 1958, employer representatives met with union leaders to discuss the issues, and letters were exchanged. Some firms

36. *ILWU*, Caucus Proceedings, October, 1957, pp. 65, 75–76, 73–75, 120.
37. Ibid., p. 88.

began planning or actually started investment programs to take advantage of the coming new conditions.

The informal talks between the employer and union representatives in late 1957 and early 1958 had made progress. In a letter to be used as a basis for further talks the union spelled out what it was prepared to give up:

We propose to discuss cargo handling operations as a whole, including introduction of new methods, expansion of present methods, removal or modification of existing restrictions which hamper output, with and without mechanization or additional investment in machinery, facilities and equipment.

In return, the union sought:

To preserve the present registered force of longshoremen as the basic work force in the industry, and to share with that force a portion of the net labor cost saving to be effected by introduction of mechanical innovations, removal of contractual restrictions, or any other means.

The PMA, for its part, agreed that the union letter was the basis for discussions, and further noted:

At the meeting of November 29 [1957] we were also in general agreement that the Union proposal for the establishment of a coastwise fund was entitled to serious consideration, although PMA was not prepared to discuss any detailed proposal as to method or amount at that time.

A rather sticky problem in the talks again concerned a measure of productivity. The employers wanted to be sure that any new costs they incurred were going to be covered by actual improvements in efficiency. They insisted that a productivity measure had to be developed "as a first and essential step for continuing and concluding our discussions." [38]

The April 1958 Caucus discussed the mechanization talks and their progress. Bridges and Thomas limited discussion by pointing out that their only recommendation to this caucus was that the talks be continued. They assured the delegates that the talks were not negotiations, and that everyone would have the right to be heard when they were ready to go to serious negotiations. The recommendation

38. *Ibid., pp. 33–35, letter from the ILWU to the PMA, dated November 19, 1957, pp. 31–32, letter from PMA to ILWU, dated April 2, 1958.*

that the talks be continued "completely independent of the coming negotiations for a new Pacific Coast Longshore Agreement" carried.

Although the 1958 contract demands were kept apart from the informal broad-ranging talks, they were in fact related to mechanization. In addition to the almost perennial demand for an eight-hour shift the union leadership sought coastwide registration. The latter was a preparatory move to the eventual modernization agreement, designed to ease the transfer of men from one port to another. The Coast Committee members frankly pointed out to the 1958 Caucus delegates that coastwide registration would infringe on local autonomy in that the former privilege of admitting members as they saw fit would vanish. The caucus approved the proposed demand by a close vote on a show of hands. The proposal for an eight-hour day had by this time been around so long that many of the delegates refused to take it seriously. The southern California delegates thought it was "window dressing" and said so. A delegate from Local 13 clearly expressed the feelings of his constituents:

We are just going on the record for a shorter day, and let's not kid ourselves. You are not going to get an 8-hour day. And if you did, you would have the rank and file up here screaming at you. Because those guys are only interested in one thing under the present setup, and that is: How much money am I going to take home? [39]

The motion favoring the eight-hour shift carried unanimously.

The 1958 negotiations proceeded as anticipated. The union leadership did not expect the employers to be ready for serious negotiations on the modernization issues; they were right. The parties spent little time on that set of problems. The union demand for coastwide registration met little opposition and was quickly settled. Harry Bridges adroitly coupled the demand for the eight-hour shift to a demand for an eight-hour guarantee to replace the four-hour guarantee then in the contract.[40] The guarantee drew the employer counterdemand for work-force flexibility that they formerly had used against the eight-hour standard shift. No agreement was reached on exchanging flexibility — involving gear priority and the willingness of

---

39. Ibid., p. 294.
40. Bridges introduced the eight-hour guarantee near the very beginning of negotiations, on May 12. The caucus had not heard the proposal. The guarantee was to provide eight hours' pay or eight hours' work with pay to every man turned to work.

the men to shift from ship to ship—for the guarantee, and the demand was dropped. The employers granted the eight-hour shift in return for the union's promise that it would not extend ship turnaround time or increase "dead" time. The 1958 agreement was an extension of the basic 1951 contract, as amended, for one year. It again stated the parties' intent to continue discussions on mechanization.

The most dramatic development of 1958 was a surprise to the top negotiators. The resistance of some of the rank and file, and local leaders, to the trend of the union's programs broke into the open. When the locals were notified of the results of the 1958 negotiations, Locals 13 and 63 (a clerks' local), both of Los Angeles–Long Beach, rejected the proposed contract changes. At stopwork meetings the membership expressed heavy support for the retention of the nine-hour day, largely on the grounds that they did not want to reduce their take-home pay.[41] On July 11, 1958, the presidents of Locals 13 and 63 sent telegrams to the union negotiating committee informing them of the strong opposition in their locals—"unanimous" and "100 per cent." Local 13 urged that a special caucus be called immediately to deal with the hours question and sent telegrams to all longshoremen's and clerks' locals to solicit their support for calling a caucus before ratification.[42]

The negotiating committee, led by the ILWU officers, decided against calling a caucus, preferring a referendum vote on the contract changes as negotiated. The ballot split the issues: the eight-hour shift was separated from the ten-cent hourly wage increase, vacation improvements, and coastwide registration. The results were an extremely narrow victory for the eight-hour day—5,630 in favor, 5,430 against—but a rather more comfortable margin for the other provisions, 6,669 for, 4,350 against.[43]

Some employers stepped up their modernization programs. Matson Navigation Company had studied costs and techniques of various unit-load systems during the mid-1950's. In 1958–1959 the company began its program leading to construction of pier and terminal facilities and ship modification to convert a large part of the Hawaii trade to a fully containerized operation. Not directly an out-

41. *The standard nine-hour day included six hours at straight-time pay and three hours at overtime rates.*
42. Union Negotiating Committee Minutes, *July 11, 1958, pp. 1–2.*
43. *From the union files, "ILWU Referendum Ballot, Coastwise Contract, 1958."*

growth of the union and PMA talks, but nonetheless noteworthy, were the studies commissioned by the port authorities of Seattle and San Francisco to modernize their ports and the accelerated large-scale port development at Long Beach. Two of the Pacific Coast subsidy lines, Pacific Far East and States Steamship, also committed themselves to extensive ship replacement programs.

In 1959 the employers increased their pressure on the union. In February the PMA, strongly backed by most of the shipowners, launched its most recent conformance and performance program. Los Angeles and San Francisco were the first targets, and the Pacific Northwest ports were included in May. As before, the program intended to eradicate late starts, early quits, deliberate slowdowns, unreasonable relief periods, and the persistent four on–four off practices. For the first time, however, the program was at least partly successful. New tactics, and rare employer cooperation, were responsible for the change. A new employer institution — the Coast Steering Committee of the PMA — was created. Dominated by the shipowners, the committee developed and supervised the conformance program. It required regular reporting of contract violations, imposed penalties for the employer tolerating the illegal practices, and instituted the "grieved ship" technique. In the latter the employer faced with an illegal work stoppage declared a "grieved ship," all gangs were released from all ships in the harbor, and no replacement gangs were ordered except for the grieved ship. Industry officials pointed to a number of brief but portwide tie-ups as evidence of wide cooperation among shipowners and claimed success in the program.

The idea of a fund to which the employers would contribute as consideration for abandonment of work rules and resistance to new methods had been tentatively accepted by the employers in the 1957–1958 informal talks. In late 1958 and early 1959 the union's position on the fund became more specific, and the Coast Committee described the approach to the caucus delegates in April, 1959. The leadership wanted fund contributions to be tied to the man-hours saved, whatever the source of man-hour savings, and valued at the basic longshore straight-time hourly rate. They argued that the use of the straight-time rate would divide the monetary benefits of productivity increase about equally between the parties; the overtime premiums, fringe benefits, and payroll taxes not required as a result of the man-hour savings would be the employers' share.[44]

The caucus opposition to the whole program was sharper now than in earlier years. The delegates were generally in favor of receiving a large fraction of the savings from mechanization. However, some delegates doubted that the employers would give up so much. Others, perhaps now convinced that they were no longer talking about "window dressing," wanted to know specifically what they would have to give up — the "price" they would have to pay for the fund. Harry Bridges' response made it clear that the union would certainly give up multiple handling and excessive manning. The caucus delegates, many apparently still smarting from the shorter workday surprise of the preceding year, did not adjourn, but instead recessed until after the coming 1959 contract negotiations. The recess was proposed by a delegate from Local 8, Portland, and strongly supported by delegates from Local 13. Despite opposition from the ILWU officers, the motion carried.[45]

Informal talks became full-fledged negotiations again in the late spring of 1959. The parties seriously attempted to settle the modernization issues. The method of determining employer contributions to the fund was the chief obstacle. The employers were still interested in tying the contributions to realized productivity changes, but they were not prepared to agree to any specific formula. Payments tied to measured productivity gains met the past employer objections to lack of performance guarantees on the part of the union. However, at the time of the 1959 negotiations, the PMA was still having trouble gathering data for measuring productivity. Fewer than half the companies responded to 1958 requests for data. The employer representatives offered to "buy time." They agreed to put into a fund one and one-half million dollars during the coming year as a token of good faith and to liquidate the union's claim to a share in benefits from any changes taking place before June 15, 1960.[46]

In the August 1959 contract the parties formalized their earlier

44. See ILWU, Caucus Proceedings, April 1959, p. 179 ff. The 1959 average hourly labor cost, excluding payroll taxes, was about $4.00, and the basic straight-time rate was $2.74.

45. Ibid., pp. 316, 323. Most of the opposition speakers to the fund were from Local 13.

46. "Coast Committee Report," in the April, 1959, Caucus, pp. 178–179; Joint Negotiating Committee Minutes, June 17, 19, 30, and July 1, 1959.

informal agreement on objectives and principles. The employers accepted the union's contention that the work force had a right to share in the gains from increased productivity, they agreed to the establishment of the fund, and they conceded that to maintain the 1958 fully registered work force was a major objective. The union recognized its obligation to guarantee the employers the right to make changes in manning and methods of work. The parties allowed one year for further study of probable changes in operations, savings in man-hours and costs to employers, the proper share of the gains to be funded, and the manner of distribution of the fund to the work force.[47]

Technically, the 1959 agreement was to run for three years. Wages and the mechanization and modernization provisions were to be reopened in June 1960, and June, 1961. The parties agreed that should the reopened negotiations fail, the issues would go to arbitration. The arbitrator's authority would be limited, however; the employers' representatives agreed during the negotiations that he could not discontinue the fund, for example, but he could determine how large the contributions should be and the method by which they were to be raised.[48] Pending final settlement, work rules and practices were "frozen," not to be changed except by mutual agreement or the grievance procedure, where it was relevant. The existing contract, in Section 14 of the 1951 agreement as amended, provided that manning scales and related matters be negotiated when laborsaving devices or new machinery were introduced. The grievance procedure, including arbitration, was compulsory if negotiations failed. Leaders of both parties agreed that all other work rules and practices were not to be changed — that is, the "freeze" would continue — except as they were negotiated out of the agreements.[49] In addition to the declarations of intent and objectives, and provisions for a fund, the 1959 agreement included a wage increase and an eight-hour-minimum work or pay guarantee in exchange for a series of new provisions to bring about greater flexibility in work-force assignment.

The July caucus wanted to explore the modernization provisions

47. Memorandum of Agreement, *August 10, 1959.*
48. Joint Negotiating Committee Minutes, *July 18, 1959.*
49. *See especially* Ibid., *May 28, July 7, 1960.*

as well as the specific changes in the contract — the eight-hour guarantee being the most important. Delegates were interested in the fund, and some wanted assurances that it would eventually go into longshoremen's pockets, not "visionary schemes." When the leadership suggested that discussion be brief — they had only allotted a day and a half for the caucus — they were met with strong opposition from all the large locals. Debate continued. Opponents of work-rule abandonment concentrated much of their effort on attacking the work-force flexibility provisions associated with the eighthour guarantee. The shifting of gangs from ship to ship had been permitted under old contracts, but the new provisions permitted the employers to shift gangs from company to company, and they relaxed gear priority rules.[50] Opponents stressed the loss of the longcherished privilege of the longshoreman to pick his own job. However, the vote on the total package — the fund, the mechanization and modernization objectives, and the other contract provisions — reflecting strong approval. Weighted by the membership of the locals, the roll-call result was 105 9/21 in favor of the package, 45 12/21 against.

Preparations, study, and dialogue between factions within each side filled the months until formal negotiations opened again in May, 1960. Although the ILWU and PMA leaders had agreed on the main points involved in the exchange of restrictive work practices for monetary employer contributions, the remaining details were not easily settled. In the union a thorny problem concerned the purpose and disposition of the fund to be created. Among the employers the tying of fund contributions to productivity was hotly disputed. In both camps, strong opposition still remained to any agreement on the whole issue.

The 1960 discussions and negotiations were a continuation of the preceding years' activities, only greatly intensified. Negotiating sessions between the union and employer representatives were more numerous. The parties met formally for more than forty sessions. The caucuses were longer, and the debate was sharper. The union leadership was not only bargaining with the employers but also, as a southern California caucus delegate pointed out, "negotiating

50. See below, p. 153–155.

with . . . the rank and file." [51] Neither set of negotiations proceeded smoothly.

The delegates to the April caucus in 1960 quickly took exception to the Coast Committee's recommendations concerning the distribution of the mechanization and modernization fund. The committee proposed that the first priority use of the employers' contributions be to guarantee weekly wages.[52] Early retirement benefits — the equivalent of the current monthly maximum social security benefit and pension — were to be used as necessary to shrink the work force to maintain work opportunities and earnings levels. Many delegates protested, favoring instead a "money . . . in our pockets" approach. A compromise — vested shares to be drawn at retirement — was proposed from the floor. The whole issue was referred to a subcommittee, with the support of the ILWU officers.[53] The subcommittee recommendations, adopted by the caucus, led to the incorporation of the principle of vesting in the union's demands.

The 1960 formal negotiations between the union and employers began on May 17. Fund contributions were the first substantial topic taken up. The union presented again its proposal that contributions be linked to man-hour savings and be valued at the basic straight-time rate. Several illustrative calculations were introduced to clarify the method. One example involved a fully containerized operation — Matson's *Hawaiian Citizen*. The container ship would require an estimated 320 man-hours to load 7,120 tons of cargo. A conventional break-bulk ship of the same approximate size would need 14,800 man-hours to load 12,000 tons. Applying the man-hours-per-ton rate of the conventional operation to the containerized ship's tonnage, and estimating the number of annual trips at twenty, the yearly-savings would be about 170,000 man-hours. Gross dollar savings would be $765,000 each year (the man-hours at $4.50, the approximate average labor cost including payroll taxes and fringes), and the fund's share would be, at $2.74 per hour, about $465,000.[54] The employers

51. *"Our Negotiating Committee is negotiating with us, the rank and file, who are up here to hear what they have been able to do with these Employers." ILWU,* Caucus Proceedings, *July, 1959, p. 268. The speaker was Pete Moore, regional director for southern California as well as a caucus delegate.*

52. *Thirty-five hours at the straight-time rate were to be guaranteed for the fully registered work force ("A" list men) who were available for work. ILWU,* Caucus Proceedings, *April, 1960, pp. 125–126.*

63. *Ibid., pp. 191, pp. 277–78, 389 ff., 480–495.*

54. *From* Documents between ILWU-PMA from May through September, 1960-up

rejected the union approach and instead proposed fund payments at an annual flat rate, amount to be later specified, or possibly a rate based on man-hours worked each year.[55]

There were a number of reasons underlying the employers' change of mind on the method of paying for work-rule abandonment. Certainly, continuing failure to develop reliable and widely acceptable productivity figures was important. More significant, however, appears to be the near elimination of the chief argument of proponents of payment only for results. During 1959 and 1960, the ship operators found that they could indeed enforce their contracts and improve dockside efficiency within the rules. Their conformance program of 1959–1960 had been successful. Furthermore, some employers had urged all along that the union and workers not be allowed the claim against industry earnings implied by any scheme of productivity-related contributions. Their hard-line view prevailed.

A union counterproposal that contributions be a specified rate per ton was curtly rejected; the suggestion that the fund be augmented by a flat amount of three million dollars for the next year, pending settlement of a formula, was set aside. After exploring the amounts of money likely to be required to fulfill the functions of the fund — wage guarantee and early retirement — the union, in effect, accepted the employers' principle of a single annual payment of a stipulated amount. Bridges suggested that the fund be twenty million dollars accumulated over four years.[56] At the end of the first six weeks of negotiations, devoted in part to wages and other minor matters, the parties were agreed on the general nature of all aspects of the fund, its uses, and method of contribution. Negotiations then were recessed for nearly a month, from early July to early August, to allow specialists to meet and work out the financial requirements of the benefits the fund was to provide.

Southern California opposition to the new program and accommodating approach reached a climax in August, 1960. Relations between the employers and Local 13 had been poor for years. The 1959–1960 contract conformance campaign had been directed against

to Caucus, October 3 *in the union's files. The pages containing the above calculations are undated, but references in negotiations place them at about May 18, 1960. The $4.50 is the 1960 average labor cost; the $2.74 is the 1959 basic straight-time hourly rate.*
55. Joint Negotiating Committee Minutes, *May 25, 1960.*
56. Ibid., *May 28, 1960.*

irregularities in all ports, but violations and problems of enforcement were more numerous and more severe in the Los Angeles area than elsewhere. Contract violations, especially job actions to protest alleged employer infractions in manning, methods of work, and discipline, continued in Los Angeles during the protracted 1960 negotiations. Settlement attempts with the local were frustrated by some of the employers as well as some of the local's leaders and members. By early August employer representatives emphasized the difficulties of negotiating in an atmosphere of demonstrated refusal to abide by the contract. On August 11, officials of Local 13 refused to recognize the new manning and methods agreement negotiated at the coast level for the *Hawaiian Citizen*, the new container ship. In retaliation, the employers broke off all negotiations on August 15.[57]

Top representatives of both sides devoted their energies to attempts to quell the southern California unrest. They agreed, on August 25, to adopt a set of stringent penalties for unauthorized work stoppages, ranging from suspension for five days for the first offense to possible deregistration — expulsion from the industry — for more than three offenses. A major innovation was the applicability of the penalties to union officials as well as to rank and file. Complaints, including work-stoppage allegations, were to be handled by the grievance procedure as before, but a new "practical" arbitrator was appointed. Following a precedent set nearly a decade earlier when a regional director of the union was appointed area arbitrator for the Pacific Northwest, the parties picked Germain Bulcke, second vice-president of the union, to be the new southern California arbitrator.[58]

Negotiations resumed on August 31. The two sides were substantially in agreement on the M&M fund and related matters. Hard bargaining on the details of rules and practices to be given up by the union then began. Within a few weeks the broad outline of the rules changes was clear — sling-load limits, multiple handling, gear priority, and manning scales were to be modified. The union was prepared to concede a great deal, but it was concerned with retaining its jurisdiction to the greatest possible extent and with contractual protection against speedup and unsafe working conditions.

57. Ibid., *August 9, August 15, 1960.* 1960 Documents, *letter by L. B. Thomas, dated August 12, 1960.*
58. Memorandum of Understanding, *August 25, 1960. See also ILWU,* Caucus Proceedings, *October, 1960, pp. 1050–1094.*

Sentence by sentence, contract language was proposed, modified, rejected, then changed and offered again. Agreement had not yet been reached when the caucus, called earlier, convened on October 3, 1960.

The final negotiating sessions were held before the assembled caucus delegates. The officers of the union were compelled to bargain as hard with their own negotiating committee members and caucus delegates as with the employers. In nearly all the final sessions of the union negotiating committee, the leadership found itself with only a slim majority, or actually in a minority, on the various proposals. In the caucus, opposition to sweeping rules concessions was so strong that negotiations were in effect suspended for the first few days. The impasse was broken only after a series of roll-call votes resulted in caucus approval of the basic principle of exchanging existing work rules for the fund, of continuing negotiations, and of taking up the specific rules and proposed contract language provisions one at a time.[59]

During the succeeding several days, the union negotiating committee reported its recommendations, often with minority reports, to the caucus delegates. After debate, and amendments of one or another sort, a union proposal was worked out. The negotiating committee then met with the employer representatives in front of the caucus. Employer objections and counterproposals forced an appeal to the caucus for changes, and the process was repeated until language acceptable to all sides was worked out. Sling-load limits were the easiest to change. The union leadership made it clear that, subject to safety and speed-up limitations, sling-load limits would disappear; the delegates accepted this with little opposition. Manning and gang size were more sharply debated. Employer demands for a free hand in determining manning were met by strong insistence in the union negotiating committee and the caucus for retention of the minimum basic gang everywhere except on mechanized operations. The most difficult issue to settle involved place of rest and multiple handling. The employers generally preferred to have no limitations on their unilateral direction of how much dockwork was to be done

59. *The key votes on this procedure came on October 9 and 10, the sixth and seventh days of the caucus. The motion to approve the basic approach passed by 152 1/2 votes in favor, 2 2/3 against. The motion to discuss and vote* seriatim *passed with 134 votes for, 21 against.* October 1960 Caucus, *pp. 654–674.*

and who was to do it. Most of the union negotiating committee members and caucus delegates conceded that multiple handling would have to be abandoned but insisted on retaining jurisdiction over all work done on the dock. The multiple-handling issue, although it prolonged the negotiations, was resolved as one side, then the other, gave a bit.

The employer side had its dissension as well. The prime movers for the modification of work rules, even at a price, were three of the larger Pacific Coast ship operators. They won over most of the reluctant firms, including the foreign lines, by the argument that the employer contributions to the fund, in addition to the wage increases, were a modest price to pay for five and a half years of stability in the industry.[60] Some firms nonetheless continued their opposition literally to the eve of the final settlement.

On October 17 the parties turned to the remaining details. The duration of the contract and the exact amount of the annual employer fund contributions were discussed, and, on the next day, they were quickly settled. The agreement was signed on October 18, 1960. Formal ratification was finished within two months. The new agreement won the support of every local except Local 13. Coastwide, 7,882 votes were cast in favor of the agreement, 3,695 against. The vote in Los Angeles' Local 13 was 1,065 in favor, 1,864 against.[61]

The contract was to run from June 30, 1961, to July 1, 1966, with specified reopening periods on matters other than the new mechanization and modernization provisions. There were to be periods of stress, especially in 1961, but they grew out of attempts to implement an agreement, not to negotiate major changes.

PROVISIONS OF THE AGREEMENT

The 1960 negotiations resulted in a series of amendments to the basic coastwide agreement and an understanding that a modernization and improvement fund, with broadly defined characteristics and

---

60. *From interviews with industry officials. Matson led the efforts for the new agreement, supported by Pacific Far East Line and States Steamship Company.*
61. *The usual contract ratification rules were in force; a simple majority of votes cast was sufficient to accept the agreement. During the October caucus Harry Bridges had attempted to blunt the opposition by proposing that a two-thirds majority be required in the event any major local did not vote in favor of the new agreement. The caucus voted to retain the usual simple majority procedure. See the October 1960 Caucus, pp. 1169–1172. The final vote is reported in ILWU, Referendum on the October 1960 Agreement.*

purposes, was to be established. The details of the benefits to be disbursed from the fund were worked out later and embodied in a supplemental agreement.

The employers gave up money — twenty-nine million dollars in all. The one and a half million dollars collected as part of the 1959 agreement was augmented by five million dollars each year for 1961 through 1965, and by two and a half million for the remaining half year of the agreement's life in 1966. The PMA and member companies collectively were responsible for the payments to the fund; individual company contributions were determined solely by the bylaws of the PMA, not by agreement with the union.[62] Within the employer group a wide range of opinion existed concerning the method by which individual companies were to pay their share. Some companies favored extension of the principle of assessment by man-hours worked for each company. This method was used in the existing pension and welfare funds and was adopted to meet the fund obligations of the 1959 agreement. Opponents pointed out that the method would doubly benefit some firms. Those companies most able or quickest to mechanize, reducing man-hours, would also pay relatively less into the fund. They favored assessment by man-hours saved. The compromise was a tonnage assessment — $5\frac{1}{2}$ cents per ton for bulk cargo and $27\frac{1}{2}$ cents per ton for other goods.[63] The ship-operating companies are responsible for the payments; in practice, the foreign lines' payments are made by the stevedoring companies. The trustees of the M&M fund, appointed by the PMA and the ILWU, assess nonmember companies at rates comparable to those paid by member companies. Although nonmember firms were not bound by the ILWU-PMA agreement, the union requires them to sign a supplementary agreement to pay the M&M assessment to the Fund. Use of the dispatch hall and other facilities is denied to any nonmember company failing to pay. Defaults in assessment payments by any member company of the PMA were to be made good by other members.

Of the three trusts set up by the parties to administer the benefits under the agreement, the only one given the power to accumu-

62. *The* ILWU-PMA Supplemental Agreement on Mechanization and Modernization: effective January 1, 1961 *(San Francisco, signed November 15, 1961), p. 4.*
63. *See Lancaster, "The ILWU-PMA Mechanization and Modernization Agreement."*

late and hold money, and assigned a specific amount, was the supplemental wage benefit trust. Eleven million dollars were to be paid into this fund over the life of the agreement. About two million dollars each year of the employer contributions were to be allocated to this trust; the exact amount could vary, depending on the needs of the other benefit trusts.[64] The provisions for eligibility and payments to workers under this fund were complex, reflecting the union's desire to protect the earnings of the registered men, and the employers' wishes to limit payments to only those persons adversely affected by productivity increases. In general, the firms wanted benefits paid only to those men whose earnings over a reasonable period of time were inadequate, and when the inadequacy did not result from a general decline in business or failure of the longshoreman to be available for work.

In brief, the plan guaranteed to fully registered longshoremen, including clerks[65] — those on the "A" list — average weekly total earnings equivalent to thirty-five hours, at the current basic straight-time rate. (In 1960–1961, this came to about one hundred dollars per week. At the 1964–1965 basic rate of $3.32 per hour, it amounted to about one hundred and sixteen dollars each week.) Benefits became payable when the average hours worked by a representative group of workers fell below 140 over a four-week period. The relevant group consists of those longshoremen or clerks who customarily work at a port, and it was further limited to about the top 70 percent of the workers, ranked by hours worked or credited during the four-week benefit period. To be eligible for benefits, individuals must also have been full-time workers, defined as men whose average hours worked during the benefit period were at least 93 percent of the representative group average. Finally, the eligible man must have earned no more than the equivalent of thirty-five hours per week at straight-time rates during the forty-eight weeks preceding the benefit period. The maximum earnings permitted was to be lowered in proportion to any decline in total trade at the port from the 1959–1960 base period.

Any longshoreman or clerk passing the stringent eligibility tests

---

64. Supplemental Agreement, *pp. 13–14.*
65. *These two groups are always in separate union locals, have their own registration lists, and have substantially different working rules. Nonetheless, the benefits under the 1960 contract are about the same for both groups. The word "longshoremen" in this section should be interpreted to include ship clerks as well.*

might still be unable to receive payment. The wage supplement was calculated at the equivalent of thirty-five hours at the basic straight-time rate, less the worker's earnings and any unemployment compensation he may have drawn during the period. A man working night shifts or on obnoxious cargo at penalty rates could work as little as twenty-five hours or so in a week during a benefit period but earn enough to eliminate his supplement benefit. On the other hand, if a large amount of manpower displacement took place, and the total cargo handled at Pacific ports was at about the 1960 level, the fund could be exhausted rather quickly. In that event, no more benefits would be paid. For example, ten thousand longshoremen drawing a supplement equivalent to only five hours' pay per week would empty the fund — at its maximum of eleven million dollars — in about one and a half years.

The union and the employers did not expect that the wage guarantee would be used until rather late in the life of the agreement, and the amount necessary was just about the maximum that the union believed likely to be needed. In the union's view, the eleven million dollars so set aside were, in effect, the "sale price" of the work rules and other requirements given up. New entrants to the industry would not be eligible for any of the benefits, and the continuation past 1966 of this part of the employers' contributions was not planned.[66]

The remaining eighteen million dollars, about three million dollars each year, were the men's "share of the machine" in the union's view. The cash was regularly made available from the general M&M fund to enable the two trust funds to meet benefit claims for death, permanent disability, and retirement bonuses. (The benefits provided by these funds are in addition to the regular industry and government retirement and disability pensions.)

The vesting benefit trust was the more important of the two administrative funds and types of benefits. Created to induce retirement, this scheme provided thirty-six monthly payments of $220 each to any eligible longshoreman who elected to withdraw permanently from the work force. For voluntary retirement with payment a worker must have been fully registered and available for work for the nine years immediately preceding the time he chose to withdraw

66. See Fairley, "The ILWU-PMA Mechanization and Modernization Agreement."

from employment. He must be at least sixty-two, and he must have had twenty-five years of service out of the thirty-five before retirement.[67] The parties also included provisions for mandatory retirement, if they thought it necessary, as early as sixty-two. Eligibility for benefits for men compelled to retire were about the same as for voluntary retirement, except that the minimum years of service were twenty-two out of the past thirty-two years for men forced to retire at age sixty-two, twenty-three of thirty-three years for men leaving at age sixty-three, and so on. Longshoremen compelled to retire early were to receive the vesting benefit of $220 each month for thirty-six months and an extra $100 per month until they reached age sixty-five.[68]

The death and disability benefits trust administered the remaining set of benefits. Eligibility and payments to qualified longshoremen, or heirs, under this part of the agreement resembled those for the vesting benefits, except that minimum years of service were fewer and benefits were linked to years of service in the industry. Fully registered men qualified for the disability benefits with as little as fifteen years of service, and they were eligible for the death benefit coverage with only five years in the industry. In all cases, minimum years in fully registered status — the "A" list — were specified. Disability benefits ranged from $2,640 to $7,920, for fifteen to twenty-five years of service, respectively. Death benefits were $2,640 for workers with five to fifteen years of service, and rose to a $5,000 maximum with each year of service between fifteen and twenty.

The retirement, death, and disability claims were paid as they were filed, essentially drawing on common funds. The benefits were subject to reduction, and even complete discontinuance, should the trustees believe that the employer contributions would be insufficient. The death and disability benefits would be reduced or eliminated first, then the retirement benefits.

The agreement provided for temporary abatement of the employer contributions to the fund in the event the union or any of its

---

67. *Minimum qualifications for years of service are spelled out in the agreement. In general, a man must have worked about 40 percent of the full-time 2,000 or so hours in the year. For the years before 1945, minimum qualifications are less restrictive. Credit is given for time spent as a union official, some military service, and illness or injury time off.*
68. *This paragraph is based on the* Supplementary Agreement, as amended, *pp. 27–31.*

members engaged in an illegal work stoppage, refused to follow arbitration awards or decisions of the joint labor relations committee, or failed to abide by the contract. The maximum allowable abatement of contributions was agreed to be $13,650 per day. The number of days to which the abatement was to be applicable were to be determined by negotiations or, upon failure to agree, by the arbitrator.

The union gave up a great deal. The agreement intended "to eliminate restrictions in the contract and working rules, as well as in unwritten but existing Union unilateral restrictions and arbitration awards which interfere with the Employers' rights dealing with sling loads, first place of rest, multiple handling, gang sizes, and manning scales." [69] Extensive revisions of the basic coastwide contract were then written into the 1960 agreement.

Fewer words were used to deal with sling loads than with any other of the work rules or practices. The relatively few words, however, very nearly eliminate restrictions on the size of the load lifted between the dock and the hold of a ship. For more than twenty years the contracts between the ILWU and the PMA had included, without change, the sling-load maxima originally adopted in 1937. The 1960 agreement continued the 1937 limits, but provided that they would apply only when manning, methods, and working conditions were the same as in 1937. In all other circumstances, according to the agreement, the loads are to be determined by the employer, subject to safety and speedup constraints. The new provisions recognized that loads built away from the docks — usually unit or prepalletized loads put together by the shipper — were not in any event subject to the 1937 load limits.[70]

The provisions dealing with multiple handling and place of rest were not only much longer than those concerning sling loads but were substantially rewritten in the first year and a half of the agreement. The crux of the issue was the conflict between the union's desire to retain jurisdiction over as much of the work as possible and the employers' wish to reduce sharply the rehandling of goods. Complicating elements were the jurisdictional claims of a third

69. ILWU-PMA, Memorandum of Agreement, October 18, 1960, section A.1.(1).
70. The sling-load provisions are contained in sections A.4–A.9 of the 1960 Memorandum of Agreement. In the Pacific Coast Longshore Agreement, 1961–1966 (San Francisco, 1962) sections 14.1 and 14.11 were changed slightly for earlier contracts — the preceding printed agreement was the 1951 contract — and sections 14.2–14.4 and 14.12 are new.

party — the Teamsters. The new agreement required about five times as many words as the previous one. They included detailed provisions intended to enable prompt settlement of any disputes concerning jurisdiction and multiple handling.

Most important of the new provisions on multiple handling was the elimination of the requirement that all cargo be built into sling loads, or broken down and placed on the dock, by longshoremen.[71] The new agreement required, as it had for decades, that all building of longshore sling loads on the dock, deboarding of cargo, sorting, moving goods about the dock and between docks, and high piling shall be done by longshoremen. The big departure from the past was that none of this work could be done unless the employer so directed. The agreement explicitly provided that goods received as unit or packaged loads, or already palletized, are to be loaded or unloaded to or from the ship as they are, or as the employer directs.

To cope with the thorny jurisdictional problem involving the Teamsters, the parties agreed that longshoremen would load and unload trucks when the goods were being transferred directly between the ship and vehicle on the dock, but only on orders from the employer and if the truck driver did not object. Truck drivers and their helpers were permitted to load or unload their vehicles, piece by piece or by unit lifts, from pallets or the place of rest designated by the employer. They could build their own loads and otherwise handle the cargo on their trucks, tailgates, loading platforms, and aprons.

The chief difficulty in implementing the agreement during its first year, 1961, involved dockwork and the jurisdictional issue. The 1960 understanding between the PMA and the ILWU appeared to claim work that had been done by Teamsters. In particular, truck drivers and their helpers were to take the whole load as it rested on the dock on terminal floor only as a unit, or to load the goods piece by piece. Longshoremen were to break down the piles of goods and set the loads to the tailgate, floor, or loading platform for the truckers to handle. A brief Teamster strike in 1961 led to four-way negotiations between the ILWU, Teamsters, PMA, and the drayage employers' representatives. The resulting agreement resulted in a bit more work being left in the truckers' jurisdiction. Teamsters could

---

71. *See sections 10–18 of the 1960* Memorandum of Agreement *and all of section 1, pp. 2–8, of the* Pacific Coast Longshore Agreement, 1961–1966.

break down piles of goods that had been piled two sling-loads high, rather than one as in the original 1960 agreement, and they were allowed more flexibility in handling the goods to load and discharge their trucks. A section in the 1960 agreement provided that cargo received by the shipper, other than unit load or prepalletized goods, was to be palletized only by longshoremen. This explicit requirement was not included in the 1961–1962 revisions.[72]

This section of the agreement protected the longshoremen's jurisdiction in that it recognized their claim to operate all machinery, equipment, and tools used to move or handle cargo on the docks. Another long-lived jurisdictional problem was sidestepped by the decision of the representatives of the PMA and ILWU to allow sailors to continue to do the limited amount of longshore work permitted them by existing practice at the time the agreement was signed.

The principal changes in the new provisions regarding gang size and manning dealt with a reduced basic gang for general cargo and the elimination of minimum manning requirements on bulk cargo and new operations. The new basic gang was the minimum complement at a hatch for general cargo — including mixed break-bulk and unitized loads — worked with the aid of mechanical equipment in the hold. It consisted of four holdmen, a hatch tender, a winchdriver, and a gang boss, and two slingmen, who worked on the dock at the ship's side. Before the 1960 agreement the typical basic gang consisted of two winch drivers,[73] two slingmen, or frontmen, and eight holdmen on loading, six on discharging, operations. For manhandled cargo, the basic gang was to be supplemented by two additional men on discharge operations and four added men on loading; in effect, it is the preagreement basic gang. However, the extra men — "swingmen" — were not to be treated as part of the gang but could be moved from hatch to hatch, and from hold to dock, as needed. There were no upper limits to the number of men to be used; the employer may add supplemental men as he saw fit.[74]

For new operations and, in effect, bulk cargo, the new contract

72. *The Teamsters' strike and settlement is described in the* PMA, Annual Report, *1959, and Fairley, pp. 677–678.*
73. *On most ships in recent years one winch driver alone is able to work the gear at a hatch; the relief operator acts as hatch tender.*
74. *See provisions 19 through 37 of the 1960* Memorandum of Agreement. *Section 10 of the* Pacific Coast Longshore Agreement, 1961–1966 *incorporates the 1960 wording with little change. Very nearly the whole section is new.*

provided that the parties would discuss the manning requirements. Failing agreement, the grievance procedure, culminating in arbitration, is to be used. The employer was given the power to put his view of the appropriate manning into effect while the dispute was being settled.

The union retained the right to challenge employer changes in all the relevant method and manning changes. In a general provision, and again in the sections revising sling loads and manning, the agreement provided that employer-directed changes are subject to health and safety considerations, and that the union may protest to forestall onerous individual work loads. The agreement repeated the longstanding, but occasionally not followed, requirement that jobs involving disputed manning or work methods are to be carried out as the employer directs. The workers' objections are then to be heard and decided in the grievance procedure. The only exceptions are disputes involving health and safety; if these are alleged, the men may refuse to work until the unsafe conditions are corrected or until the labor relations committee or arbitrator has decided the case. The union agreed not to abuse the health and safety rights.[75]

The 1960 agreement in Pacific Coast longshoring was not easy to make. Persons or groups among the employers and within the union, perhaps more rational or long-sighted than the others, very much desired to change the restrictions and inefficiencies on the docks, and to have their side gain thereby. Years of patient effort were required to overcome opposition to change within both groups, and to extract concessions from the other side. The concessions were not painless — the employers' recognition of the workers' right to explicit financial participation in productivity increase was as difficult to reconcile with ideology as was the longshoremen's giving up local union control over effort and pace of work.

On the other hand the parties did not each blindly put their fate at the mercy of the other. The employers were protected by stiffer penalties for incorrigible union officials and by clearly limited financial liability, including no liability at all if the union were flagrantly noncompliant. Even if only minor relaxation of restrictions had been the result of the agreement, it would have been nonetheless a fair bargain for the employers; their contributions to the various

75. See provisions 1.(1)d., 9, 36, and 45 of the Supplemental Agreement, 1961.

benefit funds were the equivalent of only a modest wage increase, exchanged for five and a half years of stability.[76]

The union was protected by the provisions enabling challenges to employer decisions on grounds of onerousness, health, and safety. These provisions clearly required interpretation, and further, the clarification was to be either by mutual agreement, or by arbitrators known to be nonhostile to the union and workers. In actual fact, the impressive results of the agreement were to come not so much from the contract itself as from the subsequent interpretation and implementation.

76. Total compensation including wages, vacations, welfare, and pension contributions, but excluding employer payroll taxes, were $124,406,400 in 1960; the wage bill alone was $113,461,900. The $5 million annual M&M fund contribution, thus, is the equivalent of about a 4.4 percent wage increase, or a 4 percent increase in total compensation. (Wage data furnished by PMA.)

IV / PRODUCTIVITY IN PACIFIC COAST LONGSHORING

Productivity had been controversial since the earliest days of union existence on the Pacific docks. From the late 1930s to the mid-1950s employers and some government agencies alleged poor productivity performance by Pacific longshoremen. The allegations were successfully challenged by the union. In the post-1960 years, the positions of the parties are reversed. The PMA is reluctant to concede that productivity improved substantially after the 1960 changes in rules and methods and doubts that the employer-gathered data on productivity have any validity.[1] In brief, although the descriptive evidence suggests that productivity decreased from 1934 through 1940, when the union imposed or negotiated various rules and practices, and increased after the 1960 rules abandonment, one party or the other plausibly could and did contend that the efficiency changes were negligible, or had little to do with union rules or worker behavior.

The doubt and controversy surrounding all discussion of the industry's productivity over several decades compel any investigation of the matter to be careful indeed. In this chapter and the next, a number of alternative approaches are used to estimate the more recent productivity changes in the industry and to assess the importance of the various sources of such change, including the abandonment of restrictive work practices.

OVERALL PRODUCTIVITY CHANGES

The only measure of productivity in Pacific Coast longshoring available for more than a few years on a consistent basis is also the crudest. The total man-hours worked, reported by PMA pay offices, and total tonnage handled, reported by PMA member companies,

---

1. See below, p. 115 for employer criticisms of the PMA productivity data.

are available for a seventeen-year period. Simply dividing one by the other yields a rough measure of productivity, comparable over time.

This first approximation of productivity for the industry, shown in Table 3, suggests that, with the exception of 1957, cargo-handling efficiency varied relatively little from year to year before 1960. Certainly there was no upward trend over time. In contrast, the most recent years do show a pronounced upward trend. In every year

Table 3: Crude Index of Average Productivity, Pacific Coast Longshoring, 1948-1965.

(1953 = 100)

Year	Longshore hours[a]	Total hours	Year	Total hours[b]
1948	95.7	—	1957	117.5
1949	105.3	—	1958	96.3
1950	94.1	—	1959	97.7
1951	100.2	—	1960	110.2
1952	106.4	106.5	1961	118.2
1953	100.0	100.0	1962	121.4
1954	94.7	90.2	1963	136.1
1955	—	98.6	1964	145.7
1956	—	107.5	1965	156.5

[a] Total coastwide tonnage divided by longshoremen man-hours.
[b] Total coastwide tonnage divided by total longshore, clerical, and supervisory man-hours.
SOURCE: Calculated from data in appendix, table C-1 and C-2.

from 1960 through 1965, more tons were handled, relative to man-hours, than in the preceding year. Average productivity was higher from 1961 on than in any other year for which data are available. The 1964 rate was about 45 percent above the rates for 1953, 1958, or 1959, and more than 30 percent above the 1960 rate.

A major weakness of this measure of productivity is its failure to reflect changes in the commodity or "package" composition of the cargo handled each year. "Package," as used in the industry and in this study, implies not only some sort of container but also a mode of handling. Different packages are the conventional sorts of containers — carton, drums, bales, sacks, and so on — and several varieties of noncontainer, loose pieces, or bulk, as well as packages specialized to the industry, including twenty-ton containers or vans, one- to two-ton unit loads, prepalletized loads, and so on. Different packages, and even the same package for different commodities, are handled at different average productivity rates. For example, one study indicated that small cartons of goods are loaded, on the average, at twice the tons per man-hour as large cartons; goods in bags are loaded, on the average, at twice the small-carton rate, and average tons per man-hour for loading drums of liquids are even higher than for bags. Commodity rate variation within a package — bags, for example — is illustrated by the rates for loading, for example, ammonium sulphate and carbon black; the former may be handled at nearly double the tons per man-hour of the latter.[2]

Of these commodity or package differences the most important involves bulk handling. For at least four decades in the United States, bulk goods, including grain, coal, and ores, have been handled with machinery at productivity rates ten to fifty times higher than conventionally packaged goods. As long ago as 1923, for example, grain was bulk-loaded at eighteen to thirty-six tons per man-hour in New York and Montreal; at the same time, bags of cargo were loaded at an average of 0.92 tons per man-hour.[3] About the same disparity in rates still existed forty years later; in 1960, for example, rice was loaded in Pacific Coast ports at the average rate of 1.18 tons per man-hour when manhandled in bags, and 34.5 tons per man-hour when loaded in bulk by machinery.

The difference in rates is so large that the shift to bulk methods is almost equivalent to eliminating the man-hour input altogether for the shifted goods. As a consequence, even rather small changes in the proportions of bulk and conventional cargo would vary significantly the average productivity rate. To illustrate, assume total tonnage to be handled at only two rates, and that they differ widely — plausible rates would be one ton per man-hour for all nonbulk, and ten tons per man-hour for bulk goods. If, for example, 100 tons were shifted from nonbulk to bulk handling, almost as many man-hours would be lost — a decrease of 100 man-hours associated with nonbulk, less an increase of only ten man-hours associated with bulk handling. To illustrate with more plausible numbers, if 100,000 tons were handled during some time period, 80 percent with nonbulk techniques and 20 percent bulk handling, the man-hours used would amount to about 82,000. A shift of 10,000 tons from nonbulk to bulk

2. *Taken from National Research Council, Maritime Cargo Transportation Conference,* Cargo Ship Loading, *especially appendix IV.*
3. *Brysson Cunningham,* Cargo Handling at Ports *(New York, 1924), appendix II, p. 148.*

handling would result in a loss of the 10,000 man-hours formerly required by nonbulk methods and a gain of no more than 1,000 man-hours in bulk operations. A consequence of the shift is an apparent productivity increase of about 12 percent. Similarly, a drop in the nonbulk cargo from 70 percent to 60 percent of the total is roughly equivalent to eliminating one seventh of the hours required, or an apparent productivity increase of about 14 percent, and so on.

Table 4: Indexes of Average Productivity, Bulk Tonnage Reweighted, Pacific Coast Longshoring, 1952-1965.[a]

Year	1953 $=$ 100	1960 $=$ 100	Year	1953 $=$ 100	1960 $=$ 100
1952	96.9	104.8	1959	87.4	94.5
1953	100.0	108.1	1960	92.5	100.0
1954	90.6	98.0	1961	95.6	103.4
1955	96.9	104.8	1962	105.5	114.1
1956	93.3	100.9	1963	112.6	121.8
1957	94.1	101.8	1964	124.1	134.2
1958	85.0	91.9	1965	130.0	140.6

[a] Two base years were used in order to facilitate comparisons — 1953 for the preceding tables, 1960 for the subsequent ones.

SOURCE: Appendix Table C-3.

On the Pacific Coast the proportions of bulk tonnage to the total have indeed varied over time. Bulk goods were about 20 percent of total tonnage in 1954, 40 percent in 1957, 34 percent in 1962, and so on. Clearly, any reasonable estimates of productivity must allow at least for this variety of package shift.

A second, and closer, approximation of Pacific longshoring productivity appears in Table 4. The man-hours required for bulk tonnage for each year were estimated by using the 1960 rate for all bulk goods.[4] The remaining man-hours were then applied to the nonbulk tonnage to estimate nonbulk tons per man-hour. Generally, reducing the effect of bulk tonnage variations reduces the productivity variations as well. For the years before 1960, output per man-hour fluctuated above or below the mean for the period by only a few percentage points. As the earlier calculations indicated, however, the rate increased steadily and substantially in the years after 1960.

4. *Calculated from the data in Pacific Maritime Association,* Productivity Study, Longshore Operations, Pacific Coast, 1960–1963 *(San Francisco, 1965). The PMA studies are discussed at length below.*

The figures in Table 4 are more reliable estimates of productivity than the simple ratio of tons to total man-hours used earlier, but doubts still remain. Any substantial variations in commodity or package composition would result in variations in apparent productivity similar to those associated with varying proportions of bulk tonnage. A relative increase in the tonnage handled of dense goods — logs, or iron and steel mill products — would result in an apparent increase in productivity; a shift from canned to frozen fruits and vegetables would be accompanied by an apparent decrease in average tons handled per man-hour, and so on. In the estimates of Table 4, an unknown but conceivably large fraction of the still-remaining variability in the average productivity figures, could result from such changes in commodity composition.[5] An approach more sophisticated than simple ratios of total or nonbulk tons to total man-hours would be desirable, and is made possible by data gathered for several years by the PMA.

PMA PRODUCTIVITY STUDIES

After a number of abortive attempts, the PMA succeeded, in 1960, in establishing a system to yield data bearing on productivity. Clerks in all the ports of the Pacific Coast prepared reports of quantities and man-hours used to load or unload cargo for a wide variety of goods and packages. The information was sent to the PMA, tabulated by the staff, published with some interpretation, and distributed to member companies and the union. The original intent of the studies was to provide a basis for calculating the man-hour savings and employer contributions to the M&M fund. Although this use was abandoned soon after the data collection began, the studies were continued to include four full years — 1960, 1961, 1962 and 1963.[6]

5. *These are productivity changes in a narrow, technical sense, which are not relevant to the discussion here. They usually reflect variations or shifts in demand conditions for the goods shipped, rather than modified or new production techniques or machines, or cargo-handling work practices.*

6. *Three studies were published, each with two parts: Pacific Maritime Association,* Productivity Study, Longshore Operations, Pacific Coast, 1960–1961 *(San Francisco, 1963);* Productivity Study, Longshore Operations, Pacific Coast, 1961–1962 *(San Francisco, 1964);* Productivity Study, Longshore Operations, Pacific Coast, 1960–1963 *(San Francisco, 1965). Part I of each study describes the methods, summarizes the results, and includes definitions; part II presents quantity and hours data in detail — by area, commodity, package, and by quarter for the current year and the base year. Max Kossoris, Director of the*

Industry and PMA officials were not altogether pleased with the studies. A productivity study committee, consisting of representatives of the major American-flag Pacific Coast ship operators, had been created in 1959 to oversee and evaluate productivity matters. In 1964 the committee recommended that data collection be discontinued and that 1963 be the final year for which the results were to be assembled and published. In their final evaluation in 1965 the committee disparaged the entire project, describing the data as of "such doubtful quality that the reports are probably misleading." The principal criticisms put forth were: the raw data submitted by the companies from dockside were poorly prepared and inaccurate; the productivity rates varied so widely, even when commodity, package, and pier were held constant, that they could not be trusted; and the carelessness or inconsistencies of commodity classification led to further error. Finally, the study committee believed it to be impossible to relate productivity changes to specific causes or sources of change.[7]

Although the Association's self-criticisms are not without basis, they appear to be too pessimistic. The data collection was certainly a source of some error. However, the PMA staff reclassified and audited both the raw data reports and the actual data gathering on the dock. The data for the earlier years — 1960 and 1961 — appear to have been especially carefully collected and put together.[8] Further, the biases in the data — for example, faulty classification of goods and hours, omitted hours, and so on — very likely are about the same from year to year, and, in any event, their effects may be minimized by the use of several alternative methods of estimating productivity.

The wide variability of the rates involves, in essence, statistical

Western Region of the Bureau of Labor Statistics, was PMA consultant and director of productivity research in 1959–1960, when the studies were designed and reporting initiated. The studies were prepared under the immediate supervision of Joseph H. Cox, consulting engineer. Pres Lancaster, now manager of the Contract Data (i.e., research) Department of the PMA, became Acting Director, Research, in 1960, after Dr. Kossoris returned to the Bureau of Labor Statistics.

7. The productivity study committee, in 1965, included Foster Weldon of the Matson Navigation Company, Roy Delrich of the American President Lines, and Tom Hardcastle of Pacific Far East Line. The committee's reports were not made available by the PMA, but Pres Lancaster discussed the main points of their findings and recommendations in interviews with the author. The quote is from Lancaster.

8. See appendix B, pp. 232–238, for a more thorough discussion of the PMA data and methodological and other criticisms.

reliability. Detailed information is not available describing the frequency distributions of the observations underlying the aggregated PMA productivity data. Nevertheless, the limited existing information indicates that the standard deviations are sufficiently small and the number of observations so large that the calculated productivity rate changes between, for example, 1960 and 1963, are highly reliable. To illustrate, the probability is about one in several hundred that the data would reflect an increase in average productivity for canned goods of about 10 percent, or for beer of 20 percent, if there had been

Table 5: Man-hour Savings and Productivity Changes,
Pacific Coast Longshoring, 1960-1963.

| Year | Man-hour savings | | | Total man-hours[a] | Productivity change |
	Direct labor	Clerical supervisory, and indirect labor	Total		
	– – – – –	*thousands of hours*		– – – – –	*percent*
1960	—	—	—		—
1961	910.3	576.7	1,487.0	22,777	6.5
1962 Total	1,815.9	959.9	2,775.8	21,461	12.9
Attributable to:					
1961 improvements	934.1	577.0	1,511.1		7.0
1962 improvements	881.8	382.9	1,264.7		5.9
1963 Total	2,302.5	1,532.7	3,835.2	21,855	17.5
Attributable to:					
1961 improvements	990.1	607.0	1,597.1		7.3
1962 improvements	927.9	404.6	1,332.5		6.1
1963 improvements	384.5	521.1	905.6		4.1

[a] Longshoremen's, clerks', and supervisors' hours.

SOURCES: Man-hour savings: PMA, *Productivity Study, Longshore Operations, Pacific Coast, 1960–1963,* part I, pp. 7–8. Total longshore, clerical, and supervisory hours reported: *Ibid.,* table B., p. 105. (See text and Appendix B for discussion.)

no real change in efficiency on the docks.[9] On balance, the productivity rates calculated from the PMA data deserve a good deal of confidence.

The findings of the studies for the years 1960–1963 are summarized in Table 5. Man-hour savings — the first three columns of the table — are simply the difference between the man-hours required for the current year tonnage at the 1960 productivity rates, and the man-hours actually used in the current year.[10] The direct labor man-hour savings were calculated by commodity and package; indirect labor, and clerical and supervisory man-hour savings were estimated by simple aggregates.

Direct labor hours are those used in the actual loading and unloading of cargo, including the hours used in stowing and, when required, palletizing, depalletizing, high piling, and any other handling between place of rest on the dock and the ship's hold. Direct labor man-hour savings reflect improvements in work methods, elimination of redundant manning, improved or more equipment, and similar production process changes. The direct labor man-hour savings are perhaps best understood by an illustration of the underlying calculations. For example, direct labor man-hour savings for loading rice, in 1963 relative to 1960, were about as follows:

1. Rice in bags, palletized on the dock: about 16,800 tons loaded at the 1960 rate, 0.89 man-hours per ton, would have required 14,952 man-hours. Actual man-hours used for this commodity and package in 1963 were 10,900. Thus, man-hour savings were about 4,000.

2. Rice in bags, palletized away from the dock: about 89,100 tons loaded at the 1960 rate, 0.84 man-hours per ton, would have required 74,844 man-hours. Actual 1963 man-hours used were 48,900. Man-hour savings were about 26,000.

3. Rice loaded in bulk: 179,200 tons at the 1960 rate of 0.028 man-hours per ton would have required 5,018 man-hours. Actual man-hours in 1963 were 4,900. Savings were 120 man-hours.[11]

Similar calculations were made for about sixty identified commodities and general cargo, and for about a dozen important packages.

9. See Appendix B, pp. 233–238.
10. Definitions and the relations among the various productivity measures are discussed more precisely in Appendix B, Part II.
11. My calculations from the PMA data on hours and tonnages in part II of the 1960–1963 report.

The man-hour savings for each commodity and package were added together, and loading and discharging savings combined to yield the totals shown in the table.

Indirect time consists of longshoremen's hours devoted to tasks other than moving cargo, or not worked at all. Indirect man-hour savings are related, in part, to the direct labor savings. Hours required but not worked — indirect hours by definition — as a result of equipment breakdown, waiting associated with delays in the flow of goods, shifting gangs from hatch to hatch or ship to ship, fulfilling minimum-time guarantees, and so on, are a function of employment, and would decline as direct labor requirements, relative to cargo handled, were reduced. Similarly, some of the clerical and supervisory hours are approximately proportional to direct labor employment. Additional indirect labor and clerical man-hour savings stem from productivity improvements in the indirect labor tasks — covering and uncovering hatches, rigging the gear, readying the cargo — and in clerical work methods. Indirect, clerical, and supervisory man-hour savings were calculated for the total annual volume of work; reasonably, no attempt was made to estimate such savings by commodity or package.

The overall results of the PMA studies are broadly consistent with our crude first approximations of productivity change. In general, productivity increased, over the 1960 level, by 6.5 percent in 1961, by nearly 13 percent in 1962, and by 17.5 percent in 1963. Further, by using the differences in productivity rates from one year to the next, the PMA staff was able to allocate the productivity change to efficiency improvements instituted in each of the years of the studies.

The similarity in results should not obscure the large differences in method and reliability between the simple approximations and the PMA estimates. The PMA figures on man-hour savings and related productivity increases are carefully constructed, and they exclude the spurious productivity changes associated with changing commodity composition. The simple approximations, on the other hand, include these effects. The nearness of the outcome of the simple calculations to the more sophisticated estimates derives chiefly from relative stability and fortuitous offsetting changes in the commodities handled. As a minor weakness, the PMA estimates also exclude the genuine productivity changes associated with shifts from one package to another. Package changes likely to be important in terms of longshore man-hour savings include the shifts from conventional break-bulk loads, built and broken down on the docks and in the holds, to prepalletized loads, shipper-packaged unit loads, and containers of various kinds. On these grounds, then, the PMA results understate, by some small amount, the overall productivity changes. However, the understatement is easily adjusted.[12]

The PMA studies are certainly the most ambitious, comprehensive, and most useful attempt yet made in the United States to develop data bearing on longshoring productivity. Their only substantial shortcoming is the very brief span of years included. However, the PMA data do provide a basis for estimating productivity in years not included in the studies themselves.

Careful estimates of productivity for at least a few other years are desirable for several reasons. The simple estimates introduced earlier in this chapter, even when supplemented by the PMA estimates for 1961–1963, are not enough to dispel doubt that productivity changes comparable in magnitude to the recent years have occurred before, and may be unrelated to work-rules changes. Moreover, 1963 is only about halfway through the life of the 1960 M&M agreement; it is very likely that changes in work rules and methods were still taking place in 1964, 1965, and even later. In brief, productivity estimates as careful as those of the PMA for the years before 1960 and after 1963 would be useful in order to add perspective to the post-1960 changes in productivity and to assess satisfactorily the effects of the 1960 agreement. The calculations necessary to estimate productivity for the years outside the PMA studies period have the added value of providing information with which estimates may be made of the effect of package shifts within commodity classifications and of possible overall bias in the PMA studies.

EXTRAPOLATION: NEW ESTIMATES OF PRODUCTIVITY, 1957-1964

The estimation of productivity, using rates based on PMA data, is a conceptually simple and straightforward operation. The general approach is illustrated in Table 6. The productivity rate for a com-

---

12. *Estimates of the size of the understatement — that is, of the contribution of package shifts to the overall changes — are included in the following chapter.*

Table 6: Estimated Man-hours Required at 1960 Rates and
Man-hours Saved, by Commodity, 1964.

		Inbound		Outbound	
No.	Commodity	Tons	Estimated man-hours	Tons	Estimated man-hours
1	Canned goods	341,419	365,664	485,013	538,983
2	Rice	23	35	392,031	209,648
3	Grains, other	1,455	2,235	4,918,879	238,802
4	Flour	7,344	11,280	287,251	204,954
5	Citrus	0	0	114,426	188,451
6	Bananas	291,819	413,449	929	1,263
7	Dried fruits and nuts	17,405	23,800	122,974	167,614
8	Coffee	210,782	211,942	1,870	2,542
9	Sugar	758,550	92,471	4,551	6,188
10	Foods, other	406,778	624,770	884,796	1,202,949
11	Beverages	95,953	166,110	120,737	164,151
12	Hides	621	813	130,016	225,263
13	Animal products, inedible	101,768	133,226	269,157	53,648
14	Animal feeds	19,871	26,014	544,728	168,264
15	Rubber	53,253	81,634	36,558	50,724
16	Copra	273,798	192,116	0	0
17	Cotton	1,214	1,589	298,803	396,776
18	Fibers, cordage	34,616	45,143	315	405
19	Burlap	57,858	58,008	4,051	6,084
20	Textiles, general	111,640	143,161	22,925	29,472
21	Logs	46,573	20,421	3,131,617	3,240,488
22	Lumber[a]	134,172	148,481	2,102,041	1,491,076
23	Plywood	354,533	313,861	60,996	52,548
24	Pulp	481,573	0	609,934	373,641
25	Newsprint	715,688	236,241	23,340	16,790
26	Paper products	69,763	74,570	430,344	420,172
27	Coke	0	0	1,372,305	140,889
28	Glass and products	123,068	169,228	12,051	14,654
29	Earths	2,620	3,039	218,976	335,694
30	Salt	613,967	110,474	469,889	0
31	Iron ore	229	45	2,274,733	41,866
32	Iron and steel products	1,384,879	732,630	442,562	140,546
33	Iron and steel pipe	378,829	298,263	28,630	26,577
34	Iron and steel scrap	5,939	7,775	1,543,649	410,624
35	Aluminum	22,612	15,071	77,087	51,525

Table 6 (Continued)

No.	Commodity	Inbound		Outbound	
		Tons	Estimated man-hours	Tons	Estimated man-hours
36	Copper	19,511	17,396	88,344	44,696
37	Ores, general	832,701	166,180	38,685	3,087
38	Hardware	100,917	124,410	10,750	8,732
39	Machinery and vehicles	297,030	254,544	279,094	337,540
40	Metals and products, other	67,870	60,511	69,146	45,548
41	Chemicals	280,782	114,701	772,375	642,280
42	Fertilizers	243,880	248,735	120,164	115,804
43	Potash	20	8	709,342	62,737
44	General cargo	549,881	719,871	869,460	1,057,289
45	Petroleum and by-products, dry cargo[a]	218,000	244,951	280,000	253,334
			6,674,869		13,184,318

ANALYSIS OF TABLE 6:

a. Total direct labor man-hours, estimated at 1960 rates
Total: 19,859,187

b. Estimated indirect and unattributed longshore hours (at the 1960 proportion)
Total: 9,364,878

c. Total longshore hours, estimated at 1960 rates (a+b)
Total: 29,224,065

d. Actual longshore man-hours used
Total: 21,809,338

e. Man-hours saved (c less d)
Total: 7,414,727

f. Productivity change relative to 1960 (e ÷ d × 100)
34.00 percent

[a] Modified from Engineers' data to exclude barge and tankship tonnages.

SOURCES: Calculated from the 1960 data in PMA, *Longshore Productivity, 1960–1963* and from U.S. Army, Corps of Engineers, *Waterborne Commerce of the United States*, Part 4: *Waterways and Harbors, Pacific Coast, Alaska and Hawaii*, aggregated and matched to the productivity data by commodity. See my Appendix B, pp. 238–257, for a detailed discussion of sources and methods used in developing the data.

modity, multiplied by the tonnage handled, yields the estimated direct labor man-hours required to handle the good at the base-year rate. Repeating the operation for all commodities, and summing the man-hours, results in estimated total direct labor man-hours required, for a given year, at the base-year rates (line *a* of the Table). The indirect labor hours required in the given year at base-year rates may be estimated by applying the relevant base-year ratio of indirect hours to total tonnage or to total direct labor man-hours. The latter was used in Table 6 (line *b*). The difference between total longshore hours estimated in this fashion and man-hours actually used to load or unload cargo is the man-hour savings. Man-hours saved relative to man-hours actually used is directly a measure of the productivity in the given year relative to the base year. The estimate is in fact an index number, with the various tonnages weighting the productivity rate for each good.

The productivity rates, implicit in the table, were calculated from the data in the PMA studies. Inasmuch as the detailed tonnage data — available only from government sources for the nonstudy years — were disaggregated by commodity, but not by package, only a single rate for loading and one for discharging could be used for each commodity.

Table 7 presents a summary of the results and the relevant figures underlying one set of estimates of productivity for the eight years studied. The estimates use the identical method applied in Table 6.

Although Table 7 embodies the best estimates of productivity change, given the available data, it is appropriate to point out its weaknesses, and the steps taken to overcome, or, at least, to evaluate them. The identification of the tonnages actually handled by longshoremen, choice of productivity rates, estimate of indirect hours, and similar matters involve judgment and are sources of potential error. Of the total tonnage reported by the Corps of Engineers, a large fraction is neither loaded nor discharged by longshoremen — especially liquids carried in bulk by tankships and some bulk goods, low in value relative to their weight, usually transported by barge. These goods were excluded from the above estimates and, indeed, from almost all of the estimates. Of the fifty-two commodity classifications resulting from the reconciliation of the Engineers' tonnages and the PMA productivity data, only forty-five were known or

Table 7: Man-hours Required, Man-hours Saved, and Productivity Change,[a] 1957-1964.

	1957	1958	1959	1960	1961	1962	1963	1964
	-----	-----	-----	*thousands*	-----	-----	-----	-----
Estimated direct man-hours required at the 1960 rates	15,611	14,191	15,108	16,006	15,561	15,505	17,991	19,859
Estimated total longshore man-hours	22,973	20,883	22,233	23,554	22,899	22,817	26,475	29,224
Longshore man-hours actually used	23,933	23,063	23,552	23,554	22,115	21,021	21,953	21,809
Man-hour savings	—960	—2,180	—1,319	0	784	1,796	4,522	7,415
	-----	-----	-----	*percent*	-----	-----	-----	-----
Productivity change relative to 1960 (in percent)	—4.0	—9.5	—5.6	0	3.6	8.5	20.6	34.0

[a] The "revised basic list" of commodities was used for this set of estimates — see Appendix B for details of commodity composition of the estimates and similar matters.

SOURCES: Longshore man-hours used: for 1959–1964, PMA Contract Data Department, memo dated February 9, 1966; for 1957 and 1958, PMA Contract Data Department, memo dated June 30, 1966, with hours adjusted at the 1960 proportion to compensate for the omission of Eureka and Stockton. All other figures calculated from Corps of Engineers' tonnage data and PMA productivity study data for 1960.

assumed to have been handled by longshoremen, at least in part. Within these forty-five classifications, identified in Table 6, the tonnages reported by the Engineers for at least two — lumber and petroleum — clearly overstate the quantities actually worked by longshoremen. In the estimates of Tables 6 and 7, the tonnages for these two goods have been adjusted. The illustrated estimates further assume that the productivity rates are appropriately weighted by the

Table 8: Range and Median, Eighteen Estimates of Productivity Change, Pacific Coast Longshoring, 1957-1964. (in percent deviation from 1960)

Year	Range of estimate	Median (rounded)
1957	−8.21 to −2.49	−5
1958	−12.89 to −6.63	−10
1959	−8.22 to −4.48	−6
1960	—	—
1961	1.25 to 6.51	4
1962	7.05 to 11.14	9
1963	17.95 to 22.26	20
1964	29.52 to 35.50	32

SOURCE: Appendix, table B-5.

commodity tonnages as reported by the Engineers, whereas there is some doubt that this is so. The PMA studies, for example, attributed a good deal more tonnage to general cargo than is assigned by using the Engineers' data. Many, possibly all of the commodity productivity rates very likely are biased as a result. Finally, the approach of the two tables uses the productivity rates calculated from the 1960 data; three alternative sets, from the other three study years, could have been used.

In all, a large number of different estimates were made, each reflecting different rates, weights, and assumptions. The results are summarized in Table 8; the median of the eighteen estimates is separately identified for convenience in further discussion. The many numbers and rather wide range for each year, although possibly disconcerting, nonetheless are helpful in establishing the likely outside limits of productivity change for any year and to emphasize the fact that any estimate is no more than a reasonable approximation.

Despite the range of the estimates for any one year, the direction and approximate size of year-to-year changes are clear indeed. Productivity in 1960 had increased over the preceding years by at least 5 percent. Further, there is no detectable trend in the pre-1960 years, although productivity in 1958 apparently was rather lower than in the other years. In the years after 1960, there is no doubt that productivity increased significantly each successive year — the ranges of the

Table 9: Summary, Various Estimates of Productivity Change,
Pacific Coast Longshoring, 1957-1965.
(in percent deviation from 1960)

Year	Crude estimates		Careful estimates		
	a	b	c	d	e
1957	6.2	1.8	—	—4.0	—5
1958	—12.6	—8.1	—	—9.5	—10
1959	—11.3	—5.5	—	—5.6	—6
1960	0	0	—	0	0
1961	7.3	3.4	6.5	3.6	4
1962	10.2	14.1	12.9	8.5	9
1963	23.5	21.8	17.5	20.6	20
1964	32.5	34.2	—	34.0	32
1965	42.1	40.6	—		

SOURCES AND NOTES:
[a] Uses total tons divided by total man-hours; from the data underlying Table 3, p. 111.
[b] Largely the same data as the first estimate, but eliminates the effect of bulk tonnage variations; from Table 4, p. 113.
[c] PMA estimates, from Table 5, p. 116.
[d] Of all the careful estimates, this is the preferred one. It uses the revised basic list of commodities, Engineers' tonnage weights, general cargo weighted at average general cargo rates, and the 1960 productivity rates. From Table 7, p. 123.
[e] The median, rounded, of eighteen estimates; from Table 8, p. 124.

estimates do not even overlap. Finally, productivity increased in the post-1960 period at an average annual rate of about 8 percent, plus or minus 1 percent, relative to 1960.

The facts of increased productivity in the post-1960 years are indisputable and, in one sense, not surprising. Everyone — management officials, union leaders and members, and the interested public — expected increased efficiency to result from the agreement. On the other hand, the magnitude of the productivity increase very likely was unexpected. The employers certainly anticipated an increase of at least 10 percent or so in exchange for their fund contributions. The union side expected, or sought to prepare for, larger increases in efficiency — probably 25 percent, perhaps more.[13] A well-informed and interested observer, Dr. Max Kossoris, wrote in 1960:

> So far, neither the employer group nor the union has a good measure of what the modernization program will mean in terms of man-hours saved. No one knows how fast and how far the program will move. Estimates of the reduction of man-hour requirements have gone as high as 35 percent by the end of the agreement's term. . . .

> For the industry as a whole, with gains varying widely between individual shipping companies for a variety of reasons, it probably is not unreasonable to expect a successful program to yield an improvement of 25 percent or better over the next 5 years.[14]

It was a good forecast, only a bit low.

All the various estimates, the crude and the careful alike, are brought together in Table 9. Rather surprisingly, the crude estimates appear to be reasonably accurate, especially when the effects of bulk tonnage variations are eliminated. Although the close correspondence is a bit disheartening — the careful estimates involve vastly more work than simply dividing total tons by total man-hours — it is also valuable. The crude estimates provide measures of productivity that are reasonably accurate for the years before 1957.

Several decades of productivity experience in Pacific Coast longshoring may be summarized as follows. Productivity apparently dropped during the first few years of unionization in the mid-1930s — perhaps by 20 to 30 percent. Efficiency then remained approximately constant through 1959. Only rather small fluctuations — generally no more than a few percent of the mean — took

---

13. *Hard figures bearing on expectations of either the employer or union side are hard to find. Nonetheless, the union clearly was interested in estimating the maximum likely increase in efficiency in order to prepare for the adverse manpower effects. The implicit guess, used to determine the size of the employer contributions and the various funds, was that productivity would increase — and manpower be displaced — at a rate matching work-force attrition of about 4 percent per year, or an overall productivity increase of about 25 percent during the life of the agreement. For example, see Lincoln Fairley,* "The ILWU-PMA Mechanization and Modernization Agreement: An Evaluation of Experience under the Agreement; The Union's Viewpoint," *Proceedings of the Sixteenth Annual Meeting,* Industrial Relations Research Association (December, 1963), p. 5.

14. *Max D. Kossoris,* "Working Rules in West Coast Longshoring," Monthly Labor Review, *LXXXIV (1961), pp. 7–8.*

place from year to year. In 1960, however, and in every year thereafter, productivity increased over the preceding year. By 1965, productivity was higher than ever before on the docks — 40 percent above 1960 — and it continued to rise. The post-1960 rise, dramatic enough in itself, is even more impressive when viewed against the background of decades of no change.

V / SOURCES OF PRODUCTIVITY CHANGE

Both the union and the employers expected that the mechanization and modernization agreement would increase productivity. They were less certain and less unanimous, however, about the effects and the importance of the various changes in work practices and production techniques. The union emphasized the encouragement of mechanization: the members and lower level union officials, if not those at the top, expected a large part of the increased productivity to derive from more and new machinery. Many employers, in contrast, recognizing that not all companies could mechanize to the same degree, stressed the gain from modernization, i.e., elimination of unnecessary work and men, reduction of idle time, and, perhaps, greater effort from the work force.

The PMA did not attempt to evaluate the various contributing elements of productivity change. Indeed, the Association's productivity study committee recommended discontinuance of the studies in part because, in their view, the increases in efficiency, if any, could not be related to specific sources. Despite their pessimism, the data are in fact good enough to identify and assess the factors contributing to increased efficiency on the Pacific docks.

ELIMINATION OF RESTRICTIVE WORK RULES AND PRACTICES

Although the 1960 agreement was in force almost immediately after ratification, the major changes in work practices were longer in coming. The implementation of the agreement was necessarily a slow process. The contract language required interpretation, by mutual agreement or by arbitration. Further, the elimination of many of the rules or practices involved renegotiation of a safe or reasonable work load or new manning scales, commodity by commodity, port by port.

The makework of multiple-handling rules and dockwork[1] man-

1. *In this chapter, and usually elsewhere, dockwork is defined to include all*

ning were spectacular forms of featherbedding. Although the building and breaking down of palletized loads to the skin of the dock involved work, much of it was patently unnecessary, even to the untrained eye. In addition to multiple handling, redundant dockwork manning and informal output controls in some ports limited average output even further. Moreover, dockwork man-hours were a considerable proportion of total longshore man-hours — about 18 percent of all direct labor man-hours reported in the productivity studies in 1960. In brief, dockwork restrictions, especially multiple handling,

Table 10: Dockwork Man-hour Savings and Productivity Changes, 1961-1963.
(in thousands of man-hours)

Man-hours Measure	1961	1962	1963
All dockwork[a]			
Direct labor man-hours used	1,865.6	1,592.8	1,569.9
Direct labor man-hours saved[b]	582.5	957.0	946.3
Productivity change, relative to 1960 (in percent)	31.2	60.1	60.2
Direct labor man-hours saved, all operations[b]	1,014.8	1,726.3	2,264.7
Dockwork savings relative to all savings (percent)	57.5	55.5	41.8

[a] For the goods identified in Table 13.

[b] Estimated from PMA data for total man-hour savings from all longshore operations, by commodity; includes minor package shifts but excludes the effects of a shift to bulk handling or to containers for all commodities, and to unit loads, cribs and vans in general cargo.

SOURCE: Calculated from data in the PMA productivity studies.

appeared to impose a substantial tax on Pacific Coast ocean shipping. Employers, union officials, and members all expected appreciable results from the elimination of these restrictions. Their expectations were borne out.

Despite difficulties in interpretation and implementation of some dockwork provisions of the 1960 agreement, dockwork man-hours declined sharply in 1961 and decreased further in 1962, as shown in Table 10. Allowing for volume- and cargo-composition changes, nearly 600,000 fewer man-hours were used in 1961 than would have been required at the 1960 rates, and almost a million

work done by longshoremen on the dock except the actual attaching or disengaging the load at the ship's gear (performed by frontmen) for each hatch.

fewer in 1962. By 1963, dockwork man-hour savings amounted to a productivity increase of 60 percent over 1960 for that segment of longshoring. Improved handling of almost all goods had contributed to the increase in dockwork efficiency. Dockwork man-hour savings were large, not only relative to dockwork hours used but also relative to savings from all other longshoring improvements. In fact, the dockwork savings were the chief source of productivity increase in the first two years of the agreement.

The most important source of dockwork productivity increase was the curtailment of multiple handling. Relatively little renegotiation was involved. The 1960 agreement was straightforward — palletizing and depalletizing were to be done by longshoremen, but only on orders by a supervisor. The goods most affected were those requiring palletization at some point in order to be moved easily by forklift on the dock, or by the ship's gear between the dock and the hold. Boxes and cases of canned goods, citrus fruit, other foods and miscellaneous general cargo, and bags of grain, flour, earths, chemicals and so on, are leading examples. These goods were handled in packages so small that they had to be assembled for further movement. Nine or ten or even several dozen cases, boxes, or sacks were normally stacked or piled on a pallet, and the repeated assembly and disassembly of such loads — characteristic of multiple handling — required considerable labor input. Only these goods could be prepalletized, and, hence, be seriously affected by the pre-1960 ban on prepalletization.

The 1960 agreement quickly yielded results. Goods usually palletized, and subject to multiple handling, accounted for most of the substantial amount of dockwork man-hours saved in each of the postagreement years. By 1963, their 600,000 annual hours saved were two thirds of the dockwork total.

The numbers themselves provide the best illustrations of the effects of elimination of double or triple handling (Table 11). Canned goods are an example. In 1963 about 250,000 tons of prepalletized canned goods were loaded at Pacific ports with only 4,100 dockwork man-hours. At 1960 dockwork rates, the same tonnage would have required more than 48,000 man-hours. The 44,000 man-hours saved represents a dockwork productivity increase of about 1,000 percent. Similarly, some 89,000 tons of prepalletized bagged rice would have required 15,000 dockwork man-hours with multiple handling, but

Table 11: Dockwork Man-hours Used and Saved, by Prepalletized and On-Dock Rates, Selected Goods, 1963.
(in thousands of man-hours)

Commodity, Loading	Actual hours	Hours required at 1960 rates	Man-hour savings
Canned Goods	*18.8*	*77.5*[d]	*58.7*
Prepalletized[a]	4.1	48.4	44.3
Boarded on dock[b]	14.7	26.2	11.5
Unit loads	0	1.2	1.2
(Package shift)[c]	—	—	(1.7)
Rice (nonbulk)	*0.3*	*17.9*[d]	*17.6*
Prepalletized	0	15.0	15.0
Boarded on dock	0.3	2.9	2.6
Flour	*5.7*	*19.3*[d]	*13.6*
Prepalletized	0.6	6.1	5.5
Boarded on dock	5.1	7.2	2.1
(Package shift)	—	—	(6.0)
Citrus	*24.3*	*45.8*[d]	*21.5*
Prepalletized	0	14.3	14.3
Boarded on dock	24.3	34.7	10.4
(Package shift)	—	—	(—3.2)

[a] Goods placed on pallets (by other than longshoremen) before arrival at the dock.

[b] Palletized by longshoremen at the dock or in the ship.

[c] The efficiency realized by shifting from more to less labor-intensive modes of handling; i.e., the shift of tonnage from "boarded on dock" to "prepalletized" would result in positive man-hour savings. The difference between the hours estimated at the all-package rate and the sum of the hours estimated at the individual package rates is the package shift effect.

[d] Estimated at the single, all-package rate.

SOURCE: Calculated from PMA productivity data.

actually used none in 1963. Prepalletized citrus — 22,000 tons in 1963 — required no dockwork hours, and 163,000 tons of prepalletized bagged flour needed only 600 dockwork hours, whereas with multiple handling they would have used about 14,300 and 6,100 hours respectively.

Relaxation of jurisdictional claims to piling the goods or breaking down high piles on the dock was a minor source of dockwork improvement. The 1960 agreement provided that nonlongshore truck drivers could deposit or pick up directly from the dock floor goods piled not more than "one load high." Higher piles could be made or broken down only by longshoremen. However, in 1962 the union agreed that "two loads high shall not constitute high piling," thus giving up a bit more dockwork.[2] High-piling disputes were frequent and serious, especially in southern California, in 1961 and 1962. After the "two loads rule" was introduced, the number of disputes declined appreciably.[3] The broader exemption to high piling very likely resulted in a net reduction of hours required to handle the goods. That is, the longshoremen's insistence that they alone make or break down the piles involved unnecessary work or redundant manning. Teamsters could load their trucks with about the same efficiency from high piles as from low ones.

Although eliminating multiple handling was the most important source of dockwork productivity increase, abandoning dockwork manning requirements and giving up resistance to improved machines or methods of handling were also important. Together, they accounted for perhaps one fifth of the postagreement dockwork productivity increase. Cotton loading provides an illustration of new machines and methods. The old method required six dockmen to load the 500-pound bales to four-wheelers to be towed from the place of rest to the ship's side, or four men to palletize the bales for movement by forklift. A newer variety of lift truck, a "squeeze lift," picks up the bales directly at the place of rest, without requiring pallets, and carries them to the hook. No dockmen are needed.[4] Iron and steel mill products, especially bars, rods, pipe, and similar goods, illustrate the relaxation of dockwork manning requirements. The goods often are discharged by the ship's gear, carried to the place of rest by mechanical power, and deposited on blocks set on the dock by longshore dock workers. Immediately after the 1960 agreement was signed, employers pressed for reduction in dockwork manning from six or four men to just two men to set the blocks. Their demands were met.[5] By 1963 these two commodities — cotton, and iron and steel mill products (including pipe) — accounted for al-

---

2. Memorandum of Understanding, *July 30, 1962.*
3. *See the Germain Bulcke awards of November 27, 1961, and December 12, 1961, June 13, 1962, and August 10, 1962. The latter defined the "load" as the standard maxima in the 1937 schedule of sling-load limits.*
4. *See the Bulcke award of October 3, 1960, for example.*
5. *Bulcke awards of November 10, 1960, and December 17, 1960.*

Table 12: Dockwork Man-hours Used and Saved, by Region, Pacific Coast, 1963.
(in thousands of tons of 2,000 pounds and thousands of man-hours)

Regions	1960	1963	Man-hours saved[a]	Crude productivity increase[b] (in percent)
Washington				
Tons (nonbulk)	2,638.4	3,524.8		
Dockwork hours	307.7	222.1	189.—[a]	85.0
Oregon				
Tons (nonbulk)	3,024.0	2,941.2		
Dockwork hours	204.5	83.0	116.—	140.0
Northern California				
Tons (nonbulk)	4,322.8	4,544.9		
Dockwork hours	852.4	499.0	397.—	79.5
Southern California				
Tons (nonbulk)	3,975.7	4,529.7		
Dockwork hours	1,324.7	801.1	709.—	88.5

[a] Total nonbulk tons and total dockwork hours for each region were used to calculate crude rates. The 1963 tonnage was multiplied by the 1960 rate (dockwork man-hours per ton) to estimate, very roughly, the dockwork hours required in 1963 if there had been no change in productivity. The difference between the estimated required hours and the actual man-hours appears as man-hour savings.

[b] Man-hours saved divided by actual man-hours used. The measure is "crude" because it does not allow for commodity and package differences or changes.

SOURCE: Calculated from data in PMA productivity studies.

most 160,000 dockwork man-hours saved annually, or about half the savings of all goods usually not palletized.[6]

Union delegates from Los Angeles feared the effects of the elimination of work rules, especially the loss of the multiple-handling requirements, more than any of the other locals, in part because their port was alleged to have had the most serious featherbedding. Table 12 provides a rough measure of confirmation. The southern Californian loss of dockwork man-hours was greater than that of any other region of the Pacific Coast; indeed, it was nearly half the total. Nevertheless, the loss, at least as of 1963, was not so large as had been expected. The Los Angeles region still was using 800,000 dockwork

6. See Appendix Table C–6. The category "goods often not palletized" was established to identify the goods not amenable to multiple handling.

hours annually, about the total of all the other ports.[7] It appears likely that room remains for substantial improvement.

Very nearly all the productivity increase associated with dock-work must be attributed solely to work-rules abandonment. Although investment changes could have played a role, it is very likely that any new machines would have been overmanned if there had been no changes in work rules. However, this argument is largely beside the point; little investment directly bearing on nonbulk dock-work efficiency appears to have taken place. The possibilities for investment are slight, or have not been fully tapped. To be sure, dock-work savings associated with some goods, those usually not pallet-ized and thus unaffected by multiple-handling restrictions, may be linked in part to investment. The strongest case is banana discharg-ing. Almost all the 300,000 tons or so unloaded each year are dis-charged at two facilities — one each in the San Francisco and Los Angeles harbor areas — using mechanically powered belt conveyors to move the goods from the hold directly to the railcar, truck, or more rarely, dockside place of rest. There is no doubt that dockwork hours would be much greater without than with the equipment. However, the operation was already substantially mechanized at the signing of the 1960 agreement.[8]

With respect to other goods, most of the investment that might be associated with reduction in longshoring expenses is directed at all parts of the loading or discharging operation, not just dockwork. Nonetheless, some comments are in order. Lumber loading and dis-charging do involve special lift or carrier trucks to handle the large, often unitized loads. However, much of the equipment was used at least several years before the 1960 agreement, and unitized loads

7. *The crude calculations overstate the improvements in the Northwest ports and exaggerate the differences between southern California and the other regions. The Oregon and Washington ports handle very large tonnages of goods requiring little or no dockwork — logs and lumber, for example. Further, the trend over time has been toward logs, requiring no dockwork, and away from lumber which does require some dockside labor to load. Commodity and package differences from port to port and changes over time are responsible for the substantial discrepancy between man-hour savings and productivity changes on this table and those shown in all other tables of this section.*
8. *There has been new investment since 1960 in these facilities. The amount is not known. It may be assumed that all, or none, of the dockwork man-hour savings are the result of the new investment with little effect on the main argument. Only 20,000 man-hours annually are involved, and no further dock-work improvement is possible — no hours were used in 1963.*

were already a large fraction of all lumber handled in 1960. The unitized proportion of lumber discharged, reported in the PMA productivity data, was 55.7 percent in 1960, 56.4 percent in 1963. Of all lumber loaded in 1960, 47 percent was in unit loads; in 1963, the proportion had risen to 62 percent. Similarly, newsprint is handled by unorthodox equipment — using shipboard cranes and specialized hook-on gear in most cases — but much of the technical improvement and investment took place before the 1960 agreement. In any event, all dockwork man-hours saved in handling goods even suspected of benefiting from appreciable investment changes would amount to only a small fraction of total dockwork savings. The vast majority of commodities and tons are moved over the same docks, between the same or similar ships, using the same or similar lift trucks and pallets as were used in 1960. The most important difference, analogous to a production function shift caused by a costless change in the state of the art, was the elimination of unnecessary work and redundant manning on the dock.

The evidence indicates that the abandonment of multiple handling and other dockwork restrictive rules and practices led to immediate and substantial improvement in efficiency. These rules changes were so important that dockwork man-hour savings alone would have resulted in an aggregate productivity increase for the Pacific Coast ports of about 4.2 percent in 1961, 7.4 percent in 1962, and 7.1 percent in 1963, relative to 1960.

Continued improvement in dockwork efficiency in 1964 and 1965, equivalent to a coastwide productivity increase of at least another 2 or 3 percent, very likely took place. For one reason, no substantial shift to prepalletization or unit loads took place between 1960 and 1963. It appears reasonable to expect at least a modest increase in both. Secondly, some multiple handling and redundant manning still existed at the end of 1963. A 1965 dispute illustrates the continuing problem. In Portland, Teamsters were unloading steel from their truck to blocks set on the dock by longshoremen. Local ILWU officials protested that placing the steel on the blocks, not the mere setting of the blocks, was the "load building" reserved by the contract to longshoremen. The arbitrator agreed, and found the employer guilty of violating the agreement.[9] This is not multiple

9. The Roger Fielding award of June 25, 1965.

handling, but the possibility exists that the goods in this case would have been handled with fewer man-hours had the arbitrator ruled differently.

The reductions in manning scales and consequent productivity increase in bulk operations are as spectacular illustrations of make-work elimination as the multiple handling and other dockwork changes. The overmanning on much of bulk handling was flagrant, and both parties knew it. In a southern California dispute submitted to arbitration just before the 1960 agreement was signed, the union

Table 13: Man-hours Saved 1961-1963, and Productivity Change, 1963, Bulk Cargo, by Commodity.
(in thousands of man-hours)

Commodity[a]	1961 Man-hours saved[b]	1962 Man-hours saved	1963 Man-hours saved	1963 Man-hours used[a]	Productivity change, 1960–1963 (in percent)
Loading:					
Rice	—0.3	—0.7	0.3	4.9	6.1
Wheat, barley, rye	5.2	16.4	42.9	219.1	19.6
Tallow	—1.4	0.4	1.7	3.7	46.0
Animal feeds	7.5	12.8	13.0	19.1	68.1
Coke	6.5	8.7	25.5	67.1	38.0
Ore (mostly iron)	—6.8	4.4	22.9	19.2	119.2
Basic metal, iron and steel	6.4	0.9	—0.6	2.5	—24.0
Scrap, iron and steel	4.3	10.9	12.7	27.2	46.7
Potash	6.1	13.5	19.2	22.6	85.0
Discharging:					
Sugar	13.0	8.3	22.9	57.0	40.2
Copra	30.5	51.7	34.8	111.9	31.1
Salt	6.7	36.8	60.7	12.4	489.0
Ores (mostly nonferrous metal)	—10.4	2.9	3.6	37.4	9.6
Chemicals	—0.8	—0.5	3.3	0.6	555.0
General cargo	15.0	9.1	39.7	31.0	128.0
Total	81.5	175.6	302.6	635.7	47.5

[a] Only the tonnages and hours actually reported to PMA for bulk-loading operations are used in the calculations.

[b] The difference between man-hours estimated at 1960 productivity rates and man-hours actually used in the year indicated.

SOURCE: Calculated from data in the PMA productivity studies.

insisted that six holdmen be employed for each hatch to handle scrap iron. The employers wanted none but were willing to compromise at two men. The arbitrator noted, "the sole objection of the Union was to the elimination of six jobs which had theretofore existed." He agreed with the employers, "the six men are admittedly not needed."[10] The unnecessary men were required to be taken on by the employer in this case, but the situation changed after 1960. In a more recent dispute, the local union officials sought eleven men on a scrap operation, but the employers wanted, and got, just four men.[11]

The history of loading iron and steel scrap suggests that preagreement manning scales of ten to twelve men could be reduced by 40 to 60 percent. Such reductions appear actually to have taken place. The PMA data indicate that little change occurred in 1961, but in 1962 the man-hour savings for loading scrap were about 11,000 for the year. Average productivity — output per man-hour — had increased by about 40 percent over 1960, and it increased a bit more in 1963.

An even more striking example of the elimination of "witnesses" in bulk operations occurred in nonferrous ore discharging at a Northwest port. The ore was dug out of the hold by shore-based cranes. Manning had been disputed for years, and as recently as 1959 the union had succeeded in retaining ten men to the hatch, even after arbitration.[12] During 1964 the parties negotiated the most recent manning, this time under the new agreement: just two men were to constitute the basic gang.[13] On this operation at least, an 80 percent reduction in labor input was possible without reducing output and without increased investment.

By 1963, productivity had increased a great deal for almost all goods handled with bulk facilities or equipment (see Table 13). Of the three goods exhibiting a decrease, or only modest increases in productivity, rice loading probably was not overmanned in 1960 (its 1960 rate was 50 percent above that for wheat), basic iron was han-

---

10. *Bulcke award of October 4, 1960. Bulcke had resigned his second vice presidency of the union to become an arbitrator only about two months before this award.*
11. *L. B. Thomas award of May 13, 1965, and CLRC minutes of September 28, 1962.*
12. *The union tried to require eleven men, but the arbitrator permitted only ten. The Roderick award of February 4, 1959.*
13. *Described in the Sam Kagel award of January 5, 1965.*

dled in only a small quantity in 1963, and manning for nonferrous ore discharging had not yet been renegotiated in all ports. For all other goods, output per man-hour in 1963 was 20 to 500 percent above the 1960 rates. Bulk-handling manning scales were only beginning to be renegotiated in 1961; only copra discharging reflected a significant change during the year. Substantial progress occurred in 1962; productivity for all bulk goods was about 26 percent above 1960 (see Table 14), and almost all goods contributed to the rise. Major improvements continued in 1963, when the all-bulk weighted average rate was 47½ percent above the base year.

Table 14: Man-hour Savings and Productivity Change, Bulk Operations, 1961-1963.
(in thousands of man-hours)

Man-hour measure	1961	1962	1963
All bulk operations:			
Direct labor hours used[a]	936.6	684.5	635.7
Direct labor man-hours savings[b]	81.3	175.6	302.6
Productivity change, relative to 1960 (percent)	8.7	25.7	47.5
Total direct labor man-hour savings, all operations[b]	1,014.8	1,726.3	2,264.7
Bulk savings relative to total (percent)	8.6	10.3	13.4

[a] For the goods identified in Table V-4.
[b] Total man-hour savings from all longshore operations estimated from PMA data by commodity; includes minor package shifts but excludes effects of shift to bulk or containers for all commodities, and to unit loads, cribs, and vans in general cargo.
SOURCE: Calculated from PMA data.

Increased investment could have but probably did not contribute to the increase in bulk-handling productivity. A large fraction of port investment has gone into the building of new specialized facilities, largely for bulk handling and mostly in southern California. Substantial new facilities were built in the 1960–1963 years to handle iron ore loading, grain loading, copra storage, and salt discharging, all at Long Beach. New, but far less extensive, buildings and equipment for bulk operations were built at Seattle and San Diego.[14] It is possible that some part of the productivity increases for

14. *Port of New York Authority,* Port Development Expenditure Survey; United States, Puerto Rico, Canada; January 1, 1946 to December 31, 1962 *(New*

iron are loading and salt discharging, for example, have been associated with the new investment. To the extent that new technology is incorporated in the new capital goods, or that increasing returns to scale obtain, the investment would result in increased productivity rates to both major factor inputs. On the other hand, most of the bulk tonnage is handled by techniques and equipment already in existence in 1960. There is little doubt that manning scales on existing operations would not have changed appreciably in the absence of the 1960 agreement, and that the negotiated scales for new facilities would have included "witnesses."

The effect of the added investment, incurred to meet changes in the demand for the commodity handled, would be larger output, but at about the same average productivity as before.

Analytically, the new bulk-handling investment represents the added capital in a larger input combination required in order to produce a larger output. The investment is a response to changed product market conditions, not changed relative factor prices. Assuming a homogeneous production function, no change in productivity would occur. Even with a technologically based, nonhomogeneous production function — e.g., with increasing returns to scale — the negotiated labor inputs easily could have imposed manning such that average productivity, relative to labor, was constant over all output levels. In this sense, the observed productivity increases since 1960 in bulk operations may be attributed largely to union concessions on redundant manning.

Despite the real and very large productivity increases in bulk operations, the impact of rule abandonment in this sector on the aggregate productivity increase for the whole industry has been relatively slight. In 1961, man-hour savings from bulk operations contributed only 8.6 percent of the total direct labor man-hours saved; in 1963, the much larger savings from bulk improvements were still less than 14 percent of the total. Put another way, if the only productivity increases in 1961 through 1963 had been those associated with bulk operations, the aggregate coastwide productivity increase for 1961 would have been less than .016 percent and, for 1963, only about 2.25 percent.

York, 1963), pp. 19–20. About 33.5 million dollars were invested in all Pacific ports for specialized facilities from mid-1960 through 1962 (ibid., p. 8). This includes expenditures for container docks and equipment, and petroleum depot facilities as well as dry-cargo, bulk-handling plant and equipment.

Manning reductions certainly continued in 1964 and 1965 and probably will occur in the future. The post-1960 negotiated or arbitrated manning scales still appear to be compromises in that criteria other than efficiency or safety appear to be used. In a 1963 instance, the union was prepared to reduce manning on a bulk animal-feeds operation to an eight-man basic gang. The employers sought only three men. The arbitrator ruled that five men would be "the minimum basic gang for a free-pour, self-trimming operation." It appears reasonable to assume that the scale eventually will be reduced further.[15] However, employment in bulk operations, even with the undeniable redundancy of 1960, is so small relative to total longshore employment that the complete elimination of all labor input would lead to a measured aggregate productivity increase of no more than about 7 percent. It is likely that the improvements by 1964 or 1965 were the equivalent of a 3 or 4 percent aggregate productivity increase over 1960.

Shipwork on conventional break-bulk operations is the most important single segment of longshore work. It accounts for most of the direct labor man-hours — 75 to 80 percent in 1960–1963. Unlike bulk operations or dockwork, even slight improvements in shipwork efficiency have a significant impact on overall productivity.

The measured improvements in shipwork efficiency through 1963 have been modest. (Table 15). The several hundred thousand man-hours saved in 1961 and 1962 appear large only when compared with the small absolute savings from bulk operations in those years. Dockwork man-hour savings were larger in both 1961 and 1962, and only slightly smaller in 1963. The shipwork segment of nonbulk operations contributed only about one third of aggregate man-hour savings in the first three years of the M&M agreement. Put another way, the productivity increases in shipwork were only 3 percent, 6 percent, and 9 percent for the three years, far less than the 50 and 60 percent increases achieved by 1963 in both the bulk operations and the dockwork part of nonbulk work.

Shipwork efficiency improvements have been slower in coming, and more seriously contested by local union officials and rank-and-file members in part because so many persons are involved. The contrast with bulk handling and dockwork is sharp. The "witnesses" on

15. *The Kagel award of February 8, 1968.*

Table 15: Shipwork Man-hour Savings and Productivity Change,
1961-1963.
(in thousands of man-hours)

	1961	1962	1963
Shipwork[a]			
Loading			
Direct labor man-hours used	7,729.2	7,040.8	7,832.4
Direct labor man-hours saved	199.1	257.7	633.8
Discharging			
Direct labor man-hours used	3,254.7	3,414.8	3,327.2
Direct labor man-hours saved	151.8	336.8	382.0
Total			
Direct labor man-hours used	10,983.9	10,455.6	11,159.6
Direct labor man-hours saved	350.9	594.5	1,015.8
Productivity change, relative to 1960 (in percent)	3.2	5.7	9.1
Direct labor man-hours saved, all operations[b]	1,014.8	1,726.3	2,264.7
Shipwork savings relative to all savings (percent)	34.6	34.4	44.8

[a] Shipwork hours and savings for all nonbulk tonnage reported and identified by commodity in the PMA productivity studies.

[b] Total man-hour savings from all longshore operations estimated from PMA data, by commodity; includes minor package shifts but excludes the effects of a shift to bulk handling or to containers for all commodities, and to unit loads, cribs, and vans in general cargo.

SOURCE: Calculated from the data in the PMA productivity studies.

bulk operations and persons affected by multiple-handling elimination were only a small fraction of any local's membership. Further, many of the men involved in these two categories of operations were the older, long-service men who received strong inducement to leave the labor force altogether. Shipwork gangs, on the other hand, are a large fraction of the membership of every local, and most of the men in them continued to work during the life of the 1960 agreement.

The heart of shipwork is the hold. More than half the ship gang work in the hold, and all the physical labor in this stage of cargo loading and unloading takes place below decks. Further, the hold-men derived little direct benefit from the 1960 agreement. They are the youngest longshoremen in both age and length of service on the docks; as a consequence, they were unaffected by the early retirement vested benefits of the agreement. Moreover, a great many holdmen have been limited-registered "B" men and are not protected against unemployment. The wage guarantee fund, for example, specifically excludes them.

Before the agreement union load-limit and standard-gang policies obstructed investment to the extent that they were actually restrictive.[16] In the discussions leading to the agreement, union leaders repeatedly acknowledged that their resistance to labor displacement effectively blocked the use of more machinery. Yet the leaders of the union also were concerned with the heavy manual labor still required in longshoring, especially in the hold. Harry Bridges often took the part of the holdmen.

And what do we find there? We find everybody breaking their damn back to get out of that hold. That is true in every port. And mostly your work on the Pacific Coast today is being done by people who are not members of the union [the "B" men and casuals]. They are not members of the industry. They are outsiders. Nobody wants to go in the hold. . . .

To hell with this business of eight holdmen bucking a completely mechanized operation in the hold and all kinds of people standing around on the dock or running machines and the guys down below are really taking a beating. That is not unionism.[17]

Although Bridges at first suggested, in 1956 and 1957, that increasing the hold gang might be a solution,[18] the top union leadership quickly adopted the position that mechanization would best ease the load of the holdmen. In the 1956 caucus Bridges advocated " 'one machine in every hold' and let the man be standing on the machine instead of sweating in the hold."[19] In 1956 negotiations with the employers, and even more in 1957, he explicitly linked the union's willingness to give up restrictive practices to mechanization

16. See Appendix A, pp. 214–221, for analysis of this point. In this and the subsequent sentences, more investment, capital, or machinery refers to the capital-for-labor substitution represented by movement along an isoquant. That is, capital and labor are used in different combinations in response to changed relative factor prices or lifting the restrictions to permit adoption of the least-cost combination of inputs, for any given output.

17. ILWU, Proceedings of the Longshore, Shipclerk and Walking Boss Caucus, May 15, 1956, pp. 438–439.

18. Bridges said to the 1956 caucus delegates, "If we want a program, let's have a program to double the size of the hold gangs" (Ibid., p. 438.) In the 1957 negotiations, Bridges proposed a twelve-man hold gang. The employer representatives did not consider the demand seriously, and it was dropped (Joint Negotiating Committee Minutes, May 20, 1957).

19. 1956 Caucus, p. 439.

and easier holdwork. More important, the leaders defended their rules-abandonment proposals to the union's members in large part on the grounds that the members would not only be sure of their jobs and have good incomes but also would have easier work. Howard Bodine, a member of the Coast Committee, argued,

> We need some new rules. [The first was a wage or work guarantee.]. . . . The second rule would be that no man has to sweat. That is in theory. Some people get very nervous when they get near work and they cannot help but sweat. I happen to be one of those. But I am talking about hard work. Nobody works hard. Because if the work is hard, then the machine is no good; and if the work is hard, the machine should be there doing it. That is Rule No. 2.[20]

In the preagreement discussions, the rank-and-file delegates, and even many of the members of the union's negotiating committee, sought reassurance that work-rule abandonment would not leave them victims to employer demands for more and harder work. Even after dozens of negotiating sessions with employer representatives, the union negotiating committee resolved, by a large majority, to retain existing load limits, except when mechanical equipment was used, and to allow no exceptions to basic standard manning.[21] The PMA representatives in negotiations before the assembled caucus delegates, and the union president in speeches after each negotiating session, did convince the delegates that agreement required greater flexibility for the employers — no load limits and justifiable exceptions to basic manning. However, in the final negotiations, Harry Bridges again made it clear to the employers that the union would use onerousness and anti-speedup arguments to challenge employer attempts to use larger sling loads with unchanged numbers of men and operations. He noted, "the old rallying cry of the supervisors . . . that the hook is hanging — we must meet the hook — that is out the window." [22]

In brief, the union expected mechanization to result from abandonment of the rules, not harder work. They were prepared to give up unnecessary work and jobs involving no work at all — multiple handling and the witnesses — for appropriate transition devices to soften the blow of reduced employment. They were not prepared to

20. *ILWU*, Caucus Proceedings, *October, 1957, pp. 130–131.*
21. Union Negotiating Committee Minutes, *October 2, 1960.*
22. Joint Negotiating Committee Minutes, *October 12, 1960.*

require harder or heavier physical labor for those longshoremen still on the job.

The postagreement years reflect to a great extent the conflicting expectations concerning shipwork of the union members and officials, especially at the local level, and the employers. The former were inclined to require stringent tests for "changed operations," usually some measure of increased mechanization. On the other hand, the employers tended to regard shipwork as similar to bulk operations and dockwork: they were entitled to larger output with unchanged levels of capital and labor inputs.[23] The opposed views led directly to hundreds of grievances or complaints each year, scores of arbitration hearings and awards, occasional informal work stoppages, the expulsion from the industry of one overzealous local union official,[24] and other evidence of serious conflict between the employers and the workers or the union.

Local union officials and members quickly discovered that the sling-load limits had indeed been eliminated by the 1960 agreement. Formally, the schedule of limits was retained, but it was applicable only to those operations not changed since 1937. The language of the agreement obviously required interpretation, and the parties in grievance discussions and arbitrations quickly developed the position that almost any change, however small, was sufficient to exempt the operation from the schedule of load maxima. Prepalletized loads were, of course, immediately exempt.[25] The addition of men to the hold, even though disproportionate to the load-size change, was held to be nonetheless a change in methods. For example, a 100 percent

23. *Analytically, the union view was that they were already on the production function and their rules changes were intended to permit the employer to reach the most efficient input combinations, substituting capital for labor where the rules were actually restrictive. The predominant employer view, most common in southern California, was that the production function could be shifted a bit to permit larger outputs for given input combinations; that is, the pre-1960 situation involved, for shipwork as for bulk handling and dockwork, a negotiated production function.*

24. *Pete Velasquez, a steward in Local 13 of Los Angeles, was deregistered by award of the Coast Arbitrator in early 1965. He had been guilty of eight instances of failing to use the grievance procedure and causing illegal work stoppages. Most of the disputes involved onerousness, safety, and similar issues.*

25. *Bulcke awards of October 6, 1961, March 18, 1963, and July 29, 1963. See also the summarized Minutes, Joint Meeting, Coast Labor Relations Committee and Arbitrators, August 7, 1963, p. 12 and elsewhere.*

Loading drums with a bridle.

The A-shaped special purpose shoreside gantry cranes are capable of handling containers stacked four-high on decks of ships.

Mechanized banana discharging. Shore-mounted cranes extend conveyors into the hold. Left, rail docks; center, truck-loading docks; background, refrigerated storage plant.

A post-1960 method: two prepalletized loads to one draft.

Slingmen hook bridle to pallet load of general cargo.

Loading oranges by conventional break-bulk methods.

Longshoremen handle a unitized load of cotton. Each six-bale module is made up with two-by-fours and steel wire, and weighs 3,000 pounds.

Loading general cargo with pallet and bridle.

Loading logs into a ship especially designed for this cargo. The king-size hatches are equipped with automatic covers and take full sling loads from the 15-ton capacity ship-mounted crane.

Tracked vehicle trims bulk cargo as it is loaded into the hold.

Container ship Hawaiian Monarch *at sea.*

The 1966 negotiations, last day. From left, facing camera: with folded arms, facing his left, B. H. Goodenough, Vice President Shoreside Labor Relations, PMA; with hands on table, J. Paul St. Sure, then Chairman of the Board, PMA; J. A. Robertson, Corporate Secretary, PMA; with pencil in hand, Rocco C. Siciliano, present President of PMA. Backs to camera, left to right: looking down at paper, Harry Bridges, President of the ILWU; William Ward, ILWU Coast Labor Relations Committee member for California; William Forrester, ILWU Coast Labor Relations Committee member for the Pacific Northwest.

increase in the weight of the load accompanied by a 20 percent increase in manning was a changed operation and not bound by the load limits.[26] A minor methods change — working two loads rather than three — with a six-man loading-out hold gang was enough to earn exemption.[27] Perhaps more surprising, operations and methods used for a decade or more suddenly became exempt from the load limits because they had been slightly changed over the years since 1937. In a 1956 dispute involving the discharge of sacks of coffee, the arbitrator ruled against an employer's plea of changed operations based on the dockside use of lift trucks to replace manpower. Sam Kagel at the time observed that the sacks were still manhandled in the hold and that the load limits were therefore applicable. After the 1960 agreement, the same arbitrator ruled that the identical method was a change from the 1937 operations and that the load limit no longer applied.[28] After the early rash of disputes, relatively few attempts were made to challenge load sizes on the grounds that they exceeded contract limits.

Load sizes in fact appear to be significantly larger after the 1960 agreement. The old nine-sack limit on coffee is widely exceeded with twelve, fifteen, or even twenty sacks to the load.[29] Citrus fruit and canned goods may be lifted at 3,000 to 3,500 pounds to the load.[30] Polyethelene, rubber, borax, and aluminum may be loaded or discharged at 3,000 to more than 4,000 pounds to the load.[31] The old limits of approximately 2,100 pounds appear to have been generally exceeded in the postagreement years.

The key to shipwork productivity was shifted by the agreement and its interpretation from load limits per se to manning and methods. In essence, the 1960 agreement was a change from a rigid system of draft size and manning to a system that was at least flexible upward. Formerly, the complaints, if any, originated on the employers' side and usually alleged slowdown. After 1960, the complaints

26. *Bulcke award of May 13, 1963.*
27. *Bulcke award of January 28, 1963.*
28. *Kagel award of April 23, 1956, and Kagel award of May 23, 1963.*
29. *The sacks weigh 100 to 140 pounds each. Examples of the heavier loads are included in the Kagel award of May 23, 1963, the Bulcke awards of December 7, 1962, March 8, 1963, March 26, 1963, April 25, 1963, and others.*
30. *For example, Bulcke award of March 18, 1963, Thomas award of April 28, 1965.*
31. *The Bulcke awards of August 13, 1963, July 10, 1963, May 13, 1963, and the Fielding award of March 13, 1965, include these examples.*

came from the worker or union side and charged speedup. The older system provided objective standards, requiring little or no interpretation, and were presumed to be sufficient to protect the worker. The newer method deliberately eliminated objective criteria and left to the worker and local union official the right, and task, of challenging the employer's decisions.

The consequence has been a very large increase in grievances, much greater reliance on the arbitrators to determine working methods, and the development of informal output or effort criteria. Employer and union complaints submitted to the various joint labor relations committees have increased from several hundred each year before the agreement to several thousand annually since 1960. Arbitrations, in all areas combined, averaged fifteen or twenty each year for a decade before 1960, and as late as 1959 were no more than about thirty-five for the year. In the post-1960 era there have been 150 to 200 hearings and awards annually, many involving multiple grievances. In southern California, for example, there were ten awards in 1959, thirty in 1960, seventy-six in 1961, seventy-five in 1962, ninety-three in 1963, seventy-four in 1964, and so on. In northern California, there were five arbitrations in 1959, and thirty-seven each in 1961 and 1963. In Washington, arbitrations rose from six in 1959 to about twenty each year, 1961 through 1964. The changes in Oregon have been similar in timing and magnitude. A large proportion of the complaints directly or indirectly have to do with methods of work and conventional break-bulk goods handling.

All parties agreed that the contractual protections to the worker — of challenging the employer's decisions on grounds of onerous workload or unsafe conditions — were to be applied on a case-by-case basis, and that the arbitrator should be sensitive to the specific circumstances of each job. In practice, the workers, local officials, and arbitrators tended to expect machines or more men to be used with larger loads. The men often asked for machines, but the arbitrators usually ruled for smaller loads or more men. For example, on an operation involving discharge of sacked ore in southern California, the arbitrator ruled once that the 2,700-2,800-pound loads were not onerous.[32] Later in the year, with the same load size, the same number of men in the hold, and the same number of loads in the hold at any one time, he ruled twice that two men be added and

32. *Bulcke award of January 28, 1963.*

twice that the loads be smaller.[33] For most goods, however, the ruling typically required the addition of more men. In fact, the PMA representatives complained that the arbitrators tended to require extra men almost automatically and then often applied the new scale as a precedent.[34] Furthermore, there was suspicion that even with larger loads, the men continued to work at the same, accustomed rate.[35]

Dissatisfaction with the agreement as it applied to break-bulk shipwork was clearly evident by 1963, and it continued. In the preagreement years Bridges considered adopting a program of compulsory mechanization, but he was dissuaded by PMA representatives. The union dropped its mechanization-for-rules-changes position in 1960, but in 1962 it again sought to require machines or more men for heavy loads. In 1963, Bridges pointed out:

> We intend to push to make the addition of machines compulsory. The days of sweating on these jobs should be gone and that is our objective. . . . We want to eliminate hard work by the use of machines. We are less interested in getting more men than we are in getting machines to make the work easier.[36]

The rank and file continued to complain often and loudly about their disappointed expectations of easier work. The onerousness issue reached a climax of sorts in 1965, when the union sought to establish that the hand-carrying of heavy sacks — belly packing or shoulder packing — was inherently onerous. In 1964 and 1965 a number of local grievances occurred in which the hold gang sought mechanical devices to eliminate hand- or backwork with heavy sacks but were turned down by employers. The men maintained that manhandling fifty- or hundred-pound sacks for distances of thirty or forty feet was in itself onerous. Area arbitrators ruled that the work was indeed arduous, but not onerous within the meaning of the contract. Continuous pressure, however, forced the issue to coastwide arbitration in June of 1965. The arbitrator ruled:

33. *Bulcke awards of June 30 and July 10, and awards of April 16 and October 12, 1963.*
34. Coast Labor Relations Committee Minutes, *July 3, 1963, p. 2.*
35. *Sam Kagel made this observation in an early arbitrators conference. (Notes, Conference of Arbitrators, ILWU and PMA, June 17, 1961, p. 11.) This was also used as an employer defense against charges of onerous workload; the Bulcke award of March 23, 1963, is an example.*
36. Joint Meeting, *August 7, 1963, p. 11.*

The Agreement as such does not prohibit hand handling of sacks. . . . The entire Agreement has as its object the elimination, as much as possible, the physically hard work involved in the industry. To this end the Agreement does concern itself with limitations upon, if not prohibitions, on onerousness and speed up.

There is a responsibility upon the Employer in seeking an efficient operation to also protect the welfare of his employees. He is thus required to take the necessary steps to reduce, if not eliminate, the onerousness which is inherent in a particular job. . . .

In the case of sack packing the Employer cannot simply insist that all sack packing be hand handled just because that's the way it had been done. . . .

DECISION:

1. Where it is operationally sound for four-wheelers or other types of mechanical equipment to be used, they shall be used in preference to individual sack packing provided that their use;

(a) Does not create unnecessary safety hazards by creating cramped areas in which to work;

(b) Does not create a situation where only half the men can work while the other half stand idle.[37]

The union had won at least a partial victory in their efforts to force mechanization.

Improvements in shipwork efficiency, as of 1963, were spotty (Table 16). Overall shipwork productivity was significantly higher, but not by a great deal, and a relatively few goods were responsible for most of the aggregate efficiency increase. In loading operations, logs and lumber, machinery, vehicles, other metals and metal products, cotton, and chemicals, including borax, were the goods handled rather more efficiently in 1963 by the ship gang. In discharging, bananas, lumber, newsprint, and iron and steel products, including pipe, were the biggest contributors to the aggregate man-hour savings. Most other goods were loaded or discharged at shipwork productivity rates only a little above or below the 1960 averages. The contrast with bulk operations and dockwork is great: in both those varieties of work, nearly every commodity was handled with substantially fewer hours by 1963. Although the rates may

37. *Kagel award of June 29, 1965.*

Table 16: Shipwork Man-hours Used and Saved,
Nonbulk Cargo, by Commodity, Pacific Coast, 1963.
(in thousands of man-hours)

Commodity	Hours required at 1960 rates[a]	Actual hours[b]	Man-hour savings
Loading:			
Canned goods	347.5	368.4	—20.9
Rice, nonbulk	72.0	59.5	12.5
Cotton	307.6	272.3	35.3
Logs	1,910.7	1,449.0	461.7
Lumber	1,200.1	1,113.3	86.8
Pulp	313.3	335.8	—22.5
Iron and steel pipe	47.3	27.4	19.9
Machinery, vehicles and metal products, other	188.5	150.0	38.5
Chemicals	250.0	225.0	25.0
General cargo: break-bulk	2,132.5	2,117.8	14.7
General cargo: containers	70.0	45.1	24.9
Six other goods with positive savings	310.0	290.5	19.5
Fourteen commodities with negative savings	1,319.9	1,378.3	—58.4
Total	8,469.4	7,832.4	637.0
Discharging:			
Bananas	417.9	334.4	83.5
Lumber	113.3	78.9	34.4
Plywood	158.1	136.6	21.5
Newsprint	168.6	109.9	58.7
Iron and steel mill products	326.4	303.7	22.7
Iron and steel pipe	233.3	188.4	44.9
Machinery and vehicles	117.8	100.5	17.3
Metals and products	51.5	31.1	20.4
General cargo: break-bulk	1,155.5	1,086.5	69.0
Ten goods with positive savings	270.2	226.9	43.3
Twelve goods with negative savings	698.5	730.3	—31.8
Total	3,711.1	3,327.2	383.9

[a] Hours estimated by applying the 1960 shipwork man-hours per ton, by commodity, to the 1963 tonnage reported in the PMA productivity study.

[b] Shipwork hours reported in the 1963 productivity study.

SOURCE: Calculated from the data in the PMA productivity studies.

be biased a bit, the only warranted conclusion is that, for many goods, shipwork productivity and the workload of the men involved were about the same in the third year of the agreement as in the last preagreement year.

The productivity increases that did occur in shipwork handling of nonbulk goods by 1963 were associated with increased mechanization or investment for some goods, elimination of witnesses for others, and probably simply more efficient methods, if not harder work, for the remainder. Banana and newsprint discharging are almost certainly more efficient as a result of improved ships' gear or dockside equipment used in the ship-to-shore goods movement. The man-hour savings associated with handling containers, and possibly lumber on some operations, are the result of fewer men in the basic scale, and are analogous to the elimination of witnesses on bulk operations. The savings in the other goods reflect more efficient sling-load size — especially for such dense goods as basic metal and similar heavy goods — some use of mechanical equipment in the hold, and possibly, for cotton, chemicals, and a few other goods, a bit more tonnage manhandled per hour as a result of increased pace of work.

Overall, the shipwork productivity changes are not impressive. The evidence suggests that the employers, for the most part, devoted their efforts to trying to squeeze more physical labor from the work force, rather than innovating or undertaking new investment. On the other hand, the increases achieved, even though they are associated with relatively few goods, are not insignificant. The total nonbulk shipwork man-hours saved are the equivalent of an 8 percent aggregate industry productivity increase for 1963 relative to 1960. Further, it is likely that more, but still relatively modest, increases took place in 1964 and 1965. In 1963, it was widely noted that the local officials and the arbitrators were abetting the creation of de facto load limits. The top leadership of the ILWU and PMA agreed to hold meetings in each of the major port areas with arbitrators and local representatives of the parties to remedy the problem. To the extent that they restored flexibility and the employers continued to press for harder work, efficiency would have increased.[38] Further, restoration of the

38. Coast Labor Relations Committee Minutes, *July 31, 1963;* Joint Meeting, *August 7, 1963. In early 1965 the Coast Arbitrator, Sam Kagel, suggested that the parties relax their stringent procedure for onerousness grievances. As of that date, the local union official with a grievance was required to win permis-*

1960 measured efficiency levels for those goods with negative productivity changes in 1963 would, alone, increase aggregate productivity by several percent.

MINOR SOURCES OF CHANGES IN OBSERVED PRODUCTIVITY

To a very great extent, allowing for changes in commodity composition implicitly eliminates the most important effects of package shifts or package composition. Grain, ores, coke salt, and similar

Table 17: Direct Labor Man-hour Savings, by Package and Commodity and by Commodity only, Pacific Coast, 1963.

	Loading		Discharging	
	By package and commodity	By commodity only	By package and commodity	By commodity only
Total savings for tonnages identified by commodity	1,034,404	1,229,543	719,858	754,759
General cargo (by package for both)[a]	268,794	251,763	280,720	235,997
Grand Total	1,303,098	1,481,306	1,000,578	990,756

[a] Excludes the effects of containerization in both approaches to calculating man-hour savings. The two sets of figures for general cargo differ in that the "by commodity only" estimates use fewer packages.

SOURCE: Appendix Table C-7.

goods are almost invariably handled by bulk methods when and where the tonnage involved is at all significant. Canned goods are in cases or cartons; cotton or hides are in bales, and so on. Thus the relative importance of grain or ores varies in the total tonnage handled with the proportion of bulk to total tonnage. The argument may be extended in a similar fashion to other commodities, and the consequence is that most of the package composition is, in effect, held constant. Nonetheless, it is worthwhile to explore, to the extent that the data permit, the possibility that changes in the composition by

sion from one of three top union officials before proceeding with the complaint. Kagel argued that the employers were "gimmicking"; that is they were stalling on onerousness claims and taking advantage of their right to have the work performed as the employer directs, pending settlement of a dispute.

package within the various commodity classifications have an important effect on observed productivity estimates.

The 1963 man-hour savings calculated by the PMA to eliminate the effects of all package shifts within the commodities are summarized in Table 17. The aggregate direct labor longshore man-hours saved in 1963 are from improvements instituted in all the years of the study, 1961–1963. Man-hour savings calculated to *include* savings associated with package shifts are shown in the same table (and, by commodity, in Appendix Table C-7). A comparison of the results, by commodity, indicates that for some goods package shifts did have some effect. The single-rate method overstated man-hour savings, and productivity increase, for rice, grain, and sugar, reflecting the almost total disappearance, by 1963, of nonbulk handling of these goods. Also overstated were the savings for loading citrus and discharging canned goods, reflecting the shift to prepalletized or unitized loads.[39]

On the other hand, adverse package shifts, tending to understate the productivity increase when the average commodity rate is used, also occurred. The man-hour savings totals calculated by the single rate for each commodity are understated as a result of adverse package shifts in commodities such as chemicals and iron and steel scrap, where bulk tonnage declined relative to the break-bulk packages. Similarly, the savings for lumber and plywood reflect the relatively smaller importance of unit loads in the 1963 tonnages.

On balance, the various package shifts and, within heterogeneous classifications, small commodity shifts, appear to approximately cancel out. The net overstatement for 1963, loading and discharging operations combined and for all goods, is 168,386 man-hours, or about 1.5 percent of direct labor man-hours actually used.

Overall, package shifts and changes in composition of heterogeneous commodity classifications are probably responsible for a small part of the variations in productivity as measured in chapter 4. Such changes could lead to either over- or underestimating productivity for any one year. The most likely magnitude would be about 1 to 2 percent, excluding the effects of containerization. In

---

39. *Unit loads are cartons, boxes, pieces of goods, sometimes bales, or drums strapped, banded, glued, or otherwise assembled in a single unit of roughly one or two tons. The shippers' packaged unit load is received at the terminal as a unit, loaded to the ship and stowed as a unit, and so on.*

other words, if the true productivity change from year to year were zero, the estimated productivity changes would nonetheless fluctuate, suggesting increases or decreases of, at most, a few percentage points for any year within the years covered by this study.

A fraction, but only a small one, of shoreside labor hours involved in cargo handling, and used in one or another estimates of productivity changes, resembles overhead in that it does not vary as a simple function of output. However, the overhead itself — mostly general supervisors' hours — is very small, and even the estimates of productivity based on total shoreside hours reported by the PMA do not err by more than about 0.5 percent on this account. Unlike most industrial situations, in longshoring almost the entire work force is variable from day to day. Within the limits of gear priority and the minimum guarantee, the stevedoring contractor employs men when he needs them and dismisses them when the work is finished. The hours of not only longshoremen but also clerks and lower-level supervisors are variable. Nonetheless, analogues to overhead do exist. More important, the indirect work time involved in the longshoreman's task — for example, covering and uncovering hatches — is a function of, roughly, the number of ships, but not of tonnage handled. Indirect work time would be a smaller proportion of longshore time used, and the observed productivity rates would be higher, as tonnage handled per ship is increased. To the extent that tonnage handled per ship varies over time, observed productivity may be expected to vary.

A direct measure of the "capacity" effect is possible for the years included in the PMA studies. Indirect longshore man-hours required to ready the ship — largely rigging gear and uncovering hatches — were a constant amount per ship, but varied substantially relative to tonnage handled and direct labor man-hours required (see Table 18). In 1963, a good year in that tonnage was larger than in the immediately preceding years, man-hours saved as a result of the capacity effect associated with working more tons per ship was the equivalent of about a 2.5 percent aggregate productivity increase over 1960.

In 1959 the ILWU and PMA agreed to increase the minimum work or pay guarantee for longshoremen from four to eight hours. In exchange for the improved guarantee the union conceded substantial relaxation of the gear-priority requirements. Most important

Table 18: Man-hours Used to Ready Ships, Ships Worked, and Man-hour Rates, Pacific Coast, 1960-1963.

	1960	1961	1962	1963
Indirect longshore man-hours used to ready ships	2,679,800	2,701,900	2,597,400	2,532,300
Direct labor man-hours	15,077,400	14,460,400	13,260,400	13,745,000
Hours to ready ships as percent of direct labor	17.9	18.7	19.6	18.4
Tonnage reported in productivity data	24,744,000	25,065,000	23,545,000	27,199,000
Man-hours per ton to ready ships	0.109	0.108	0.110	0.093
Number of ships[a]	12,007	11,801	11,632	11,109
Average Man-hours used to ready ships	223	229	223	228

[a] Dry-cargo ships of twenty-three feet or more draft reported as arrivals or departures by the Corps of Engineers for the major and medium Pacific ports — Seattle, Tacoma, Portland, Longview, Vancouver, Coos Bay, San Francisco, Oakland, Stockton, Los Angeles, Long Beach, and San Diego.

SOURCES: PMA productivity studies and Corps of Engineers, *U.S. Waterborne Commerce*, various years.

was the agreement that men could be shifted from dock to dock, even over a wide area. Before 1959 the men could refuse to shift even to a nearby dock. After the concessions, shifts to places miles away from the starting employment site could be ordered. For example, longshoremen dispatched to a Portland pier may be moved by the employer to a Vancouver site, six or more miles downriver, and so on.[40]

Greater flexibility was also extended to curb the individual long-shoreman's claims to specialization. Gang members may be ordered to shift from the hold to the dock, as frontmen, and they know that their refusal to shift will be penalized.[41] Similarly, small amounts of general cargo work may be required of a specialty gang. The prevailing interpretation since 1960 holds that the principal task required of a gang, but not necessarily every small bit of work they do, must be appropriate to their specialty.[42] Gear priority still exists, and

40. *The Fielding award of May 5, 1965, is one example.*
41. *For example, the Bulcke award of September 30, 1961.*
42. *From the Fielding award of January 19, 1964.*

the employer must take care not to violate it, but the limits to flexibility in task reassignment largely have been removed.

The effects of changes in the minimum guarantee and assignment flexibility would appear as variations in idle, or "dead," time — hours paid, but not devoted to any productive task. The data indicate that idle time declined sharply in 1961, not earlier, and remained fairly constant thereafter (see Table 19). The independent contribution of the relaxation of rules limiting work-force flexibility

Table 19: Other Indirect Longshore Man-hours Reported and Rates per Ship and Ton, Pacific Coast, 1960-1963. (in thousands of man-hours)

	1960	1961	1962	1963
Indirect longshore man-hours: other[a]	1,763.6	1,351.0	1,232.3	1,198.9
Hours as percent of direct labor hours	11.7	9.3	9.3	8.7
Hours per ship	136.0	115.0	106.0	108.0
Hours per ton	0.071	0.054	0.052	0.044

[a] Time used to ready cargo, in breakdowns, waiting, dead time, and miscellaneous indirect.

SOURCE: PMA productivity studies.

is certainly less than the several percent productivity increase implied by the decline in indirect hours. First, idle hours would vary with direct labor hours, assuming no change in job-assignment rules, reflecting the smaller gang sizes on bulk operations, dockwork, and similar improvements in direct labor efficiencey. Second, idle hours would vary with total port activity. With no changes in flexibility rules, an employer would be able to reduce idle time as the tonnage handled per ship or the number of ships at the dock increase.

All told, the union concessions on assignment flexibility and the offsetting longer minimum guarantee probably very nearly balanced each other through 1963. The data would support the proposition that perhaps the greater flexibility was associated with a 1 percent or so aggregate productivity increase in 1963, relative to 1960, but not much more.

INVESTMENT

There is relatively little quantitative information available concerning investment in the industry. Even worse, the available information is not directly applicable; although it deals with ships and ports, the data cannot be used to identify capital stock changes directly bearing on only the ship-loading and unloading segment of the goods movement.

Substantial amounts of investment have been devoted to port improvement on the Pacific Coast. In the seventeen years from 1946 through 1962 nearly one third of a billion dollars had been spent to construct new facilities and to improve existing ones. The rate of in-

Table 20: Port Improvement Expenditures, Pacific Coast, 1946-1962
(in millions of dollars)

Years	Investment in special facilities	Total expenditures	Average annual rate	Pacific Coast as a percent of all U.S.
1946–55	$43.9	$123.6	$12.4	19.2
1956–57	9.4	43.4	21.7	15.2
1958–60[a]	19.2	50.2	20.1	15.3
1960–62[a]	33.5	104.3	41.7	24.6
Total	$106.0	$321.5		

[a] Midyear 1960.

SOURCE: Port of New York Authority, *Port Development Expenditure Survey* (New York, 1963), p. 21.

vestment has increased over time but, until 1960, not much faster than the rate of price level change. In general, port improvement expenditures for the Pacific Coast have been about the same share of total U.S. port expenditures — 15 to 20 percent (see Table 20) — as Pacific ports ocean trade is of total U.S. ocean commerce. Only in 1960–1962 was the West Coast's share significantly larger. A high level of investment in Pacific ports clearly has occurred, and appears to be continuing. However, port investment very likely has had only a slight effect on longshoring productivity.

Several points bearing on the relatively weak link between port investment and productivity deserve mention. First, Pacific Coast port investment had been overwhelmingly concentrated in the Los Angeles–Long Beach area. Of the $321.5 million in coastwide expenditures from 1946 through 1962, about $222.5 million, or nearly 70 percent of the total, were spent in southern California. A large fraction of the southern California total was devoted to construction of new general cargo facilities in Los Angeles; all told, twenty-three new shedded berths and eight open berths were built during the period.[43] Although longshore productivity improvements were greater in Los Angeles than elsewhere, the role of port investment probably was not great. The disproportionate contribution to the aggregate productivity increase appears to be easily explained by the area's notoriety for unusually restrictive work practices before the 1960 agreement. Except for Los Angeles harbor, expenditures for new or improved general cargo facilities have been slight.

Second, almost all of the remaining port expenditures on the entire Pacific Coast were devoted to bulk-facilities construction. Most of the southern California expenditures, other than the Los Angeles improvements, were applied to the construction of new bulk-handling facilities in Long Beach. Of the remaining ninety-nine million dollars spent over seventeen years in all other Pacific regions, a large proportion was used to build bulk-handling facilities in Stockton, Portland, and other ports, and to open an altogether new minor port at Sacramento.[44] Although this investment is not insignificant, all the methods used to estimate productivity changes, except the crude ratio of total tons to total man-hours, very nearly eliminate any effect of new or improved bulk-handling installations. The tens of millions of dollars spent for these facilities almost certainly improved efficiency in handling the goods involved, but they contributed little to the overall productivity increase as measured in this study.

Finally, perhaps the greatest hindrance to linking port expenditures to longshore productivity is the high probability that most of the expenditure on general cargo facilities has nothing to do with the efficiency of the loading and unloading of ships. Nearly all the port investment for other than bulk facilities are to provide deep water berths or to build terminals, warehouses, transit sheds, and the like. Most of the expense in berth construction has to do with enabling the ship to discharge or load cargo directly from a land-based structure, rather than lighters or barges. The only requirements, from the point of view solely of ship loading, are a reasonably level and unobstructed land or dock surface and enough area to stack the goods to be loaded without physically interfering with the

43. Port of New York Authority, Port Development Expenditure Survey, pp. 20–21.
44. Expenditures for the seventeen-year period were $16.2 million in San Francisco, $11.0 million in other San Francisco Bay ports, $14.6 million in Stockton and Sacramento, $27.3 million in Portland, $19.4 million in Seattle, and $9.6 million in other Washington State ports. Ibid., p. 21.

flow of goods to or from the ship's gear. In general, a well-maintained but fully depreciated fifty-year-old pier would suffice as well as a new berth costing several million dollars. Almost all the expenditure on terminals, transit sheds, and similar construction is intended to protect the goods in transit, to provide for more efficient assembly for subsequent shipment of the cargoes, and so on. Very little has to do with the efficiency with which the goods may be picked up at the last place of rest, carried to the ship's side, hoisted aboard, and stowed in the hold.[45]

Investment by ship-operating companies resembles port investment in that there has been a lot of it, and most of the investment is not related to cargo loading or discharging. The five principal U.S. companies operating ships in the U.S. Pacific Coast ocean commerce invested nearly two hundred million dollars in new ships, buildings, and other property and equipment in the 1958–1965 period.[46] (See Table 21.). Total investment allocable to the U.S. Pacific Coast trade for the period by all companies is difficult to determine, but it probably is at least twice, but no more than three times, as much. However, much of the investment by the Pacific firms appears to be wholly independent of changed working practices and costs as dockside; the comparable group of U.S. firms engaged primarily in the Atlantic and Gulf Coasts added more, both absolutely and relatively, to their capital stock. Furthermore, only a small fraction of the investment in a conventional ship would affect cargo loading and discharging — the costs associated with the ship's hoisting gear, variations in hatch size, and apparatus controlling speed and ease of opening and closing, and possibly, some hold modifications. About half the investment during this period by the five Pacific companies, and nearly all the investment by other ship-operating companies, was for conventional ships.[47]

45. Proponents of most of the new port facilities usually argued that they were necessary to avoid ship waiting associated with too few berths, to improve the cargo assembly and storage areas, and to provide more efficient flow of goods from the storage areas to land transportation. None of these improvements would have much effect on the efficiency of hoisting goods to and from the ship, or stowing or breaking-out in the hold.

46. The five companies are those for which financial statements are publicly available — American President Lines, Matson Navigation Company, McLean Industries, Pacific Far East Line, and States Steamship Company. The companies, their importance in the industry, and other attributes are discussed in the industry section of the next chapter, pp. 172–178.

47. Subsidized ship construction for 1956–1964 amounted to about $98 million in costs for the companies included in the Pacific group; companies in the

Table 21: Apparent Investment in Ships and Other Capital Goods[a]
Five Pacific Companies and Six Atlantic Companies, 1957-1965.
(in millions of dollars)

Year	Pacific trade companies[b]		Atlantic trade companies[c]	
	Assets	Change from previous year	Assets	Change from previous year
1957	—	—	435.1	—
1958	347.7	—	461.0	25.9
1959	331.9	—15.8	470.0	9.0
1960	343.4	11.5	547.4	77.4
1961	354.0	10.6	563.9	16.5
1962	482.8	128.8	613.2	49.3
1963	516.1	33.3	734.2	121.0
1964	476.2	—39.9	736.4	2.2
1965	530.4	54.2	761.0	24.6
Net change, 1958–1965	182.7		300.0	
Net change, 1960–1965	187.0		213.6	

[a] Estimated by summing the assets of the companies, excluding current assets, before depreciation.
[b] American President Lines, Matson, McLean, Pacific Far East Lines, and States Steamship.
[c] American Export Isbrandtsen, Delta, Grace, Lykes, Moore-McCormack, United States Lines.

SOURCES: Published financial statements of the firms; available in *Moody's Transportation Manual* and Standard and Poor's *Reports*, various years.

An important variety of investment is, unfortunately, the most difficult to quantify. Capital-goods expenditures for materials-handling equipment used on the dock or in the hold, such as those for specialized hook gear and similar tools or improvements directly used in cargo loading and discharging, are of interest in assessing the sources of productivity change. Regrettably, the most that can be said is that some expenditure for this type of investment, perhaps a large fraction of the industry total, are included in the capital stock figures for the Pacific trade companies mentioned above. In addition, ship-operating company officials and union spokesmen concur that the small, independent stevedoring companies have undertaken very little of any kind of investment, including that for material-handling machines and similar goods.

Atlantic and Gulf trade group incurred costs for ship construction totaling about $390 million in the same period. Ship construction data is reported by company in U.S. Congress, Joint Economic Committee, Subsidy and Subsidy-Effect Programs of the U.S. Government, 89th Cong., 1st sess. (Washington, 1965), pp. 46–47.

Negative comments notwithstanding, some of the investment of the Pacific Coast firms involved improvements that clearly did affect productivity. A very large proportion of the change in assets not attributed to subsidized construction of conventional ships was incurred by the nonsubsidy companies operating in domestic commerce. Most of this expenditure involved containers and the equipment to handle them.[48] The shift of general-cargo tonnage from break-bulk methods to containers was an important source of productivity increase, and the only one clearly related to investment.

Containers are large, rigid boxes filled by the shipper or terminal operator; they are handled through the entire journey from point of origin to destination, with special equipment, as a unit. Although the PMA study definition includes "containers, over five tons," most of the containers now in use weigh about twenty tons when loaded. The special equipment required includes not only very large gantry cranes and specialized trucks, or jitneys, at dockside but also extensively modified ships.

The effect of the new method is significant only in the most recent years. The first container ship began operations at Pacific Coast ports in 1960, and approximately 290,000 tons were discharged and loaded in containers that year. Total container tonnage reported by the PMA rose to 409,000 in 1961 and 418,000 in 1962. If the 1962 net increase in volume of 128,000 tons had been handled at the average break-bulk productivity rate for the year, an additional 106,000 direct labor man-hours would have been required. Treating this as man-hours saved would add another 0.8 percent to the total productivity increase in 1962, relative to 1960.[49]

Container tonnage increased greatly in 1963; about 1,012,000 tons of containerized goods were loaded and discharged at Pacific ports. Applying the same approach used for the 1962 data, the net

48. *According to an industry official, Matson's expenditures for their container ships and related expenditures were about $35 million through 1964. Sea-Land, a subsidiary of McLean Industries, apparently incurred expenditures of $75 million or so from 1959 through 1965, but part of the expenditures were for Atlantic Coast facilities and ships not used in the Pacific trade. As a rough approximation, perhaps half the capital-goods expenditure of Sea-Land is allocable to the Pacific trade.*

49. *This is approximately the PMA approach, with the exceptions that the PMA estimates are based on all container tonnage, not just the net increase, and no attempt was made to relate the shift-to-container man-hour savings explicitly to relative productivity changes. See PMA, Productivity Study, 1961–1962, p. 12, and 1960–1963, p. 9.*

increase in volume, about 722,000 tons, would have required a net addition of about 582,500 direct labor man-hours. Had these been included in total direct labor man-hour savings, and assuming that indirect, clerical, and supervisory hours vary as a constant proportion of direct labor hours for any given year, then 1963 productivity, relative to 1960, would have been about 4.4 percent higher. That is, the 17.5 percent increase shown in Table 5 would be about 21.9 percent if it included the package shift to containers.

The effect of containerization for 1964 certainly must be at least as much as in 1963, and probably is a bit more. At most, the shift to containers could have been responsible for about one fourth of the 1964 productivity increase of 32 or so percent. The maximum effect of containerization may be approximated as follows. Recognizing that, in 1964, the only containerized routes were in domestic commerce,[50] the maximum tonnage capable of being put in containers in that variety of trade may be estimated. From total reported domestic cargo tonnage, the following were excluded: an estimate of barged goods to Alaska, outbound rice, beverages, and animal feeds, and inbound sugar, salt, and chemicals — all are handled in bulk — and lumber, vehicles, and iron and steel mill products. About 1,730,000 tons remain. Assuming that all this tonnage were handled in containers, the net increase in containerized tonnage, for 1964 over 1960, would be 1,440,000 tons. At the average nonbulk, all-cargo rate, and adding on estimated indirect hours at the 1960 proportion, the assumed maximum container tonnage would have required about 1,700,000 man-hours, or a bit less than one fourth of the man-hour savings estimated for the year.

SUMMARY: SOURCES OF PRODUCTIVITY CHANGE

The overall productivity increase in Pacific Coast longshoring, above 1960, was about 20 percent by 1963 and about 32 percent or so by 1964. A small part of the observed productivity increase is attributable to minor package or commodity-composition shifts and to more efficient utilization of indirect labor time as a result of increased port activity. The combined effect of minor package shifts and "capacity" were man-hour savings the equivalent of an aggre-

50. Matson, in the Hawaiian trade, and Sea-Land, in intercoastal and Alaskan trade, were the only ship operators with containers and the appropriate facilities.

gate measured productivity increase of at most 2 percent in 1963, and possibly as much as 5 percent in 1964.

The most important sources of productivity change were the elimination of restrictive work rules and practices. The abandonment of redundant manning on bulk and similar highly mechanized cargo-handling operations was responsible for spectacular increases in measured output per man-hour for that variety of longshoring. Despite the very slight importance of bulk-handling employment to total longshore man-hours, the elimination of witnesses nonetheless was the equivalent of a more than 2 percent productivity increase in 1963, and probably a 3 or 4 percent increase in 1964. The elimination of multiple handling was much more important to the overall improvement of performance. The precipitous decline in dockwork man-hours matched the impressive changes in bulk operations manning, and contributed the equivalent of a 7 percent aggregate productivity increase in 1963. Continued improvements could have led to the equivalent of as much as a 10 percent increase in overall productivity by 1964. The elimination of sling-load requirements, basic break-bulk manning reductions, and relaxation of informal work restrictions led to modest increases in efficiency, no more than 10 percent by 1963 for that part of the longshoring work. However, the man-hours employed in this segment of longshoring are so large a fraction of total employment that the small improvements were the equivalent of an 8 percent aggregate productivity increase in 1963, and perhaps 11 or 12 percent by 1964.

Investment — the substitution of capital for labor — was important, but less so than work-rules abandonment. Substantial investment occurred in new bulk-handling facilities and equipment. Although the shift from break-bulk to bulk handling of alfalfa, rice, wine, and similar goods is clearly substitution of capital for labor, the method used to measure productivity in this study generally excludes the effects of this sort of change. Further, the investment in bulk facilities appeared to be associated with changes in demand for the goods shipped, rather than a cost-inspired change in relative factor inputs. Containerization represents a much clearer case of the role of investment. The rapid growth of container cargo was associated with man-hour savings equivalent to an aggregate productivity increase of a bit more than 4 percent by 1963, and could have been as high as 7 or 8 percent by 1964.

VI / EFFECTS OF PRODUCTIVITY CHANGE ON THE WORK FORCE AND THE INDUSTRY

The modification of work rules and abandonment of resistance to new methods involved some compensation to the longshoremen and added costs to the industry. The compensation and effects on the work force are examined in the first section of this chapter, and the financial consequences of the 1960 agreement for the industry are taken up in the second section.

EFFECTS ON THE WORK FORCE

By 1964, Pacific Coast longshoremen were about as numerous, a bit younger, and more highly paid than before the 1960 agreement. The union and employers expected some changes in the composition of the work force, and, as a result of negotiated increases in the basic wage, they expected average earnings to improve. Few anticipated the frequent and large additions to the work force that actually occurred.

The size of the total work force in Pacific longshoring has been almost constant for nearly two decades. In 1949, for example, there were a few more than 15,000 men registered as longshoremen, ship-clerks, and walking bosses. In 1960 the total, 15,700 was only a few percent higher. The net change in work-force size during the 1960s was very small. The total work force was smaller by about 200 men in 1964, but the number of registered longshoremen — about 85 percent of the total in most years — increased very slightly.

The stability of recent years, however, has to do only with size; the composition of the work force was changed substantially and unexpectedly. The older longshoremen quickly took advantage of their newly won rights to a retirement bonus under the 1960 agreement. In San Francisco, the leading Pacific port, attrition was five percent of the work force in 1961 and nine percent in 1962.[1] On the entire Pacific coast by late 1963, about 1,600 longshoremen had withdrawn from the work force under the provisions of the 1960 agreement. Another 400 had died by the middle of 1963. At the termination of the agreement, in June, 1966, a total of 1,913 longshoremen had retired under the vesting or disability bonus provisions of the agreement, and 695 deaths had been covered by the improved death benefit provisions.[2] The withdrawal of 2,600 registered longshoremen represents an attrition rate of slightly less than four percent per year for the life of the agreement. The heavy concentration of withdrawals in the earlier years — three fourths of the retirements and deaths had taken place by October, 1963 — represented much higher attrition rates, nearly seven percent overall in 1962, for example. Although the total withdrawals over the five and a half years of the agreement had been estimated accurately by the parties in 1960, the early and sharp curtailment of the registered longshore work force, largely by voluntary retirement, was unexpected. Among the results, certainly unanticipated, were severe manpower shortages on the docks.

The union and employers underestimated the sizes of the expected productivity increases and early work-force attrition, but their pessimistic expectations about the volume of trade in the post-1960 years were even farther from the mark. At first, during 1961 and early 1962, no serious problems developed. Although work-force withdrawals were large, the volume of trade was approximately stable, and productivity increases more than offset the contraction in the number of workers. Then the volume of trade began to rise. In 1963, tonnage increased sharply over the 1960–1962 level. In 1964, cargo volume was 20 to 25 percent above 1960, and in 1965, about 40 percent higher. Productivity increases had been so large that, in 1964, a labor force about nine percent smaller than the 1960 level could do the work, but the shrinkage of the original registered list had been

1. *Attrition was higher in San Francisco chiefly because it had been growing less rapidly than many other ports. During the depression and World War II, San Francisco clearly was the leading port in tonnage handled, men employed, and so on. By the 1960s, however, Los Angeles–Long Beach had grown to very nearly equal the San Francisco Bay Area in tonnage and men.*
2. *From ILWU Research Department,* Estimated Status of M & M Funds, *mimeographed, prepared for use by the Longshore, Shipclerk and Walking Boss Caucus, April 4, 1966.*

15 to 18 percent. By 1965, despite the large increase in efficiency, as many longshoremen were needed as had been required in 1960.

The employers and the union became increasingly aware of manpower problems during 1962. Although the timing differed from port to port, the dispatch halls in every major region experienced growing difficulty in filling all the employer requests for longshore gangs. Portland, Longview, and the smaller ports in Washington were reporting gang shortages in 1961. The San Francisco Bay Area experienced shortages in 1961, and they were more severe in 1962 when the employers reported 8,762 gang-days short.[3] In southern California, on the other hand, 1961 was not a period of shortage — only 1,825 gang-days were reported short. In 1962, however, shortages in that rapidly growing area became more severe, and they peaked in 1963, when 9,628 gang-days were reported short. In December 1962 the employers and the union agreed to add one thousand men to the registration rolls. In fact, nearer to two thousand new men were registered during 1963, and it was apparent that the numbers were still insufficient. Men continued to be added during 1964. By the end of that year, about one fourth of the registered longshoremen were new; they had been admitted to the rolls after the 1960 mechanization and modernization agreement was signed.

The substitution of a large number of younger new men for the older long-service workers ought to have reduced the average age of the work force. The median age did drop slightly, from about fifty in 1960 to forty-eight years by mid-1964 (see Table 22). However, by early 1966, the median age had crept back to fifty. The high median age of the longshoremen continues because the withdrawal of the oldest men of 1960 has been balanced by the aging of the large numbers of nearly old longshoremen during the life of the 1960 agreement.

The top-heavy age structure is the result of a serious dilemma

3. The employer requests for gangs — ten to twelve men on conventional breakbulk work — that the dispatch hall is unable to fill on a given day are reported as short for that day. The number of gangs short each day, summed over the available workdays during a month or year, are the gang-day shortages cited above. The figures used in this paragraph are published in the PMA Annual Report, 1961, 1962, and 1963. A good description of the method of measuring gang shortages, their importance relative to total work time and involuntary unpaid idle time — gang-days idle, for example — appears in U.S. Congress, Study of Harbor Conditions in Los Angeles and Long Beach, pp. 63–69 and 90–96.

for the industry, and especially for the union. New, or added workers are necessary from time to time to handle unusually heavy cargo volume. But, once admitted to the industry, the workers stay.[4]

The post-1960 age-structure problem of Pacific longshoring has its roots in the situation caused by World War II and the immediate postwar period. Most of the men in the industry at the outbreak of the war had had seven or more years of experience; only experienced

Table 22: Age Distribution, Registered Longshoremen, Shipclerks, and Walking Bosses, Pacific Coast, 1949, 1960, and 1964.

Age Group	1949	1960	1964
66 and over[a]	1,201	831	321
60–65[a]	1,482	2,402	1,959
50–59	3,958	4,669	4,852
40–49	4,561	4,245	3,950
30–39	3,222	2,354	2,680
29 and under	666	1,198	1,734
Total	15,090	15,699	15,496
Median age	47	50	48

[a] For 1949, 60 to 64, and 65 and over.

Sources: 1949 data: ILWU, *Age Distribution of Longshoremen, Clerks and Walking Bosses as of 1949*, dated October 23, 1953.
1960 data: ILWU, *Longshoremen, Clerk and Bosses, Registered But Not Pensioned*, June 29, 1960.
1964 data: PMA, machine tabulation, as of July 1964.

men were registered in 1935, and few new men were added before 1941. As the cargo volume grew rapidly to meet the wartime needs, unprecedented expansion of the work force, and union membership took place. Of the longshoremen and clerks still registered and active in early 1966, more had been admitted in the 1940–1944 period than in any other five-year span.[5] Further, by using only the active survivors rather than the number of initial entrants, this approach greatly understates the magnitude of the wartime entry to the indus-

4. According to Lincoln Fairley, "The basic reasons for the high average age of longshoremen has been the high degree of security on the job and high earnings so that there has been no turnover until death or retirement." From his letter of June 26, 1967.
5. In 1935–1939, 790 longshoremen were registered; in 1940–1944, 3,278; 1945–1949, 1,930; 1950–1954, 2,397; 1955–1959, 2,931; 1960–1964, 1,923. ILWU Research Department, Ages of Longshoremen and Clerks, by Year Entered Industry, typed table, dated March, 1966.

try relative to later years. Moreover, the war and postwar new registrations were older men (as shown in Table 23), partly as a result of the wartime unavailability of young men, and partly from admitting, during the war and postwar period, workers with previous experience in the industry. The effect was the addition of a large number of middle-aged men to a work force and union already middle-aged. By 1949, three fourths of the waterfront work force were

Table 23: Median Age, by Year Entered the Industry, Longshoremen and Clerks, Pacific Coast, 1966.

Period entered the industry	Men registered in 1966:	
	1966 Median age	Median age at final year-of-entry period[a]
1960–1964	30	28
1955–1959	39	32
1950–1954	47	35
1945–1949	52	35
1940–1944	57	35
1935–1939	56	29
1934 and earlier	61	29

[a] The difference between 1966 and final year-of-entry period — 1964, 1959, 1954, and so on — was subtracted from the 1966 median age.

SOURCE: ILWU Research Department, *Ages of Longshoremen and Clerks, by Year Entered Industry*, table dated March, 1966.

forty years or older, and only about four percent were under thirty years.

Although there was redundancy in some ports, and shorter work weeks as the unemployment was shared, the men would neither leave voluntarily nor would the membership support an involuntary work-force reduction. Harry Bridges testified before the Congressional Committee in 1955,

And I went down and advocated the addition to the work force after Taft-Hartley. Then in 1949 I went back and tried to get them to lay off a thousand people. They had been working 3 or 4 years and making around an average of 25, 26 hours a week; my own home port. . . .

When I marched in with the idea of laying off a thousand men, I am just telling you not one single person voted for me. . . . We had just been through a strike. This was the spring of 1949, and they said, "This is a fine thing, for you to come around after all of us have stuck together and fought together, and propose now a thousand of us be thrown away." [6]

During the subsequent decade, new and younger men were admitted, but the work force steadily grew older. The middle-aged cohort of, for example, 1949, moved into the fifty to sixty age group, attrition was low, and the volume of cargo passing through the ports did not permit work-force expansion. After 1960, accelerated attrition removed many of the oldest workers from the active rolls, but it did not cure the age-structure problem. The even larger group of men taken on during and immediately after World War II became the new old men on the docks by 1966.

Top-heavy age structure notwithstanding, the 1960 agreement did bring about work-force composition changes. The men over sixty-five have largely vanished, and the ranks of the sixty to sixty-five age group were thinned by the inducements to voluntary retirement provided by the agreement. Most of the men who left before 1966 were industry veterans from the early days of the union during the 1930s, and they were indeed rewarded for long and faithful service. At the other end of the age range, young men have again appeared in substantial numbers on the docks, after decades of virtual absence. Although still only 11 percent of the work force in 1964, the number of men under thirty was three times the number in 1949. The 1960 agreement, and fortunate rapid growth of the volume of trade, have tapered the top and smoothed the bulges of the longshore age distribution.

Although the 1960 agreement did discriminate between the fully registered longshoremen and the "B" men with limited registration, the fears or gloomy predictions of critics were not borne out. Pessimists in 1960 or 1961 sympathized with the plight of the "B" men and cited their poor prospects as evidence of callousness or worse on the part of the union leadership. A rather extreme view drew the bleak picture of broken promises and elimination from the industry as the "B" men faced, not full registration, but "what seems most likely, their gradually being starved out of the waterfront."[7] It never happened.

The "B" men had been brought into the industry specifically to

6. Study of Harbor Conditions, p. 329.
7. Harvey Swados, Radical's America, pp. 60–61.

provide a reservoir with which to meet peak labor demand. As "A" list attrition and the demand for labor permitted, they could expect to move into the permanent work force. Prior to the 1959 closing of the registration lists, the "B" men in the various ports typically had worked for some time — a few months to a year or more — in their probationary status, and had then been admitted to full registration and union membership. New "B" men were added to replace those moved up. The expectations of the 1960 "B" men differed chiefly in that attrition and labor demand were a good deal more uncertain than they had been before.

Without doubt, the 1960 "B" men, mostly younger men with only short service on the waterfront, would have borne the first and heaviest unemployment had the demand for labor declined sharply after 1960. But manpower shortages, not surpluses, developed. The "B" men continued to work much as before the agreement. In one sense, however, the "B" men of 1960 were in fact eliminated. Most of them were removed from the limited registration lists in 1963 and were promoted to full registration.

The record of the industry with respect to "B" men has been good, perhaps better than should be expected. There has been no tendency to create a large, growing, or permanent second-class work force. Over the years "B" men have been about 15 percent of the total registered work force, and their hours have been about 10 percent of the total. The figures refer to the status, not the individuals. Thousands of "B" men were promoted to full registration in the ten years before and five years after 1960, and limited registration has become well established as the means of entry into the industry.

The hours and earnings of the "B" men as a group are lower than the averages for the "A" men. In 1964, for example, a "B" man worked an average of 1130 hours compared with 1650 hours for an "A" man.[8] The differences stem largely from the peak-demand, full-employment dilemma. Ship arrivals tend to be bunched, not a smooth flow over time, aggravating the seasonal and other peak needs for longshore labor. The "B" men are the principal source of manpower to meet the peak needs, but, to maintain their hours and earnings at even 50 to 60 percent of full time, their numbers have to

8. *Rough averages calculated from PMA Contact Data Department, "Longshore Manhours, Pacific Coast, 1954–1965," memo dated June 30, 1966, and from registration figures of the PMA mid-1964 machine tabulation.*

Table 24: Wages and Earnings, Pacific Coast Longshoremen,
Selected Years, 1941-1965.
(in dollars)

Year	Basic Rate[a]	Average Hourly Earnings[b]	Average Hourly Compensation[c]
1941	1.00		
1945	1.37		
1950	1.92		
1955	2.27		
1956	2.45		
1957	2.53	3.75	
1958	2.63	3.58	
1959	2.74	3.65	4.01
1960	2.82	3.80	4.17
1961	2.88	3.87	4.49
1962	3.06	3.85	4.74
1963	3.19		4.96
1964	3.32		5.16
1965	3.38		5.39

[a] Straight-time basic rate for longshoremen, excluding skill differentials.

[b] Wages paid to longshoremen divided by total hours paid; includes overtime, skill, and penalty-cargo premiums.

[c] Includes wages, payments for vacations, payments for health and welfare benefits and insurance, and M&M fund contributions; excludes employer-paid payroll taxes.

SOURCES: U.S. Department of Labor, Bureau of Labor Statistics, *Wage Chronology: Pacific Coast Longshore, Industry*, 1934–65, Bulletin 1491 (Washington, 1966); and PMA data.

be limited. The genuine peak labor needs then must be filled with outsiders — casuals. Since 1950, casuals, drawn from the ranks of unemployed warehousemen or seamen, or referred daily by the local offices of the U.S. employment service, again have been used in most Pacific ports. By 1958 they accounted for about 7 percent of total longshore man-hours, and in 1962, 9 percent of the total. Expansion of the "B" men pool reduces the importance of casuals — they furnished less than 6 percent of the hours in 1964 — but it also reduces the hours and earnings of the "B" men. The problem apparently has no solution; the flow of work cannot be completely regularized.[9] The creation of yet another variety of registration for extremely temporary longshoremen would be farcical.

9. *A lot of research has been directed at the problem of more efficient ship scheduling and manpower dispatching. One good illustration is National Research Council,* San Francisco Port Study, Vol. II, pp. 57–64, and 93–115.

Wages and earnings in Pacific Coast longshoring have increased since the 1960 agreement, but not unduly. The post-1960 changes are comparable with the increases of the preceding years, and are about the same as wage changes in other sectors of the economy. The basic straight-time hourly rate in longshoring increased by about 20 percent in the five-year period ending in 1965, a relative increase similar to that occurring in the preceding decade (see Table 24). Basic wages increased a bit more, 24 percent, from 1955 to 1960, and a bit less, 18 percent, from 1950 to 1955. The relative increase in recent years was, of course, much less than the changes during the 1940s, when the basic wage rate rose, in part keeping pace with rapid price-level increases, by an average of 8 to 10 percent per year.

Average hourly earnings declined in 1958, chiefly as a result of the elimination of one overtime hour from the standard workday, and had just barely recovered the 1957 level by 1960. The increase in compensation — including welfare and M&M fund contributions, but excluding employer-paid payroll taxes — since 1960 has exceeded the relative change in the basic rate, rising by about 24 percent by 1964, and 29 percent by 1965. All of the greater relative increase in compensation is attributable to increased employer contributions to pensions, the M&M fund, and other welfare benefits. The increased pension contributions were about twenty-two cents per hour by 1965, or the equivalent of a bit more than a 5 percent increase over the 1960 average hourly labor costs.[10] M&M fund contributions averaged about seventeen cents per hour during the period, or the equivalent of a 4 percent increase over 1960. Other welfare improvements amounted to only seven cents per hour by 1965, less than 2 percent of the 1960 average hourly labor cost.

The longshore wage and earnings increases since 1960 have been about the same as in the rest of the economy. The absolute increase in the longshore basic rate from 1960 to 1965 was identical to the motor freight nonsupervisory employees' change in average hourly earnings, but with 1960 as the base, the longshoremen lagged slightly, in relative magnitudes, behind the truck drivers. The longshore increase was 19.7 percent, the motor freight employees gained 22.2

10. *The costs, in cents per hour, of the improvements in pensions and welfare benefits since 1959 or 1960 were taken from a memorandum prepared by the ILWU research department, "Table of Increases in Wage Package, 1961–1966," dated April 4, 1966.*

percent. Construction workers won larger absolute earnings increases than did Pacific Coast longshoremen, but the relative increase over 1960 was about the same as for the dock workers. Production workers in manufacturing continued to fall behind construction and transportation workers with only a 15.5 percent increase from an appreciably smaller base earnings rate.

Table 25: Wage Changes, Pacific Coast Longshoring and Selected Other Industries, 1950-1960 and 1960-1965

Production workers	1950–1960		1960–1965	
	Dollars	Percent	Dollars	Percent
Pacific longshoring[a]	0.90	47	0.56	19.7
All manufacturing	0.82	57	0.35	15.5
Contract construction	1.22	65	0.61	19.8
Other transportation[b]	0.88	61	0.56	22.2

[a] Longshoreman's basic hourly rate.

[b] 1950-1960; Rail and bus transportation. 1960-1965: Motor freight workers.

SOURCES: Longshore basic rate, see Table 24. All others: U.S. Department of Commerce, Office of Business Economics, *Business Statistics*, 1965 (Washington, 1965), pp. 81–84.

EFFECTS ON INDUSTRY REVENUES AND PROFITS

Assessing variations in the economic well-being of the industry is not an easy task. Data on revenues and profits for stevedoring contractors are not publicly available. Although some information for ship operators is published, it is not in concise and easily usable form. Scores of companies from about two dozen countries operated hundreds of ships in U.S. Pacific Coast ocean trade in the years covered in this study. At best, aggregate industry revenue and similar data are obtainable only by adding the figures from the many countries and companies. In fact, the situation is even worse. Most of the companies devote only a small fraction of their fleets to, and derive a correspondingly small part of their revenues from, the U.S. Pacific trade. Separate data for just this one small segment of their total volume are in most cases unobtainable. Nevertheless, despite the difficulties, some rough approximations for the industry can be attempted.

Five American-flag ship-operating companies — American President Lines, Matson, Pacific Far East, States Steamship, and

McLean — owned only about 15 percent of the ships in the trade at U.S. Pacific ports in any one year, but they were responsible for slightly more than one fourth of the sailings during 1955–1965.[11] The five companies were involved almost exclusively in Pacific Coast trade during this period, and they were almost the only companies thus specialized. In addition, the five American companies are a good proxy for evaluating the effects on all the firms of the industry of the post-1960 changes in cargo handling because most of their ships are loaded and discharged by longshoremen directly employed by the ship-operating company or its subsidiaries. Unlike all foreign and most U.S. ship operators, Matson, American President Lines, and Pacific Far East Line operate their own terminals in one or more of the major ports. Longshoring cost variations are thus directly reflected in the costs, earnings, and profits of the ship-operating companies.

A continuous series of revenues and profits for the five companies is possible only from 1957. Two of the companies, States Steamship and McLean, were formed in that year, or only slightly earlier. Although some data from their predecessor companies are available, they are not comparable over all the years. Revenues for the five companies appear in Table 26, together with comparable data for six other U.S. companies engaged in ocean shipping principally in the Atlantic. The non-Pacific trade companies are included in order to contrast the trends over time.

The general trend in revenues through 1964 is about the same for both groups of companies. From their post-1957 low — 1958 for the Pacific trade companies, 1959 for the others — gross revenues in 1964 had increased by about 25 percent for both groups. Comparisons of the 1965 and 1966 figures yield very different results. The Pacific trade companies continued to enjoy growing revenues, whereas the Atlantic and Gulf companies suffered an appreciable decline and only modest recovery. The Pacific companies were 35 percent above

11. *American President Lines includes its subsidiary, the American Mail Lines, and Matson includes its subsidary, Oceanic Steamship. The assets, revenues, and so on for McLean Industries, for most of the period studied, consisted chiefly of property and business of its ocean-ship-operating subsidiary, the Sea-Land Corporation. Sea-Land is a container-ship firm operating ships in the intercoastal and Pacific Northwest-Alaska trades. The number of ships in the trade, sailings, and other industry data are covered in more detail in Chapter 1, pp. 5–11; especially Table 1, p. 7.*

Table 26: Gross Revenues, Five Pacific Companies and
Six Atlantic Companies, 1957-1966.
(in millions of dollars)

Year	Pacific[a] Companies	Atlantic[b] Companies
1957	346.2	503.8
1958	296.1	440.8
1959	309.5	422.3
1960	328.3	430.4
1961	310.4	414.9
1962	337.4	467.2
1963	374.5	484.0
1964	370.8	537.4
1965	403.8	467.1
1966	468.9	542.9

[a] American President Lines, Matson, McLean, Pacific Far East, States Steamship.
[b] American Export, Delta, Grace, Lykes, Moore-McCormack, United States Lines.
SOURCES: Published financial statements of the firms; available in *Moody's Transportation Manual* and Standard and Poor's *Reports* various years.

their post-1957 low in 1965 and 58 percent above it in 1966. The six non-Pacific companies were only about 13 percent above their post-1957 low in 1965 and 30 percent above it in 1966.

Several factors account for the relatively poor performance in 1965 and 1966 of the non-Pacific companies. Most important, the Atlantic and Gulf ports were partially shut down in early 1965 by a longshoremen's strike. The impact of the strike was least in the North Atlantic ports, where the strike lasted only a few weeks, and greatest in the Gulf ports, where most of the cargoes were delayed for about two months. Although a large part of the cargo was only slowed in its journey through the ports, there is no doubt that at least some of the goods movement was lost altogether. The strike took place in January through early March; an examination of the monthly tonnages indicates that in the immediate poststrike months unusually large amounts of cargo were handled. In the later months of the year, the Atlantic and Gulf ports appeared to handle their customary volume. Although cargo diversion is difficult to show, the tonnage figures suggest that a bit of diversion or loss actually occurred. Calculations using the figures for the first ten months of the

year indicate that tonnage was up 4 percent over 1964 in Pacific
ports, up less than 1 percent in the Atlantic ports, and down 4 percent in the Gulf Coast ports.

Secondly, the war in Vietnam may have had some small effect,
favoring the Pacific ports. The expansion of the United States military commitment in Vietnam did not directly account for the revenue differences; much of the increase for the Pacific trade group was

Table 27: Foreign Trade, Atlantic, Gulf, and Pacific Coasts,
Selected Years, 1954-1966.
(in thousands of tons of 2,000 pounds)

Year	Atlantic		Gulf		Pacific	
	Tons	Percent	Tons	Percent	Tons	Percent
1954	64,452	62	27,569	27	11,549	11
1957	134,814	68	42,938	21	21,020	11
1958	101,514	63	42,995	27	16,221	10
1960	96,626	57	50,602	30	21,710	13
1963	102,884	53	62,810	32	28,191	15
1964	109,105	51	73,738	35	30,329	14
1965	111,347	51	73,372	34	32,370	15
1966	115,389	48	87,754	36	38,705	16

SOURCES: United States Department of Commerce, Bureau of the Census, *United States Foreign
Trade: Waterborne Foreign Trade Statistics; Summary Report FT 985*, Annual
summary for the various years.

accounted for by the two companies engaged chiefly in domestic
trade. Further, the Atlantic and Gulf companies and ports also participate directly in moving cargo to Vietnam. The Vietnamese war
may have increased the Pacific group revenues relatively more than
the others as a result of the general expansion of Pacific basin trends.
But the relative increases of Pacific ports were most likely slight. On
balance, revenues of the companies engaged in Pacific Coast commerce reveal a steady and substantial growth over time. Despite the
relatively favorable showing of 1965 and 1966, the evidence is not
sufficient to conclude that the post-1960 revenue increases were unusual, or attributable to improved productivity.

The hypothesis that the reduced costs associated with the post-
1960 productivity and cost improvements led to expansion of the total volume of Pacific Coast ocean shipping may be tested more directly by examination of the tonnage data. In theory, reduced costs

Table 28. Profits,[a] Five Pacific Companies and
Six Atlantic Companies, 1957-1966.
(in millions of dollars)

Year	Pacific[b] companies	Atlantic[c] companies
1957	18.0	51.9
1958	6.2	41.2
1959	12.6	24.6
1960	7.7	16.8
1961	9.9	16.8
1962	11.9	27.4
1963	15.0	30.2
1964	22.7	37.6
1965	28.8	21.5
1966	41.9	38.7

[a] After federal income tax.

[b] American President Lines, Matson, McLean, Pacific Far East, States Steamship.

[c] American Export, Delta, Grace, Lykes, Moore-McCormack, United States Lines.

SOURCES: See Table 26.

would induce a large volume of shipping by the transfer of cargo from competing ports and, perhaps, by slightly increased demand, in the destination region, for the goods being shipped. The tonnage data for foreign trade neither supports nor rejects the hypothesis. The total volume of trade at Pacific ports had increased a bit relative to total U.S. trade, raising the Pacific ports' share from the 13 percent in 1960 to about 16 percent in 1966 (see Table 27). On the other hand, the expansion was no greater than the growth of trade at the Gulf Coast ports. To the extent that Pacific ports are substitutes for any other U.S. ports, surely those other ports must be on the Gulf Coast. The most reasonable conclusion is that no diversion of cargoes to Pacific ports is evident in the six years after 1960.

The change in profits is a very different matter. The five Pacific trade companies have enjoyed substantially increased after-tax profits (see Table 28). More important, the growth has been impressive when judged by relevant criteria. First, the profits of the Pacific trade companies have grown relatively much more than have those of the companies in Atlantic and Gulf trade; the 1964 profits of the former were more than three times the post-1957 low, those of the latter only double. Second, profits as a fraction of revenues have consistently improved in recent years for the Pacific companies, increasing from 2.1 percent and 2.3 percent of revenues in 1958 and 1960 to 7.1 percent and 8.9 percent in 1965 and 1966. The East Coast companies did less well. Their profits were 3.9 percent of revenues in 1960; profits rose slightly to 4.6 percent and 7.1 percent of revenues in 1966.

Table 29: Profits as a Return to Stockholders' Equity, Five Pacific and Six Atlantic Companies, 1957-1966.

Years	Pacific companies	Atlantic companies
	percent	*percent*
1957 (partial)	9.0	10.0
1958	3.7	7.2
1960	4.2	2.9
1963	5.9	4.7
1964	10.4	5.6
1965	10.9	3.1
1966	13.9	5.4

SOURCES AND NOTES: see Table 26.

Finally, the most relevant criterion — profits as a return to stockholders' equity — reflects a much more favorable performance by the Pacific trade companies than the other firms. Both groups of companies did well in 1957, earning 9 and 10 percent on equity,[12] for the Pacific and Eastern companies, respectively. Both suffered poorer returns in 1958. The Pacific companies recovered a bit by 1960, when profits were 4.2 percent of stockholders' equity, and improved every year thereafter. The return on equity reached new highs for the group in 1965 and 1966 of 10.9 percent and 13.9 percent (see Table 29). The Eastern companies present a sharp contrast. They earned much smaller returns on stockholders' equity than did the Pacific group in every year after 1960, and at no time did they approach their 1957 level of performance.

The revenue and profit evidence suggests that the employers of Pacific Coast longshoremen derived substantial benefits from the 1960 mechanization and modernization agreement. Their profits grew appreciably, more than would be associated solely with im-

12. *Book value of ownership shares plus retained earnings and other surplus accounts.*

provement in revenues, and their profit rates indicate a marked improvement relative to both their own past performance and the record of other U.S. ship-operating companies. Although quantitative evidence is not available, it appears reasonable to assume that the foreign and other U.S. companies in Pacific trade enjoyed financial improvements comparable to those of the five identified firms.

To the industry, the five-million-dollar annual contribution to early retirement and other M&M fund benefits was a modest price to pay for the significant increase in cargo-handling efficiency. Some rough calculations outline the magnitude of the firms' improved well-being, but the roughness of the approximation cannot be over-emphasized. The productivity estimates of the earlier chapters indicate that total man-hour savings were about ten million in 1964, and a conservative guess for 1965 would be that about eleven or so million man-hours were saved, relative to 1960. At average labor costs of $5.40 per hour (see Table 24), the man-hour savings were worth about $59.4 million in 1965. Using profit figures, the five major Pacific companies would have earned about $18 million less in 1965 if their return on stockholders' equity had been at the 1960 rate. Assuming that these five companies accounted for about one third of the cargo volume at Pacific ports — their 28 percent of sailings understates their share of tonnage to some extent — the industry's profits were about $54 million higher in 1965 than would have been the case at 1960 rates. Both these figures probably exaggerate the financial improvements associated with work-rule abandonment. The 1965 average hourly labor cost perhaps would not have been so high had there been no increases in productivity; some of the increased profit is attributable to the larger volume of business — the more efficient use of capital stock — associated with general prosperity or the Vietnam war, and so on. Nonetheless, the application of every conceivable capital cost and similar argument would still leave a very substantial annual savings to the industry as a result of the elimination of restrictive work practices.

VII | A NEW AGREEMENT AND A SUMMING UP

As the 1960 agreement period neared its end, the important results of its major innovations were widely known, at least in approximate form, to interested employers, union officials, and members. On the union side, members and officials knew the industry was doing well — volume of trade, revenues, and profits all had increased a good deal in the recent years. The Vietnam war was recognized to have been important, but the war chiefly meant uncertainty as to how long and how well the industry would fare in the future, not that the profits already earned were unreal. Although the work force had not declined, many within the union shared the belief that they had "sold too much for too little" in 1960; the attractive state of the industry's finances was persuasive evidence. For their part, the employers knew that they had done well by the 1960 agreement, but that there were still work-rule concessions to be sought. For the first time, the possibility was real that substantial technical improvement, perhaps even widespread mechanization, could and would be applied to break-bulk cargo. Some of the provisions of the 1960 agreement — the basic gang and break-bulk shipwork manning — had turned out to be less flexible than was desired. Finally, everyone knew that there were still a lot of old men on the waterfront.

In brief, both parties knew that some catching up was in the cards, and that some of the problems leading to the 1960 agreement were still with them. In these circumstances, the union and employers prepared for and began negotiations for a new agreement.

THE 1966 AGREEMENT: REAFFIRMATION, EXTENSION, AND CATCHING UP

The 1960 agreement expired on June 30, 1966. Earlier in 1966, both parties formally prepared their demands and positions. The Longshore, Shipclerk and Walking Boss Caucus was called for April 4, 1966, to meet in San Francisco. The caucus proceedings ran a good deal more smoothly than in 1960. Following established procedure, the caucus heard the leadership's proposed demands and arguments, accepted some, modified others, and introduced their own demands by resolution. As always, there was a good deal of debate, but little acrimony. After nearly two weeks of meetings and discussions, the union side was ready for negotiations, and the negotiating committee so notified the employers. The longshore caucus adjourned, to be recalled later when negotiations were near completion.

On June 24, 1966, the caucus reconvened, for three days, to hear a progress report on negotiations. The union and employers were near agreement on wages, the manning issues, and pensions; the host of smaller points had been touched only lightly. The caucus heard the report, debated a bit, but decided to postpone action until a near final agreement could be brought before the delegates. Negotiations continued into early July, and the results were put before the reconvened caucus on July 11. Debate was extensive, at times with a touch of heat — eight days were filled with statements, questions, analysis of illustrative problems of implementing the proposed contract changes, and the like. In the end, however, the caucus supported, by a vote of fifty-two to thirty, the memorandum of understanding reached by the union and employer negotiating committees.[1] The union's membership ratified the new agreement, by coastwide balloting at the end of July, by 6,488 votes in favor of the new agreement, 3,985 against.[2]

The union and its members went after a large wage increase, and they got it. The union's initial demand for an increase of fifty cents per hour on the basic rate for one year was countered by an employer offer of fifty cents spread over five years. The parties settled for a five-year contract, with an immediate increase of fifty cents to the basic hourly rate, an additional twenty cents at the end of three years, and another twenty cents the year after that. The wage increase was the largest, in absolute terms, ever negotiated by the union. Further, it was the costliest part of the entire package of wages, pensions, welfare, and M&M benefits. The initial wage jump, about 15 percent above the old rates, brought the average longshoreman to an effective hourly rate of at least $4.36 in 1966. In the final year of

1. *ILWU*, Proceedings of the Longshore, Shipclerk and Walking Boss Caucus, *July 18, 1966.*
2. The Dispatcher, *Vol. XXIV, No. 16 (August 5, 1966).*

the new agreement the minimum effective hourly rate will reach $4.81.[3]

The substantial wage increase may be viewed as part of the catching up and prepayment to the younger longshoremen for the work-rules relaxation and associated productivity increases, both those already accomplished and those yet to come. It benefits only the active worker, not the old men already pensioned or about to be pensioned. Although denied the vested benefit of the men old enough to retire, the younger worker retains a financially attractive occupation made even more attractive by the 1966 wage changes.

Overall, the 1966 agreement was very much a continuation of the principles and institutions of the original mechanization and modernization agreement of 1960. The M&M fund, for example, was continued both in name and methods. The purposes were narrowed a bit, and the benefits increased, but otherwise the fund and its administration were much the same as under the earlier agreement. The motivation, too, was unchanged. In 1966, there were as many men aged fifty-seven and older as there had been in 1960. Furthermore, even stronger inducement apparently was required to persuade them to leave the work force; a substantial number of those eligible under the old agreement still had not voluntarily withdrawn. As before, the M&M fund, with its vesting, disability, and death benefits, was part of the gain to the union in exchange for continued and additional work-rules relaxation.

At the start of negotiations, the union proposed that the vested benefit to be paid to men retiring with twenty-five or more years of service be approximately doubled, to $15,000 from the old $7,920. As in the 1960 agreement, the disability provisions would permit disabled men to withdraw from the labor force with fewer years of service and with benefits scaled down from the full vested benefit amount at twenty-five or more years to a small fraction of that amount at fifteen years of service; only the amounts in the old agreement, not the method of prorating nor the parity at twenty-five years of service, would be changed. The union also sought continued provision for early retirement at increased benefits, and mandatory

3. *ILWU*, Caucus Proceedings, *April 5, 1966, and June 24, 1966. In the last half of 1966, the lowest paid day of eight hours would include six hours at the basic straight-time hourly rate of $3.88, and two hours overtime at $5.82 per hour. Penalty-cargo rates, skill differentials, more overtime hours, and the like would increase the average hourly earnings even more for many men.*

retirement with benefits in addition to the improved vested amount. One major change in the M&M fund was the elimination of the wage guarantee. It had not been used in the preceding five years, and neither the union nor employers foresaw a need for its continuation. The union sought no change in the death benefits of the existing contract.

In negotiations the employers agreed to the continuation of the fund and annual contributions. The horse-trading of the bargaining table resulted in larger benefits, but not so large as the union first demanded. As in 1960, the size of the total and annual contributions were determined by first settling the amount of the benefits and then estimating their costs by an actuarial study of the eligible workforce.

The results of the negotiations, in brief, included vested benefits of $13,000, payable at retirement in a lump sum or in monthly installments of $216.67 or $270.84, over five or four years respectively, to men sixty-two years or older with twenty-five or more years of service in the industry. No special benefits for early retirement, voluntary or compulsory, were provided. The formal mandatory retirement age of sixty-eight years was not changed, but the 1966 agreement did provide for compulsory earlier retirement if a mutually agreed work-force contraction were necessary. When agreed on by employers and the union, or ordered by the arbitrator, the men qualified for the vesting benefit may be removed from the registration lists and the industry, in reverse order of age, from sixty-eight to sixty-three. If more men must go, the agreement provided that the parties were to negotiate how many, the age classes, and the extra payment, if any, to the men involuntarily forced out.

The emphasis of the agreement, however, was on inducement to voluntary withdrawal of the older men. The substantially increased vested benefit was part of the inducement. Markedly improved pensions were another part. The union demanded an increase in the monthly pension from $165 to $250, and reduction of normal retirement age from sixty-five to sixty-two. The amount was whittled down, and the age for full pension set by compromise in negotiations. The final agreement provided a full pension of $235 per month to men at age sixty-three, with prorated smaller amounts for men with less than twenty-five years of service, payable to those retiring on or after July 1, 1966.

The sharp improvements of the 1966 agreement carried a danger with them — eligible workers might postpone retirement, hoping to do even better under the next agreement. Clearly, the men who were qualified for the benefits under the 1960 agreement improved their position a great deal by remaining in the work force until July 1, 1966. The new benefits were not only larger than before, but they accrued only to the men leaving the work force under the new agreement. No provision was made for adding to the vested benefits of the men already retired, nor were their pensions increased. The employers and the union recognized the danger in 1966, and sought to mitigate it by providing penalties for failure to withdraw when eligible. The worker remaining on the active rolls loses $83.33 for each month he remains in the work force past the date he becomes qualified for the full vesting benefit, up to a maximum of $3,000.

Manning was the central issue in 1966, and the negotiations, caucus debate, and final results had some of the flavor and were a continuation of the spirit of the 1960 events and agreement. Manning took up most of the time in negotiations and was the subject of most of the discussion in the caucus. As before, the employers sought flexibility and elimination of men whom they regarded as unnecessary. Also as before, the union granted concessions reluctantly and only in exchange for solid gains on other demands.

The experience of the two sides during the life of the original mechanization and modernization agreement was influential in shaping their subsequent positions. Shipwork and the basic gang were the chief focus for concern. Highly mechanized operations and most of the dockwork had been no problem during the period 1961–1965; the redundant men were eliminated and a wide variety of new manning scales had been negotiated or arbitrated under the 1960 agreement. Improvements in break-bulk shipwork, with its great reliance on manual labor, had been less satisfactory; indeed, both sides were dissatisfied. The employers saw that the productivity changes in shipwork had been only modest. The workers and union knew that the work still was often arduous. Finally, technical improvements being introduced in 1965 and 1966 suggested that, even in break-bulk cargo handling, mechanization in one form or another could and would replace the traditional labor-intensive methods.

In negotiations, the employers demanded the widest possible

flexibility in break-bulk cargo handling, including the elimination of any and all men if they were not actually necessary for most of the time for the job at hand. They wanted machine operators and other men to be assignable to manual work as well as skilled work, and from dock to ship, from hatch to hatch, and so on, with the work to be done determining the requirements. The union renewed its demand, maturing during the preceding five years, for compulsory use of machines, especially where heavy loads were involved. Its position clearly intended to exclude wherever possible the heavy handwork of belly packing or shoulder packing. Urged by the caucus, the union also adopted the stand that there be no decrease in the basic gang.

Most of the negotiations in May and June were taken up with the manning issues. Tentative agreement had been reached by June 24, and the progress report was given to the caucus. Final agreement was reached within the next two weeks; the results were presented to the July caucus. Although debated at length, no substantial changes were made by the delegates.

The new agreement changed a bit the existing contract language defining the basic gang.[4] The gang boss, traditionally used in some ports, but not others, could be eliminated if he does not or cannot perform his supervisory and other duties; the latter are specified by mutual agreement between the employers and the union. The old requirement of a winch driver and a hatch tender was replaced with "skilled deck man or men as required." The required four holdmen must include, by the new agreement, two skilled machine operators. The contract language requiring that the basic gang be supplemented by two men for discharging and four for loading operations involving hand-handled cargo was slightly changed to apply more clearly only to cargo hand-handled piece by piece.

Although the agreement retains a basic gang, the parties were explicit in reaffirming the general mechanization and modernization principle that unnecessary men may be eliminated by mutual agreement or arbitration, and that the new agreement eliminates the "basic gang" as a barrier. For example, in operations using machines to stow or remove cargo loads, the employers may request review of

4. *The manning provisions are sections 10.1 through 10.9 of the ILWU-PMA, Pacific Coast Longshore Agreement, 1961–1966, as amended July, 1966. The contract amendments were reported verbatim in a special supplement to* The Dispatcher, *Vol. XXIV, No. 15 (July 22, 1966).*

manning and, under the new agreement, could win elimination of all holdmen except the machine operators; under the 1960 agreement, the holdmen would have remained. The 1966 major change — elimination of the basic gang (except for wholly manhandled cargo) — was effected largely by deleting the contractual protection for existing operations and explicitly granting the employer the right to seek review of all manning and that "the Employer shall not be bound or limited by the basic gang structure provided in 10.2."[5]

A technical innovation of the last years of the old agreement — the "robot" or "cage" — provides another illustration of the new approach to manning in shipwork. The "robot" is a large, partially enclosed metal platform attached to the running gear. It is capable of being turned and positioned on the dock and in the hold by remote control. The loads, usually palletized, are placed and removed from the cage by forklift or other machines. The robot eliminates the need for the two frontmen on the dock and for holdmen to position loads and to attach or remove the hook or hook gear in the hold. Robot operations were overmanned in 1965 and early 1966, as the parties negotiated but failed to agree to revised manning scales. The issue had been submitted to arbitration but had not been resolved when the 1966 new contract negotiations began. The arbitrator's authority expired with the termination of the old contract, and the parties negotiated the issue as a separate provision in the new agreement.

The theme of much of the new agreement — flexibility — applies clearly to the manning of robot operations. The contract specifies that skilled men for deck, dock, or hold are to be hired as needed. Frontmen and the gang boss are explicitly eliminated; they are wholly redundant. Although two longshoremen are required for whatever unskilled work is left, the contract and related discussion leave no doubt that should they be found unnecessary, the employers will ask for, and win, their removal. In its explanatory statements to the membership, the union's negotiating committee pointed out, concerning robot operations manning, "Under this section, to go to the extreme possibility, the employers may be able to get down to a gang that has no frontmen, no more men that the machine drivers in the hold, and possibly no gang bosses."[6]

5. Section 10.3(a) of the 1961–1966 agreement, before amendment; section 10.3 of the contract, as amended in July, 1966.
6. The Dispatcher, Vol. XXIV, No. 15 (July 22, 1966).

In addition to elimination of the last traces of actual or potential redundant manning, the employers won still greater flexibility in task assignment of the work force. The first steps toward greater flexibility had begun before 1960 when dockmen were split off and could be moved from hatch to hatch, without the ship gang. Flexibility increased in 1959, when all gangs could be shifted a good deal to fill out the eight-hour guarantee. In principle, the 1960 agreement brought still more flexibility as it created a large group of "swingmen" who could be assigned to shipwork as well as dockwork. The 1966 agreement very nearly has completed the process. It abolished the distinctions, and nontransferability, between shipwork, dockwork, and swingmen. All unskilled workers are now "longshoremen," not dockmen or swingmen and the like. The agreement provides explicitly that longshoremen may be shifted from dock to ship, to railcars or barges, and back again, as the employer directs. As the nature of an operation changes — for example, from machine stow to hand-handling, or vice versa — the employer may add or reassign men as required by the actual task at hand. The parties did provide one exception: each port may establish a new list giving preference for the easy jobs, usually dockwork, to men whose age or partial disability justifies preferential treatment. In caucus discussion, a member of the Coast Committee told the delegates that the new provisions did away with the "sick, lame, and lazy" board. The sick and the lame would be taken care of with the new preferential lists, but the "lazy" would probably have to go in the hold.[7] The existing preferential lists for dockwork were abolished.

As partial consideration — the M&M fund, higher wages, and similar benefits were the rest of it — for giving up the rules remaining in 1966, the union won a number of points. One was the compulsory use of machines. The employers formally agreed to mechanization as desirable for both parties, and that they would add machines and adopt new methods, subject to further negotiation of "ground rules." The experience under the 1960 agreement suggests strongly that the parties themselves, perhaps helped a bit by the arbitrators, will in fact implement the principle wherever possible. A second variety of union gain included reaffirmation and expansion of the practice of drawing skilled men from the ranks of the unskilled

7. *ILWU*, Caucus Proceedings, *June 26, 1966.*

longshoremen by employer-operated training programs. Finally, the union won the right to reclaim jurisdiction over any and all work on the docks or ships — including work done by Teamsters, carpenters, and other skilled and unskilled work — provided that they do so without jurisdictional disputes with the other unions involved.

Although the 1966 caucus delegates were as interested in manning and held views resembling those of the 1960 and earlier caucuses, there were differences. As before, there were strong statements in favor of "holding the line" on the basic gang. Also as before, some of the delegates regretted the passing of the old ways and resented the machines. Containers and huge gantry cranes had changed the work and broken up the gangs in many areas. The robots and other mechanization continued the threat. Old-fashioned unskilled longshoremen were fast becoming unnecessary, and many longshoremen were discomfited by the feeling of not being needed at all. Unlike the earlier caucuses, however, the delegates in 1966 appeared disinclined to oppose further mechanization. They did not all like it, or its consequences, but they nonetheless accepted the inevitability of change. In 1966 the focus shifted even more than before to sharing the economic and other benefits of technical improvement and productivity change.

The wage guarantee fund was created by the 1960 agreement to protect minimum earnings of the fully registered work force. It was never needed or used during the life of the agreement. For some time prior to the new contract negotiations, the union and many of its members had assumed that the $13 million accumulated by mid-1966 would be theirs to allocate. The claim was made early in the 1966 negotiations, and quickly conceded by the employers. The issue of fund disposition was not difficult; the general tone of the various resolutions submitted by the locals to the caucus and the views of the leadership coincided. The fund had been established to protect only the fully registered longshoremen who remained active during the agreement period. The "B" men were not protected because they were only probationary or temporary workers, and the older men had their vesting benefits. The caucus resolved, with little debate, to divide the fund equally among all longshoremen and clerks who were fully registered, on the "A" lists, on July 1, 1960, and were still active — a fully registered longshoreman, clerk, foreman, or walking boss — on June 30, 1966. Those men who received any benefit from the vesting or disability provisions of the M&M plan were excluded from the wage fund distribution.

The actual disbursement was a time-consuming administrative chore. Complete lists of eligibles had to be prepared and wide publicity given in order to attract all who had a legitimate claim but possibly had been otherwise overlooked. All together, months were required, and the payout came only at the end of the year, on December 30, 1966. At that time, those longshoremen who had wanted for a long time the "money in their pockets" finally got it. The checks were for $1,223 for each man.

Negotiating a new contract was an easier matter in 1966 than in 1960. The issues at stake were neither so complex nor so novel as in the earlier years. The precedents had been established; the M&M fund to share the benefits of increased efficiency, protection of employment opportunities to the existing work force and, on the union side, giving up rigid rules in favor of continual negotiations and arbitration to protect pace of work and safety. The 1966 agreement reaffirmed the basic principles and was a tidying up of some of the loose ends left in 1960.

The new agreement, to run until mid-1971, extended the benefits and principles of the old contract. A new cohort of longshoremen and clerks was made eligible for the retirement or disability bonus, and the extension established that the 1960 arrangement was not an accidental and ephemeral settlement. The employers recognized that sharing the gains and protecting the work force were continuing obligations, not limited by a specific five-year agreement; the union demonstrated that the elimination of unnecessary men or inefficient practices in every sector of longshoring was not a temporary concession.

FROM OPPOSITION TO ENCOURAGEMENT OF THE MACHINE: A SUMMING UP

The ILWU, over the years, had won a strong position on the Pacific docks. It gained extensive control over the labor supply, pace and methods of work, and manning. The union successfully eliminated all traces of worker allegiance to specific companies and changed the employment relationship from the conventional one in which the firm hires, directs, and discharges workers to one in which the union participates in all of these functions.

Job control grew out of the nature of the industry and the union's determination to strengthen itself and to settle effectively the many grievances of the members. The hiring hall and work force control were required by the need to decasualize the labor market, to establish uniform conditions in the industry, and to limit the size of the work force as a prerequisite for further economic advances. The work rules were sought to protect the health, safety, effort, and employment opportunities of the work force. Most of the motives are not rare; almost all effective unions seek higher wages and protection of health, safety, and effort standards. However, only the unions in competitive industries and in inherently casual labor markets are compelled to establish job control to accomplish these tasks. Further, some of the motives — decasualization, uniform conditions, and work-force size limitation to maintain employment and wage levels — are necessary only in casual labor market and competitive industry circumstances.

In Pacific Coast longshoring, the specific rules were a direct outgrowth of the technical and similar conditions of the industry. The wide variety of tasks differing in goods handled and characteristics of the docks and ships afforded opportunities for employers to vary their output and effort demands. The short duration of jobs and wide geographical dispersion of the work places provided scope for employers, unscrupulous or harassed by market pressures, to insist on excessive effort or unsafe conditions and be done with the job before review or redress could be won. Rigid and detailed rules, enforced by local militance and threat of the "quickie" strike, were an appropriate response.

On the face of it, modification of a large part of union job control was not an inevitable necessity during the late 1950s. In fact, however, pressures for change were great, their sources varied and numerous, and they affected both the union and the employers.

The employers were interested in, and occasionally insistent on, easing restrictions. Employer pressure for modification of work practices and union control of labor supply varied over time, but nonetheless was continuous from the very beginning of the collective bargaining relationship up to the signing of the 1960 agreement. In the earlier days the employers fought long and bitterly every encroachment in job control. The union-run hiring hall was first granted by an arbitration board, not by the employers, and employer opposition did not cease until thirteen years later. Sling loads, pace of work, and idle time were seriously contested for seven years after 1934, then, after a brief respite during World War II, fought again for another three or four years. Employer attempts to roll back completely all elements of union job control ended with the collapse of the Waterfront Employers Association in the 1948 strike, but management pressure continued for greater productivity through elimination of informal work restrictions. Within a few years of the 1948 debacle, in 1952, the then-new PMA began its first publicized contract conformance program and attempts to gather productivity data for use in bargaining. Within four more years, the first steps leading directly to the elimination of the restrictive work rules in 1960 already had been taken.

Product-market pressures and the possibility of substitution of capital for labor were elements in softening the union's resistance to change. The American-flag segment of the Pacific Coast shipping industry had never been strong, except during war. Profit margins chronically were narrow, and, important to the demand for labor, the coastwise and intercoastal branches of ocean commerce were clearly vanishing. The last general-cargo carriers in those branches of trade were withdrawing from the industry even while the mechanization and modernization agreement was being negotiated. Mechanization, including specialized ships and gear for some cargoes, and more important, containerization, were recognized as cost-induced substitution of capital for labor. The union could continue to block mechanization, but the consequence, if successful, would have been the elimination of companies and jobs from the industry. With or without union resistance to new methods, given high or increasing relative wages, the demand for longshore labor would shrink. If the union opted for accepting mechanization, it was at least possible that industry demand was sufficiently elastic to bring about employment levels as high or higher than those accompanying a policy of continued resistance.

Government interest in the industry was influential in bringing change, both through pressures on the employers for improved performance and threats to the union to modify its control over labor supply and work methods. Most of the U.S. ocean shipping industry is dependent on the government, through the subsidy programs, for survival. Advised by the Maritime Administration or the important congressional committees that a tougher line on costs or more imagination in pursuing efficiency were desirable, the ship operators were compelled at least to try. The threats of government interference with the union's high degree of job control were credible. The union-run hiring hall and closed membership lists were in principle contrary to the public policy proclaimed by the Taft-Hartley Act, and in practice, at the edge of legality. Only slight changes in the law or its interpretation were necessary to destroy both. Restrictive work practices were difficult to defend in public. The immediate precedent of the New York–New Jersey commission created to restore order to the New York port area docks was uneasily noted by Pacific Coast employers and the union. The expressed interest of congressional committee members in desiring evidence of improved output conditions on the Pacific docks was seriously taken.

Within the union, the age structure of the work force was an unusual but relevant factor in bringing about change. The presence of a huge group of elderly dock workers blocked the registration and full union membership of young men who actually were doing most of the work in the holds of the ships. Further, many of the old men did little work at all, and their absence would not have been missed. The union leadership was aware of the irony: a strike to maintain featherbedding would have depended, in large part, on the support of the younger men who did not benefit from the restrictive practices and who, in many cases, were not even members of the union.

On the union side, additional motives for abandoning work rules were the need for greater uniformity in practices in the various ports and the desire of the top leadership to limit local autonomy in a number of aspects. Work rules and practices varied in the ports, and at several times during the decade preceding the 1960 agreement the locals appeared to be competing with each other in relaxing rules to attract cargo to their ports. At almost every longshore caucus one local or another sought support for a resolution to adopt coastwide uniformity in manning requirements or other work rules. The officers of the union were disturbed by the divisiveness of nonuniform work rules; in fact, the program leading to the 1960 abandonment of the restrictive practices was initially introduced to the caucus in 1956 as a statement addressed to a local's resolution reaffirming coastwide uniformity in basic manning scales. Local autonomy further promoted divisiveness by the refusal of some of the larger locals to admit registered men from ports with slack demand for labor. Many of the smaller ports had experienced sharp declines in port activity. The longshoremen from these ports brought almost perennial complaints to the annual caucuses of their low hours and earnings and their desire for some of their members to be admitted to the more prosperous locals.

Finally, the abuse of local autonomy weakened the union's ability to win substantial overall improvements in wages or to make other gains. The recurrent failure of the ILWU's officers to force contract compliance in the Los Angeles local undercut the union's position in negotiations year after year. The 1958–1960 agreements strengthened the position of the top leadership in that coastwide transfer of longshoremen between locals were eased and permission from the ILWU was required before men could be added to the local registration rolls. The definition and enforcement of work practices have been shifted from the local leaders to the arbitrators, many of them former union officials at the regional or coastwide level.

The pressures for change were important, but they were not alone decisive. Perhaps crucial was the fact that the work rules could be abandoned without significant penalty to the union or its members. The necessity for detailed and rigid rules was disappearing during the decade following the 1949 settlement of the industry's last great strike. By the late 1950s, the parties had developed a grievance procedure of increasing scope and effectiveness. The key device was "instant" arbitration. In each major port, an arbitrator was always on call. Arriving at the scene of a dispute within minutes or, at most, a few hours, the arbitrator was authorized and expected to hear the evidence, decide the merits, and order compliance on the spot. A written award followed later.

In the context of growing good relations between the employers and the union, the grievance procedure showed promise, fulfilled after 1960, of providing a flexible substitute for rigid rules. Effort, health, or safety were grounds for challenge to any employer's changes in methods or output standards. The workers raising the challenge in good faith were not required to work until the matter had been settled; they could stand by, or under the clarifications of 1966, be assigned to "work around" the disputed cargo until an agreement or arbitrator's decision resolved the dispute. The union did not give up job control or return to the employer unilateral discretion in effort and pace of work when it consented to the elimination of work rules. It did change the nature of job control.

To the extent that the rules were motivated by employment opportunities, the union did change its objective; but here, too, the change was without penalty, and the vital elements of control were left undisturbed. Under the old rules the union could have held, although it never clearly did, the size of the work force to be itself a goal — a larger work force is preferred to a smaller one. This view, if ever held, has been abandoned. But protection of employment opportunities for the union's members, the fully registered men, was not given up. For the short run, the wage guarantee and accelerated attrition provided the safeguard. Over a longer period, the continuation of control over the size of the work force, continued provision of a buffer labor pool to meet peak demand, and reaffirmed jurisdiction are the protection. Finally, the work-force attrition was not harsh. The many men old enough to retire, and who would not have had much longer to work even without special benefits, were well cared for by the vested severance bonus.

Within the industry and the union, the consensus is that the approach, the agreements negotiated by the parties, and the post-1960 implementation offer little that other unions or industries might follow. This is, to a great extent, true. The essence of the 1960 agreement, and its subsequent modifications, was the exchange of many and detailed work rules for guarantees that giving up the rules would not result in undue hardship to the union and its members.

But few unions have so much to give up. The typical industrial union in the United States, for example, has almost no job control at all. Hiring is management's prerogative; thus, work-force size and selection of individuals are beyond union control, or even participation. Job assignment, reassignment, methods of work, and manning are similarly almost wholly management prerogatives, with only slight modification by the industrial union. Seniority is applied, with greater or less weight, to identify the individuals — but not to determine how many — to retain jobs, or to move to better ones. To protect effort or output standards, the industrial union has, at most, the right to maintain given manning or other conditions, provided the techniques or production methods are not changed. The steel industry contracts (Section 2B in the U.S. Steel agreement) are an excellent illustration of this point. The agreements provide, in effect, that the local working conditions may be changed only when equipment or methods of operations are changed. In fact, most industrial unions do not even have this right.[8] Craft or former craft unions often have a bit more than industrial unions, but still a good deal less than the ILWU. The compositors in printing have had the makework of "bogus" (unnecessary duplication of work set up elsewhere), and the printing pressmen have had manning requirements, occasionally restrictive in some jurisdictions. The widely publicized rail-industry controversy of nearly ten years' duration turns largely on a single practice — excess manning by firemen.[9] The various construction crafts have or had rules specifying, in part, the tools or techniques to be used or not to be used, but usually not manning. And so on.

On the other hand, the ILWU-PMA experience is useful as an example in some respects. It is an excellent illustration of the bargaining principle of exchanging concessions, not demanding moral or similar rights. That the union gave up a great deal is, at this point, obvious and does not need repetition. On the other side, the employers recognized and conceded arrangements to satisfy the workers' and union's fear of increased effort for unchanged wages and of displacement of the currently employed work force. They further conceded the principle of explicit financial benefits to the work force in partial exchange for increased efficiency. In all, Pacific longshoring appears to provide an illustration of classic bargaining — each party was made better off, none worse, as a result of the exchange.

Further, to the extent that some of the circumstances have parallels elsewhere, the longshore example is appropriate. Large severance bonuses and reduced retirement age, backed up with flexible mandatory retirement provisions, are applicable to any industry with a

---

8. See, for example, Jack Stieber, "Work Rules and Practices in Mass Production Industries," Proceedings of the Fourteenth Annual Meeting, Industrial Relations Research Association *(December, 1961), pp. 404–412.*
9. A good summary of the rail industry and the attempt to eliminate restrictive practices appears in Robert D. Leiter, Featherbedding and Job Security *(New York, 1964), pp. 70–100.*

work force composed in large part of older workers. (Among others, the railway industry appears to fit these specifications.) Employer-sponsored training and upgrading of unskilled men already in the industry, together with reaffirmed jurisdiction to the union, are similarly widely applicable.

Finally, the ILWU provides an additional demonstration of the flexibility of an industrial or multioccupational union when contrasted with a union with narrow occupational jurisdiction. Unlike the firemen in the railway brotherhoods, longshoremen displaced by the elimination of redundant manning, or by any other rule abandonment or technical change, may become skilled machine operators or clerks without involving other unions or jurisdictional problems. Moreover, the union's existence is not threatened by even the total elimination of unskilled longshoremen; whoever is working on the Pacific Coast docks, without regard to his skill or job title, will still be a member of the ILWU.

FUTURE PROSPECTS

Three forecasts are required to assess the future in Pacific longshoring — work-force attrition, productivity change, and the volume of trade in the years to come. By far the easiest to predict is work-force attrition. Very nearly as many men will be eligible for the M&M fund benefits during the five years after July 1, 1966, as were eligible during the preceding five and one-half years. All in all, about 2,700 men should withdraw by mid-1971, assuming fewer deaths (there are fewer very old men than before) and more eligibles retiring than in 1961–1966. The latter assumes that the penalty reduction in benefits will in fact induce the eligible men to leave promptly.

Productivity change certainly should continue. The elimination of work rules and restrictive practices will go on. The relatively few redundant men of 1966 will be eliminated; the displacement of dock workers by prepalletizing and other unit load practices will continue. Continuing productivity increase should be the result. More important, however, are the favorable prospects for continued investment in containerization as well as new and growing investment in mechanization of the remaining break-bulk cargo work. Work-rule abandonment shifted the production function and resulted in sharply improved profits to the firms, but provided little incentive to undertake new investment. But, the once-and-for-all shift in the production function was nearly completed under the first agreement of 1960. Future productivity increase will possible only by substituting capital for labor, perhaps accompanied by technical innovation. Labor costs certainly will rise relative to capital costs, and the union members will continue to be most interested in eliminating the heavy physical labor of the job. The result will be competitive market pressures and frequent grievances from the workers. The laggard employer will be coerced; failing to mechanize, he may be eliminated altogether from the industry.

Containerization will be an important part of continued investment and mechanization. The use of containers had not in any sense reached its limits by 1966. The techniques had been applied almost wholly to domestic commerce, whereas a large fraction of foreign trade appears to be in every respect suited to containerization. The Pacific Coast trade with Japan, for example, involves distances and number of major ports comparable to the already containerized U.S. intercoastal trade. Several companies have announced their intention to provide container service in the Japan routes. There is every likelihood that much of this large and growing segment of the Pacific Coast's ocean commerce will be handled in containers within a few years of 1966.

As a result of all changes, productivity should increase at least at the same rate as during the 1960–1965 period, perhaps a bit faster. By mid-1971, efficiency should be 40 or 50 percent above the 1965 level.

Trade volume is the most difficult to forecast. Domestic trade and the civilian part of foreign trade should continue to grow at about 6 or 7 percent each year over the five years after 1966, assuming continued near full employment in the United States and economic growth comparable to the recent experience in Japan and the other Pacific countries. The trade generated by military activity abroad probably will decline during the five years, but very likely could be replaced by reconstruction or development aid. In brief, trade volume through Pacific ports will continue to grow, but probably at a rate below the rate of productivity change.

Given the three forecasts, a number of expectations reasonably follow. The industry should continue to do well. Costs will outstrip productivity during the first year or two of the 1966 agreement —

more than half of the the five-year wage increase was effective immediately. But the downtrend in labor costs per ton then will resume. Revenue and profits should reach new record levels, the former each year, and the latter by the second or third year of the new agreement.

The size of the work force will contract a bit, but not much. More important, the composition will continue to change. Although the work force, already old in 1966, will still be old in 1971, the median age will drop a bit from about fifty years to perhaps as low as forty-five years. The substantial attrition associated with the departure of the older men will be met by admitting almost as many new and younger men to the work force and the union. By 1971 nearly half of the union's membership will consist of the men taken in since the first modernization agreement was put into effect. But a large fraction of the remainder will be the several thousand men aged fifty-seven years and older — the last of the World War II and immediate postwar massive addition to the membership. Looking to 1971 and beyond, it appears very likely that this last cohort of disproportionately large numbers of older men will expect severance benefits comparable to those paid the old men retiring during the more than ten years from 1961 to mid-1971. Their numbers probably will require some provision for their orderly and prompt withdrawal from the work force. On the other hand, the younger men will be more numerous than ever before, and they are likely to press for higher wages and easier work as their "share of the machine." Their impatience with anything resembling an "old man's contract" may be hard to restrain.

In its thirty years of existence, the collective bargaining relationship on the Pacific Coast docks has accomplished much and has itself been changed a great deal. The work of the longshoreman has been transformed from casual and hard physical labor, at average wage rates but below average earnings, to partially mechanized work, with a substantial proportion of it skilled, and at high wages and higher earnings. Pacific Coast longshoremen are no longer the transient, ill-paid *lumpenproletariat* of many ports and times past. Their jobs are secure, their status high, and occupations attractive. The queues of job seekers are good evidence of the job's desirability. At every opening of the registration lists, ten or twenty men apply for every vacancy on the rolls. In 1959 in San Francisco, for example,

9,000 men applied for 750 places on the "B" list; in 1963, about 10,000 applied for the 1,000 places. In 1966, 23,000 inquiries were received and 15,000 actual applications filed for the 700 openings on the San Francisco lists.

The union and employers both also have been transformed. The formerly militant and fiercely aggressive stances have given way to peaceful, almost cooperative relations. Hostility, suspicion, and rigidity have been changed to accommodation and flexibility. The men, too, are changing. The original union members are almost all gone from the waterfront. The employers and firm managers in 1966 are not, in most cases, the men who were present in the days of struggle. The third generation of leadership is taking over in the employers' association, and new men are appearing on the union side as well. The long-time president of the PMA, J. Paul St. Sure, retired in mid-1966 and died soon after, in September. Not only most of the old-timers but their successors are passing from union leadership. Two of the three members of the Coast Committee at the negotiation of the 1960 agreement have died — Howard Bodine in April, 1966, and L. B. Thomas in January, 1967. Indestructible Harry Bridges still leads the union he created more than thirty years ago, but he is being joined by new men.

VIII AFTERWORD

Developments in the period from the first writing of the preceding chapters through mid-1969 have continued the general trends already described. Pacific Coast trade has continued to grow. The 58,801,000 tons handled by PMA member companies in 1968 was an increase of more than one-third over the 1965 tonnage and was almost twice that handled in 1960. The increase is the result of continued rapid economic growth of the U.S. Pacific region and the Pacific basin countries; only a small part of it is directly attributable to the war in Vietnam. In 1964, for example, the Pacific Coast trade with the entire Southeast Asian area, including the Philippines, Taiwan, Indonesia and Malaysia as well as Vietnam, was about 2,284,000 tons, or about 7 per cent of all Pacific Coast foreign trade for that year. In 1967, trade with Southeast Asia was about 3,081,000 tons, still only 7 per cent of the year's coastwide total foreign trade. Even if the entire increase were military cargo, the 800,000 or so tons involved is relatively insignificant. Over the same three years the increase in trade with Japan was 9½ million tons of dry cargo, and trade with India, Australia and Canada increased by about 3 million tons.[1]

Employment has been maintained at high levels. The slight drop in man-hour input in the few years following 1960 was recovered by 1965, and man-hours continued to rise slowly through 1968 (see Table 30). The total number of longshoremen on the rolls was about the same in 1968 as in 1960 or 1965, but the individuals have changed as new men were added to replace those leaving through retirement, death or disability. In San Francisco, 720 "B" longshoremen were registered in May 1967, drawn from the thou-

---

1. *The PMA-handled tonnages are from PMA data; see Table 30. The foreign trade figures are dry cargo tonnages, adapted from data in U.S. Department of Commerce, Bureau of the Census, U.S. Waterborne Foreign Trade, FT 985, January–December, for the various years. The military cargo carried in ships operated by the U.S. Armed Forces are not included in any of the tonnage data.*

Table 30: Tonnages and Man-hours, Pacific Coast Longshoring, 1960, 1965-1968

| Year | Tons Handled (Thousands) | | Man-hours (Thousands) | | |
| | Bulk | Total[a] | Longshore | | Shoreside |
			Casual	Registered	Total[b]
1960	10,772	29,814	1,812	20,765	28,877
1965	16,813	42,713	1,729	21,890	30,097
1966	18,009	48,341	2,727	23,269	32,575
1967	20,412	53,702	2,320	22,585	31,684
1968	20,824	58,801	3,593	20,828	32,385

[a] Includes adjustment of logs and lumber data; board feet were converted to tons by the formula: 1000 board feet × 1.8 = 2 tons.

[b] Includes clerical, supervisory and miscellaneous man-hours. The 1960 figures are adjusted to include estimated man-hours for Eureka and Stockton.

SOURCE: PMA Contract Data Department, letter and tables July 24, 1969.

sands of applicants of late 1966; the ILWU and PMA agreed to add 125 clerks and another 400 longshoremen to the "B" list in 1969. In Los Angeles, 200 longshoremen were added in 1966, and 68 clerks in 1968. In Portland, the parties agreed in 1968 to add 300 longshoremen; 100 were actually registered in 1968 and the rest were to be admitted in 1969. In the Puget Sound area, 101 new men were added in 1968 and 143 were to join the work force in 1969. In the smaller ports, Stockton registered 42 longshoremen and 35 clerks in 1967, and Eureka added 43 men in 1968, with 30 more to be registered in 1969.

Despite the addition of 1300 longshoremen and clerks, and agreement to add 900 more, registration has continued to be a problem. The number of new entrants has fallen behind demand, and the use of casuals has increased sharply as a consequence. The 3½ million man-hours worked by casuals in 1968 was almost 15 per cent of all longshore man-hours used, far higher than the average of 6 or 7 per cent of the earlier years in the decade. In part, the problem results from the continuing reluctance of longshore locals in all ports to admit new men. Although they eventually agree, their caution and the time required to solicit and examine applicants typically result in the admission of fewer men than needed at the time the registration process is completed. More serious is the two-and-one-half year impasse in Los Angeles. Although the leaders of ILWU Local 13 and PMA representatives agreed to add more men in 1967, the PMA challenged the Local 13 "sponsorship" requirement. Unlike locals in all the other ports, the Los Angeles unit has required all applicants for registration to be "sponsored" or recommended by a member of the Local. The PMA has been unwilling to add men under this method, and Local 13 has refused to give up the practice.

Table 31: Productivity Indexes, Pacific Coast Longshoring, 1965-1968

Year	Total Tons Per Man-hour[a] (1960 = 100)	Allowing For Bulk Tonnage Variations[b] (1960 = 100)
1965	142	136
1966	148	147
1967	170	166
1968	182	184

[a] All tonnage reported by PMA divided by total shoreside man-hours. This index is comparable to the figures in Table 3, p. 111.

[b] Man-hours required at 1960 rates were estimated separately for bulk and all nonbulk tonnage. Total shoreside hours and tonnages adjusted for underweighting of logs and lumber were used. This index uses a slightly different method, but is roughly comparable to the ones in Table 4, p. 113.

Productivity has continued to increase rapidly. The trade and employment figures indicate that in 1968 longshoremen on the Pacific Coast handled almost twice the tonnage with a work force only slightly larger than in 1960. Rough estimates of efficiency (see Table 31) show that productivity in 1968 was more than 30 per cent above the 1965 level and more than 80 per cent above 1960. Although the techniques of the careful estimates of chapter 4 were not applied,[2] the findings of that chapter suggest that the crude measures are good first approximations.

The most interesting source of productivity change since 1965, even if not yet the most important, is containerization. The use of

2. *For two reasons: the detailed tonnage reports of the Corps of Engineers are available only after an average lag of two years or so; second, the Engineers have changed their commodity classification system so drastically that my commodity reconciliation data and computer programs for aggregating the data would have to be completely rewritten. For purposes of a brief afterword, the detailed, careful estimates would require too much work for too little improvement in the productivity measures, and for too few added years.*

containers has grown steadily, accompanied by expansion of container terminal facilities and ships. In 1963, the Pacific Coast ports handled about 1 million tons of containerized cargo, all of it in the trade with Hawaii, U.S. Atlantic and Gulf ports, and with Alaska. In 1964, about 1½ million tons were handled, all of it still in the three main branches of domestic trade. In 1966, containerized cargo was about 2¼ million tons, reflecting in part the continued steady but unspectacular growth in domestic trade, and, in larger part, the inauguration by Sea Land of container service to Vietnam, the Philippines and Okinawa. The 1968 volume was about 3½ million tons. Although more than half the increase is attributable to growth in domestic and trans-Pacific military traffic, a major breakthrough was the opening of containerized trade with Japan. The Matson Navigation Company and a consortium of four Japanese companies — Mitsui O.S.K. Lines, the Japan Line, Kawasaki Kisen Kaisha and Yamashita Shinnihon — began service in the last quarter of the year, operating two and four ships respectively, between Japan and two California ports, Oakland and Los Angeles. Sea Land began eastbound nonmilitary container service in December, with eight ships carrying goods from Japan to Seattle and Oakland.

The continued growth of container tonnage is a certainty. The full-year cargo volume carried by companies already in the trade will substantially increase the figures for 1969, and new entrants will add even more. A six-company Japanese group is planning large scale service between Japan and the Northwest ports, and a U.S. company, Seatrain, will enter the Oakland-Hawaii container trade in mid-year. The first two of a fleet of ships, owned by the Johnson Line, will begin container service between the Pacific Coast and Europe in 1969, and more will follow in 1970. All in all, Pacific Coast container tonnage should amount to 5½ to 6 million tons for the year.[3]

Despite the growth in container tonnage, containers were not the chief source of productivity change, at least for the years through 1968. If all the goods moved in containers that year had been handled as conventional break-bulk cargo at the 1960 average rate, about 5 million man-hours, including indirect, clerical and supervisory labor, would have been used. Although not insignificant, the

3. The tonnages are my estimates. See appendix B, pp. 232–45, for a brief description of the method and sources of data.

man-hour savings represent a productivity increase of only about 15 per cent, relative to 1960, or less than one-fifth of the overall estimated increase during the 1960–1968 period. More important were the continuing benefits from work rules relaxation, already identified for the earlier years. Manning scales continued to be revised downward, accompanying the expanded use of machines, including, for example, the "robot" hook gear for break-bulk goods, and improved gear on special operations. The growth in prepalletized and other unit loads almost certainly has continued to be important. It is clear, however, that containers have grown in importance as a source of productivity change, especially since 1965, and they almost certainly will be the principal source of change in the years to come.

Labor relations during the first two years of the 1966 agreement were essentially a continuation of the experience of earlier years. The grievance procedure continued to be heavily used to settle the hundreds of small disagreements between workers and employers on the docks. The number of arbitrations dropped from 118 in 1965 to 42 in 1968 in the Oregon ports and rose from 73 to 117 between 1966 and 1968 in southern California, but, overall, the coastwide annual rates were roughly the same as earlier in the decade. The principal larger issues were registration of new men, already discussed, and the employment of "steady men." The ILWU and PMA agreed in 1966 to permit skilled men, for example, straddle-truck drivers to become steady employees of one or another firm.[4] Some ILWU locals resisted the implementation of this provision, generally without success, and continued to press the top leadership to reach agreement with the PMA to limit the numbers of steady men.

The tranquillity in labor relations was disturbed in 1968 and 1969. Dissatisfaction with developments in working containers, aggravated a bit by concern with pensions and wage rates, led the ILWU to seek a reopening of the contract in late 1968 and to call a brief, very limited, but official work stoppage in early 1969. Container "stuffing and stripping"[5] was the principal issue. The ILWU sought to reaffirm or reclaim jurisdiction. Related problems con-

4. *Section 9.43 of the ILWU–PMA,* Pacific Coast Longshore Contract Document, July 1, 1966–July 1, 1971.
5. *These rather inelegant terms are necessary to avoid confusion in discussing containers. The industry appears to be adopting the following as standard usage: "loading" is the movement of the container from the dock to the ship, and "unloading" is the reverse. "Stuffing" is placing cargo in the container itself, and "stripping" or "unstuffing" is taking the cargo out.*

cerned the wage scale, fringe benefits and working conditions applicable to container station workers.

The issue is complicated by the fact that within the ILWU itself, jurisdiction over off-dock warehouse work had been given to separate warehousemen's locals, and, more serious, two unions, the ILWU and the International Brotherhood of Teamsters, claimed the right to organize workers in warehouses off the docks. Building and breaking down loads on the dock had been within the jurisdiction of ILWU longshore locals for decades, but the inauguration or expansion of container operations led to the movement of much of the cargo preparation, including container stuffing and stripping, to other terminal areas and warehouses. In many cases, these were in the harbor area, but not clearly on the docks. Some employers proposed a narrow definition of "dock" and began to employ non-longshoremen to do the work.

Differences in costs were a large part of motivation. Contracts negotiated by ILWU warehouse locals and the IBT locals provide lower wage scales, less expensive fringe benefits, and working conditions generally less costly to employers than those of the registered longshore work force. In 1968, warehousemen working on containers were paid $4.08 per hour under one ILWU warehouse contract, and the rates ranged down to as little as an alleged $1.50 per hour in one southern California nonunion warehouse. In contrast, the basic longshore rate under the Pacific Coast Longshore Agreement was the equivalent of $4.36 per hour for an 8-hour day. The M and M retirement bonus, as well as more generous pension and other welfare benefits increased the longshore-warehouse labor cost differential by an additional 50 cents or more per hour. Warehousemen earned shift differentials of as little as 5 per cent of the straight-time hourly base rates, whereas longshoremen worked nights at the full overtime rate (one-and-one-half times the base rate) — the equivalent of another few cents to more than $1.00 per hour, depending on the amount of shiftwork involved. Travel time from the dispatch hall to the job site, and stricter rules involving shifting men between jobs of different skills or clerical work also added to the cost differential.[6]

6. *Longshore wage rates are from the ILWU–PMA*, Pacific Coast Longshore Contract Document, July 1, 1966–July 1, 1971, *Sections 6.1, 6.2 and pp. 94–111. Warehouse rates and other cost items are from ILWU, Longshore Caucus,*

The situation was complicated further by the informal and gradual delegation to the locals of the task of looking after jurisdictional matters. The ILWU Executive Board and the Coast Labor Relations Committee exercised general supervision, established basic principles and participated in meetings with employers, especially PMA members, to deal with coastwide jurisdictional issues. The locals applied the principles, aided by regional directors and using the grievance machinery and arbitration when dealing with PMA members. The locals negotiated agreements for container work with non-PMA companies on a port-by-port basis.

By 1968, the results were dissimilar local contract provisions and practices, and a growing tendency to use nonlongshoremen to work containers. One large non-PMA company, Sea Land, employed members of the Teamsters' union to stuff and strip containers near the docks in Oakland and Los Angeles. Six Japanese ship operating companies had also signed with the IBT for similar work in Los Angeles. In Stockton and Seattle, the ILWU warehouse Locals 6 and 9, not the longshore Locals 54 and 19, did much of the cargo preparation on and near the docks. In Longview, on the Columbia River, and in Los Angeles, ILWU longshore Locals 21 and 13 had negotiated agreements covering container work providing wages, fringe benefits and working conditions different from the coastwide Longshore Agreement and from each other. Similar local agreements were pending in other ports. A final aggravation was associated with the opening in autumn, 1968 of new container berths in Oakland. Negotiations with PMA member companies over jurisdiction, wages and conditions of work had failed, in part because the lower cost provisions of the IBT and ILWU locally negotiated agreements were introduced by the firms as evidence of competitive market conditions that had to be met.[7]

Summarized Minutes, *October 21, 1968, Morning Session, p. 9; Afternoon Session, pp. 4–5, 10; October 22, 1968, Morning Session, p. 3; October 23, 1968, Afternoon Session, p. 1.*

7. The IBT contracts are discussed in the Caucus Minutes, *October 21, 1968, Afternoon Session, p. 2 and October 28, Morning Session, p. 7.* The warehouse agreements and longshore local agreements are described in the Minutes, *October 21, Afternoon Session, p. 10; October 22, Morning Session, pp. 3–5 and Afternoon Session, pp. 2–5, 7, 10.* A summary of the various problems and of the Bay Area negotiations is included in the Minutes, *October 21, Morning Session, pp. 8–9 and Afternoon Session, pp. 6–7; October 23, Morning Session, p. 6 and Afternoon Session, pp. 1, 5.* There were a number of nonlongshore contracts in the harbor areas, but most important in these

The Coast Labor Relations Committee of the ILWU called a meeting of the Longshore, Shipclerk and Walking Boss Caucus in October 1968 to deal with the container issues and pension parity. The Coast Committee reported the development of local contracts, disparate wages and fringes and the threats to jurisdiction. The CLRC asked for authority to open negotiations with the PMA for a uniform coastwide contract. The caucus established a negotiating committee and instructed it in effect to negotiate two contracts — one to bring all container stuffing and stripping on the docks under the PCLA and the other to be a coastwide container terminal contract requiring the use of the longshore work force. For the latter the committee was further instructed to demand a wage scale of $4.30 per hour, roughly equivalent to the longshore basic rate then in effect, and it was given the power to call a coastwide stoppage of work on container ships. The caucus also instructed the negotiating committee to seek revisions in the pension program, to move up the deferred wage increases already in the Longshore Agreement, and to provide a contract reopening in 1970 for wage negotiations. Although important, pensions and wages were subordinated to the container issues.[8]

Negotiations were opened in November 1968. The PMA agreed to hold talks on the container issues, but refused to discuss pensions and wages on the grounds that they were already covered by a contract with some two and a half years yet to run for wages and even longer for pensions. The PMA representatives offered a proposal, in December, providing that container workers be "utilitymen," permitted to do clerks' work and miscellaneous tasks as well as longshore work, and that they work a standard 8-hour day at $3.76 per hour, with a 20 per cent shift differential. After two more months of discussions, the two sides agreed that the registered longshore work force would be used in container stations on and off the dock, that

negotiations was the one between Sea Land and the Teamsters' union, covering container stuffing and stripping on and near the Oakland waterfront.

8. *ILWU Caucus, Summarized Minutes, October 31, Afternoon Session, mimeographed document, "The Amended Recommendation of the Coast Committee and the Amended Program of Action on Containers and Vans," and ILWU Caucus, Demands and Instruction to the Coast Negotiating Committee from the October 1968 Caucus, mimeographed, no date. The pension issue had been a source of discontent among the pensioners for several years. The improved benefits of the 1966 agreement covered only those men who retired after July 1966. The disparity rankled, and pensioner pressure on the Caucus led to the 1968 demand for pension parity.*

stuffing and stripping on the dock was longshore work covered by the PCLA, that container station workers would be utilitymen, and that the men would be steady employees of the various firms. The parties disagreed on the use of clerks and walking bosses, performance of a limited amount of container work on the dock by nonlongshoremen and on applicability of the definition of "dock" to the new Oakland container stations. The PMA further introduced registration problems, especially those in southern California, as an issue to be resolved, and asked for either the $3.76 hourly wage rate, or for a two and one half year transition period within which to bring all container work under the more costly provisions of the Pacific Coast Longshore Agreement. Mediation in February 1969 was unsuccessful; the negotiations were halted on March 6.[9]

The ILWU called a coastwide stoppage of container work on March 17. By March 24, 16 ships had been tied up, half of them in the San Francisco Bay area. The shutdown was not intended to be a coastwide strike; exceptions were permitted for military or war cargo, and the 90 per cent or so of longshore work involving cargo in conventional packages was not affected. The PMA challenged the stoppage through the grievance procedure, and, in a hearing not attended by the ILWU representatives, Coast Arbitrator Sam Kagel ruled that the longshoremen must resume work on containers. The union ignored the ruling. The PMA took its case to the courts; and on March 31 the U.S. District Court ordered the ILWU to comply with the arbitrator's ruling. The stoppage continued. The District Court then subpoenaed a number of the ILWU officers for a contempt hearing. The ILWU ordered work on containers to resume on April 7 and the hearing was postponed indefinitely.[10]

While the ILWU-PMA negotiations were being held, the ILWU and the Teamsters tried to resolve their jurisdictional problems. In early December 1968, the ILWU negotiating committee met with Einar Mohn, director of the Western Conference of Teamsters, and other top Teamster leaders. The group created a joint subcommittee to continue talks, and the subcommittee met several times in December and January. On April 10, Frank Fitzsimmons,

9. *A summary of the negotiations are included in ILWU, Longshore Caucus,* Summary of Container and Pension Negotiations, *April 12, 1969, mimeographed, pp. 1–8.*
10. Ibid., pp. 12–13.

general vice president and senior executive officer of the IBT, addressed the ILWU biennial convention in Los Angeles, declaring his interest in strengthening the mutual support and friendship between the two unions. The two unions have announced that there is no jurisdictional dispute between them, but that the meetings will continue to settle matters of joint concern.

The Longshore Caucus convened again April 12, 1969. The delegates were briefed on the failure of negotiations and on difficulties of the limited work stoppage. In the first few days, all proposals for a bargaining position were rejected, reflecting in part the delegates' frustration with the ineffectiveness of a limited strike and in part their continuing local indifferences in outlook and interests. On April 17, one detailed proposal was adopted by a narrow majority, 74 9/14 for, and 69 5/14 against. The close vote prompted a motion to reconsider with debate to be "off the record" in an attempt to win strong support for one position or another. After a day and a half of off-the-record talks, the delegates still failed to agree. A special subcommittee was elected to meet evenings and over the weekend to reconcile the remaining differences in points of view. The subcommittee reported to the Caucus on April 21, and disagreements in debate on the floor led to the election of yet another subcommittee, which reported back the next day with majority and minority reports. The majority report was adopted, and the negotiating committee appointed.[11]

The Caucus instructions were stringent. The negotiating committee was again directed to negotiate a container freight station contract requiring the use of the registered longshore work force. All container stuffing and stripping, except manufacturers' loads, was to be done on the dock or in dock areas to be mutually defined on a port-by-port basis under the Pacific Coast Longshore Agreement, and to provide the same basic fringe benefits. The wage demand was $4.60 per hour, roughly the equivalent of the basic longshore rate effective on June 28, 1969. The Caucus reaffirmed the ILWU's negotiating position of the preceding November that clerks were to be used to do clerks' work, night work was to be paid at overtime rates of one-and-one-half times the basic rate rather than the more modest shift

11. ILWU, *Longshore Caucus*, Summarized Minutes, *especially April 16, Morning Session, pp. 3–4, 6–7; April 17, Morning Session, p. 3, and Afternoon Session, pp. 1–2; April 21, Afternoon Session, pp. 1–3; April 22, Afternoon Session, pp. 1–2.*

differential proposed by the PMA, the 8-hour work-or-pay guarantee was to apply, and container station workers were to be referred from the dispatch hall. The employers were conceded the right to retain as many steady employees as needed. In the event of failure of negotiations, the negotiating committee was given authority to hold a coastwide referendum on cancellation of the Pacific Coast Longshore Agreement. The referendum would not be a strike vote, but it certainly could be regarded as a necessary first step toward such a vote.[12]

Negotiations with the PMA were reopened on April 25, and tentative agreement was reached in July. Container stuffing and stripping on the dock are to continue as longshore work, performed by registered longshoremen under the terms of the Pacific Coast Longshore Agreement. Container freight stations, special sites on the docks or in the harbor area, are to be manned by the registered longshore work force as steady employees of the various firms. The hours worked in container stations are credited toward the M and M bonus, but the wage rates, $4.30 per hour for an 8-hour day in 1969, rising to $4.50 in January 1970, are below the PCLA basic rate (averaged to an equivalent for an 8-hour day). The PMA agreed to the ILWU demand to raise pensions for men retired before 1966 to the level of those retired or about to retire under the current agreement; monthly benefits will increase from $165 to $235 maximum, in stages to 1971. The demand for a wage reopening in 1970 was dropped.

The issues in dispute between the ILWU and PMA were and will continue to be serious, but not critically so. They are problems in implementing an agreement that is basically acceptable to both sides, not fundamental disagreements. Jurisdiction will be a more serious and persistent problem within the ILWU and in relations between the ILWU and other unions. The loss of jurisdiction over container work in the harbor areas would have been intolerable to the ILWU, but maintaining jurisdiction over container freight stations raises tough, new problems. The competitive pressures of lower labor costs in non-longshore warehouses will be a galling constraint; it will be difficult to push or hold wages and benefits for container

---

12. *The Caucus instructions are summarized in ILWU, Longshore Caucus,* Majority Report, Caucus Subcommittee Recommended Plan of Action on Containers, Pensions and Wages, *April 21, 1969, mimeographed, and ILWU Negotiating Committee Proposals for On and Off-Dock Container Freight Station Contract, November 26, 1968, mimeographed.*

work much above the levels prevailing elsewhere. And there will be an "elsewhere;" the ILWU will almost certainly be unable to win jurisdiction over *all* container work. Warehouses with container work already organized by the IBT, warehouses far inland, organized or not, and the container stuffing and stripping performed while the container is attached to a truck bed, all will be out of reach. More serious, the lower wages and benefits elsewhere will, by restraining the levels at the ILWU-organized stations, make container work unattractive to the registered longshoremen and may threaten the conditions of the PCLA itself. There is no easy solution to the dilemma.

As of this writing, the tentative agreement between the ILWU and PMA has not been ratified. If ratification fails, or if it is a close vote, as appears likely, the issues may have to be renegotiated. Whatever the outcome, there has been no hint of returning to the restrictions of the past. It is probably impossible to do so. Problems there will be, but productivity will continue to increase, and longshoremen will continue to work at increasingly skilled and well-paid jobs.

APPENDIXES

A | THEORETICAL ANALYSIS OF RESTRICTIVE WORK RULES

The literature dealing directly, or even only in passing, with the theoretical analysis of restrictive work rules or practices is limited. Almost all monographs or major studies having to do with production, production functions, union effects on costs and efficiency, and the like, ignore work rules, or mention them only very briefly.[1]

Unlike most of the existing literature, this appendix attempts to relate the rules in force in an industry directly to the theoretical concepts. In the first section, work rules are examined using nonmathematical comparative statics. The actual rules recently in force in Pacific longshoring are related to the conventional analytical tools of neoclassical economics. In the exposition, some testable hypotheses emerge and are applied to the data generated by the Pacific longshore experience. The second section is more general. It relates the work rules previously described to each other, attempts to derive unequivocal conclusions with respect to the resource allocation effects of the rules, and relates the rules to rational union behavior.

WORK RULES AND THE PRODUCTION FUNCTION

Work rules or practices are restrictive if they require the employer to hire more labor than he would have hired in the absence of compulsion, at a given wage rate. The verb "to hire" was deliberately chosen over "to use" or "to pay for." The essential distinction is that men appear physically at the workplace and are paid, whether they perform useful work, unnecessary work, or do not work at all. If the rule or arrangement requires payment, but is not related to

---

1. *The best and most relevant articles or passages in books are: Lloyd Ulman,* Rise of the National Trade Union, *pp. 536–566; Norman Simler, "The Economics of Featherbedding,"* Industrial and Labor Relations Review, *XVI (1962), 111–121; Paul A. Weinstein, "Featherbedding: A Theoretical Analysis,"* Journal of Political Economy, *LXVIII (1960), 379–389; and Wassily Leontief, "The Pure Theory of the Guaranteed Annual Wage,"* Journal of Political Economy, *LVI (1946), 76–79.*

physical attendance at the workplace, it is a component of the wage or system of payment, not a work rule. By definition, work rules are constraints on the production function.

Although it may appear obvious, the fact that work rules are not all the same needs emphasis. Some rules specify the number of men to be employed, others the output levels; some require unnecessary work, others the use of inefficient methods, and still others payment for no work at all. Some rules are intended to maintain or reduce effort levels, others are aimed at expanding or maintaining employment. Indeed, a very large number of work rules and practices associated with unions in the United States and other countries have been described in the literature, each differing in objective or details of method. Not surprisingly, no single simple theoretical proposition encompasses the variety. Some rules impose constraints on part, but not all, of the production function. Other rules appear to transform the entire production function.

Three main varieties of restrictive rules appear to be clearly distinguishable — those requiring a fixed quantity of labor input, those requiring labor input to be a fixed proportion of other inputs or of output, and those involving negotiated nonoptimal input proportions.

Rules requiring firms to employ a fixed quantity of labor input — in effect, wage-or-work guarantees — empirically are rare. In Pacific Coast longshoring, gear priority, including narrow job definition and specialization, and the minimum guarantee are the nearest approach to this variety of work rule. An employer needing, for example, only a few man-hours of work at a hatch often was required to employ a whole standard gang for the minimum guarantee of at least four hours. Gear priority prohibited the temporary transfer of other employees to do the work. In effect, the employer would be compelled to take from forty to seventy man-hours, or none at all. A second illustration is the wage guarantee in force from 1961 through 1965.

Fixed-quantity rules constrain only part of the production function. Figure 1 represents a conventional production function; the lines q_1 through q_4 are successively higher levels of output. The lines $(w_1/w_2)_1$ and $(w_1/w_2)_2$ are representatives of two sets of isocost lines, whose slopes reflect relative factor prices. The expansion path, for example line r_2 associated with $(w_1/w_2)_2$, is the locus of the least-cost combinations of inputs to produce the various levels of output. If $(x_1)_0$ is the absolute amount of labor required to be employed, the least-cost input combinations now available to the firm or industry are indicated by the intersection of the various output curves with the line $(x_1)_0b$. For all outputs less than q_3 the imposition of the rule would require inefficient input combinations, given factor prices $(w_1/w_2)_2$.

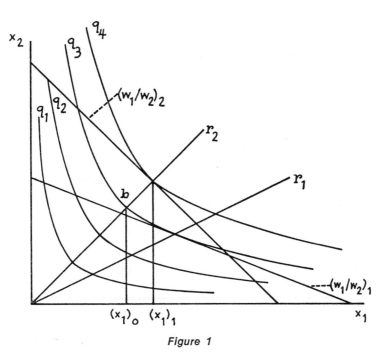

Figure 1

In Figure 2, AC_0 represents industry average costs[2] when all factors are variable; AR is the industry demand curve for output. The imposition of the lump-of-labor rule changes the cost function as suggested by AC_1. The decreasing segment reflects largely the spreading over a larger output of the constant lump-of-labor cost. AC_1 coincides with AC_0 at q_3 and all larger outputs. Assuming a competitive industry, the equilibrium output and factor inputs are un-

2. *Both figures assume infinitely elastic supplies of both factors and a first degree homogeneous production function; that is, a proportionate increase in all inputs yields the same proportionate increase in output. Given relative factor prices, total costs are proportionate to output and average costs are constant.*

changed from the nonrule solution; employment at $(x_1)_1$, associated with equilibrium output of q_4, is higher than the required minimum.

However, alternative outcomes are possible. AC_2 in Figure 2 represents the same information as AC_1 with the single exception that factor prices are higher in terms of output price. The horizontal segment of AC_2 represents costs associated with outputs on the ex-

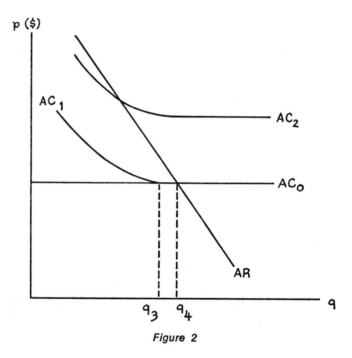

Figure 2

pansion path. Unlike the preceding illustration, the output associated with the rule in this case is smaller, average costs higher, and labor input larger than would have been the result without the rule.

The chief implication of the analysis, as far as it is developed here, is that it is impossible to conclude a priori that the imposition or negotiation of a fixed minimum quantity of input is necessarily inefficient.

The evidence in Pacific longshoring suggests that the fixed quantity of input rules did not result in inefficiency. The wage guarantee to the permanent, minimum work force was never used; employment was at all times above the minimum during the life of the provision. That is, the situation resembled that described by AC_1, output q_4 and input $(x_1)_1$. The evidence with respect to minimum fixed labor input to the hatch is only slightly less clear. The rigid, no-shifting-of-gangs provisions were abandoned in 1959. No significant increase in productivity was apparent immediately after the rules change. Further, the minimum tonnage per hatch that could be handled efficiently — corresponding to q_3 in Figure 1 — was about 40 to 100 tons for typical break-bulk cargo, whereas the average tonnage per hatch actually handled was approximately 350 tons in the relevant years. This suggests that a large proportion of the total tonnage was unaffected by the minimum fixed labor input.

The finding that no adverse effect resulted from this variety of union-imposed restriction is not surprising. The principal motive for a wage-or-work guarantee is to force the employers to regularize employment and not, for example, to extract the largest possible wage income from the industry. The guarantee is successful, in the eyes of the negotiators, if the employers are able to reorganize production so that no idle labor input is required.

The above analysis differs from the discussion of fixed-quantity rules by Norman Simler[3] in that it emphasizes that the employer very likely will be able to reach the output level at which the required labor may be used as part of the least-cost input combination. Simler, on the other hand, assumed that the rule required more than the least-cost input of labor up to a given output far larger than that associated with the long-run technological optimum scale. A consequence, in addition to higher costs and prices, is a contraction in the competitive industry output reflecting a backshift in the industry supply of output curve as marginal firms are forced out.

The former approach is more likely. In the longshore industry, as in other casual-labor-market industries and in seasonal industries in which the guaranteed annual wage has been sought, the chief motive to the lump-of-labor requirement is to force the employer to regularize employment. It appears very unlikely that the union would pick an absolute labor input level so large that the employer would seldom reach a technically efficient output level. Simler's assumption is not implausible — a union in a declining industry conceivably would attempt to impose such a large absolute quantity requirement — but

3. pp. 113–116.

other assumptions are equally or more plausible. Unions in declining industries are certainly concerned with employment, but their rules and policies probably will require fixed factor proportions or similar devices, not absolute total quantities of labor input.

An empirically more important variety of work rule requires that labor vary as a fixed proportion of other inputs or of output. In Pacific Coast longshoring, the pre-1960 contract between the union and the employers specified minimum gang size and maximum draft size — the weight or number of pieces of a commodity to be hoisted by winch or crane for movement between the dock and the hold of the ship. Further, informal practices controlling the pace of work, both on the dock and in the hold, were imposed unilaterally by the union members at the local level. The consequence was, for many operations, that output was proportional to labor input.

Analytically, the fixed-proportion rules exclude or transform part of the production function. In Figure 1, assume that line r_1 represents the locus of the rule-imposed maximum output, or capital-input, proportions. At relative factor prices greater than $(w_1/w_2)_1$, for example $(w_1/w_2)_2$, costs are minimized only by using those input combinations represented by line r_1 for all output levels; combinations on the production surface to the left of r_1 are excluded by the rules, those to the right are more costly. If the production function implies constant returns to scale, the inputs and output are related to each other in fixed proportions.[4]

Assuming relative factor prices to be sufficiently high, the effects of the fixed-proportion rules are to require, unambiguously, inefficient input proportions and higher unit costs for all output levels. The elimination of the rules, if they were restrictive, must be accompanied by increased capital input and increased productivity.

The employment effects of fixed-proportion rules cannot be predicted without knowledge of demand conditions for the industry's output. If output demand is inelastic, the rule-imposed employment level will be higher than nonrule employment, given relative factor prices. On the other hand, a very elastic output demand would lead to smaller employment, as higher costs force output reductions suffi-

---

4. *In the main, the analysis and conclusions in this section are similar to the discussion in Lloyd Ulman, pp. 539–540, Paul Weinstein, pp. 384–386, and Norman Simler's analysis of his "Type II" rule, pp. 117–119.*

ciently large to overcome the employment-increasing effect of smaller capital input and lower labor productivity.

The most restrictive work rules in Pacific longshoring fit neither of the two preceding categories. Multiple handling and manning on special operations are leading illustrations. The former would be fixed-proportion rules if no concessions were made; but the rules were in fact compromised. Manning on special operations had been settled by compromise for decades before the 1960 agreement. The requirements that fourteen men be used at a hatch if one technique — including a given input of capital — were used, but permitting reduction to ten men with a more capital-intensive technique, and so on, cannot in any sensible manner be called fixed-proportion rules. On the other hand, the rules clearly were restrictive — as few as six, four, or even two men could do the work with the capital goods manned by ten men. The history of the establishment of manning, effort, and output standards for most of the nonbreak-bulk work suggests a third variety of work rule — the negotiated production function.

The rule denies the entire technologically based production surface to the firms and industry, but it permits a good deal of capital-for-labor substitution. In effect, the rule shifts the production function such that all possible combinations of factor inputs are associated with smaller outputs than without the rule.[5] The negotiated production function is analogous, allowing for the difference in direction, to a production function shifted by a change in human knowledge or technology.[6]

Figure 3 illustrates, with only one isoquant, a likely interpretation of the negotiated production function. Technological conditions are reflected in the pre-shift isoquant q_1; the curve $(q_n)_1$ represents the factor input combinations permitted to the industry, by negotiations, to produce output q_1. A priori predictions of effects of the rule are difficult because they require further assumptions about the

5. If $Q = f(x_1, x_2)$ is the production function based on technology, then the production function constrained by institutional arrangements negotiated or imposed by the union would be $Q_n = \phi[f(x_1, x_2)]$, such that for any given pair of nonzero values for x_1 and x_2, $Q_n < Q$.
6. Note, for example, the "efficiency parameter" and discussion of its effects in the constant-elasticity-of-substitution production functions estimated in K. Arrow, H. Chenery, B. Minhas, and R. Solow, "Capital-Labor Substitution and Economic Efficiency," Review of Economics and Statistics, XLIII (1961), 225–250.

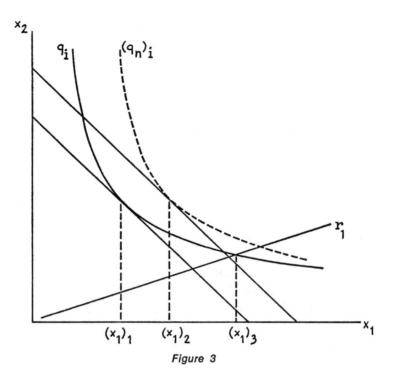

Figure 3

shape of the negotiated production function. Generally, average costs under the new rule are likely to be intermediate over the relevant output range — higher than with no rule, lower than with fixed-proportion rules. Employment effects further depend on output demand elasticities. If demand is inelastic at all three cost levels, and the negotiated production function approximates the shape and position described in Figure 3, employment with negotiated production function rules will be intermediate — higher than nonrule, lower than with fixed proportions.

The negotiated production function may be interpreted as a rational device used by a union, given factor prices, to exploit the possibilities afforded by an industry output demand function with variable elasticity. Rigid adherence to fixed-proportion rules results in lower-than-otherwise employment levels if the resulting costs yield an equilibrium output at an elastic portion of the output demand function. At the other limit, costs based solely on the technological least-cost input combinations may yield equilibrium output at an inelastic portion of the demand function. Employment, and the aggregate wage bill, will be largest with some intermediate sort of restriction on input combinations — for example, a negotiated production function. An even more compelling case may be made for abandonment of fixed proportions if the technologically based production function exhibits increasing returns to scale; in this case, even with rather inelastic output demand, employment would be increased by abandoning the fixed-proportion rules.

An interesting implication of the negotiated production function rule is that its elimination may result, for a given output level, in reductions in employment and costs and increases in productivity, with no significant increase in investment. The lifting of the constraint simply eliminates the redundant labor inputs, and all inputs are more efficient than they were before the change.

The three analytical views of restrictive work rules could have been developed a priori, but their relative importance, approximate effects, or, especially for the negotiated production function, the nature itself of the rules would have been impossible if there had not been work-rule abandonment. Of the three views, the negotiated production function and the fixed-proportion rules are the more relevant to the practices in Pacific longshoring. The former is perhaps most important. The actual behavior of the parties in dockwork and special operations manning are accurately described by no other theoretical approach. The results of rule abandonment confirm the view: the observed very large increases in productivity, with existing techniques and capital stock, are consistent only with movement from a point off to a point on the technologically based production surface. Much of the improvement in shipwork efficiency by 1965, although it was not great, was similar in nature — the same output with the same capital stock, but fewer men. Overall, the largest part of the productivity increase between 1960 and 1965 was associated with relaxation or abandonment of the negotiated production function rules.

The fixed-proportion rules also were important and especially applicable to conventional break-bulk shipwork; both the preabandonment description and postabandonment experience confirm the aptness of the analytical view. Before 1960, output in this variety of longshoring varied proportionately with labor input; productivity was constant. The abandonment of the rules did not, of itself, result in dramatic productivity increases. Although employers at first expected results as if the rules were of the negotiated production function variety, their experience subsequently revealed the need to invest in order to improve efficiency. The technical developments and investment programs, by 1965 and 1966, support the view that movement along the production function had begun in belated response to the abandonment of the constraints formerly imposed by fixed-proportion rules.

The effect of work-rule abandonment on the industry production function — the preceding consider only component parts — merits a brief exploration. The experience of the industry after 1960 confirms two propositions: first, the various work rules were in fact restrictive, and second, the predominant effect of the rules was to constrain production possibilities in the fashion best described by the negotiated production function.

In the absence of work-rule abandonment, or before 1960, a skeptic could have argued that the various rules of Pacific Coast longshoring were not restrictive. Gear priority and the minimum guarantee affected only very small outputs, and any adverse effect could be overcome easily by the appropriate arrangement of the flow of work. Manning, load limits, and other rules and practices, to continue the argument, are only apparent, not real, restrictions. Changes in the proportions of capital to labor in some handling practices had occurred often — shifts to bulk handling, for example — and the labor inputs in such cases perhaps could be regarded as those required for safe and efficient operations. The lack of change in break-bulk operations was proof of the technological difficulty of adapting the work to capital-intensive methods, not of obstruction by the rules.

In the aggregate, the overall industry experience before 1960 could be interpreted as illustrated by Figure 4. Over the years, wages increased steadily relative to the cost of capital.[7] The relative factor-price changes are shown by lines $(w/w_2)_1$, a low price of labor relative to the price of capital services, and $(w/w_2)_2$, reflecting the more recent much higher relative price of labor. During this period, output

---

7. *Direct evidence of the cost of capital and the size of capital stock is not available. However, ship-operating-company profits, as an indicator of the cost of capital, suggest that it was approximately constant during the decade of the 1950s. Wages increased by about 50 percent during the same period.*

per unit of labor input was very nearly constant, varying no more than 6 percent about the mean between 1950 and 1960, holding constant the effect of bulk-tonnage variations. The isoquant q_0 reflects the unchanged labor input required by the observed almost constant output per man-hour. Consistent with the facts, the production function exhibits a low elasticity of substitution of capital for labor.

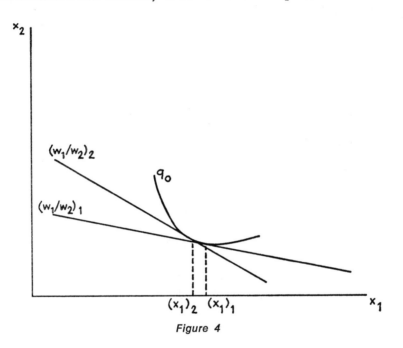

Figure 4

However, the data after 1960 are inconsistent with the foregoing; they suggest a very different sort of production function. Wages relative to the cost of capital probably increased, but not by much.[8] Output per unit of labor input rose very sharply and labor costs per unit of output dropped sharply. Considered by itself, this information is consistent only with the inference that the production function exhibits a high elasticity of substitution of capital for

8. *This is the most conservative assumption, and is made only for the argument. more reasonable assumptions would be that, at best, relative factor prices did not change between 1960 and 1965, or, more likely, wages decreased a bit relative to the cost of capital. The evidence of Chapter 6 indicated that wages rose at about the same annual rate as they did between 1950 and 1960, whereas the profit rates of the Pacific ship-operating companies were much higher in the post-1960 period than before.*

labor — the relatively flat isoquant q_1 of Figure 5. The isoquants illustrated in the two figures are not two output levels from the same production function. The output levels in the two periods in fact overlap; tonnages handled in the 1960 through 1963 period were about the same as in the high volume years during the 1950 to 1960 decade.

In brief, the results of work-rule abandonment definitively

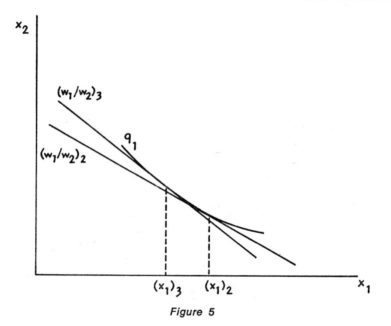

Figure 5

eliminate the possibility that the pre-1960 results were efficient adjustments along the industry production function; further, their most reasonable interpretation is that the pre-1960 production function was in large part negotiated. In the aggregate, a given output could be produced, by 1965, with a labor input 40 percent smaller and with a capital stock only slightly larger than four years earlier. Factor inputs prior to 1960, for the aggregate, could not have reflected the technologically based production function — by definition the locus of the most efficient input combinations. The most reasonable interpretation is that they were governed by institutional arrangements, the "negotiated production function," and that the abandonment of the rules was analogous to a technological change or innovation that shifted the production function.

The once-and-for-all shift of the industry production function very likely was completed by 1966 or 1967. Future productivity increases will take place only with increased investment — that is, they will reflect, for the first time since the beginning of unionization by the ILWU, movement along the technical production function.

WAGES VERSUS WORK RULES: A LOOK AT RATIONAL UNION BEHAVIOR

Brief introspection plausibly suggests that work rules and wages must be rival goals — given employment, one may be gained only at the expense of the other. Such introspection implicitly regards work rules simply as arrangements imposing higher labor costs and assumes that labor cost is uniquely related to employment. The conclusions of brief introspection are in part incorrect. Tighter analysis indicates that, within limits, a union may increase aggregate income to its members by the imposition of work rules; in other words, at a given wage rate employment may be expanded, or at a given level of employment the wage may be increased with the imposition of work rules. In brief, a union desiring a given employment level for whatever reason, or interested in maximizing wage income to the work force, may win higher wages or a larger aggregate income with work rules than without.

The analysis proceeds as follows. For some industry, assume

(1) $p = p(x_0)$, a conventional demand function for industry output, with negative slope throughout;

(2) $R = x_0 p = R(x_0)$, the total revenue function; it has some maximum or approaches asymptotically some maximum limit;

(3) $x_0 = f(x_1, x_2)$, a conventional industry production function, with monotonically decreasing marginal rates of factor substitution for any given level of output;

(4) w_1 is the wage rate, the factor price of labor; it is either a parameter, implying an infinitely elastic supply of labor at the identified value, or, in some cases, a decision variable for the union; and

(5) w_2 is the factor price of capital, a parameter. The supply of capital is infinitely elastic at some positive price.

For any industry, an equilibrium condition is

(6) $(\partial x_0/\partial x_1)(1/w_1) = (\partial x_0/\partial x_2)(1/w_2)$, implying cost

minimization for the firms and industry, assuming the second-order conditions are satisfied.

Further, for a competitive industry, equilibrium requires

(7) $R - w_1 x_1 - w_2 x_2 = 0$; that is, industry profits are zero at some nontrivial (nonzero) output.

The expansion path is a function of the inputs satisfying the first order conditions of (6) and may be written

(8) $x_2 = \phi(x_1, w_2/w_1)$, or, for clarity in the subsequent exposition,

(9) $x_2 = \phi[x_1, (w_2)_i/(w_1)_j]$, where the subscripts i, j identify specific values for w_2 and w_1 respectively.

Our interest is primarily from the labor market point of view. The relevant relations may be easily expressed as functions of labor input. Substituting the expansion path into the production function, (3), and the result into the revenue function, (2).

(10) $R = R_{ij}[f\{x_1, \phi[x_1, (w_2)_i/(w_1)_j]\}]$; that is, revenue is a function of labor input.

Capital cost is $w_2 x_2$, by definition. Defining revenue net of capital cost as R^* using equation 10 and substituting the expansion path, (9), for capital,

(11) $R^* = R_{ij}[f\{x_1, \phi[x_1, (w_2)_i/w_1)_j]\}]$
$- (w_2)_j\{\phi[x_1, (w_2)_i/(w_1)_j]\}.$

For the competitive industry, the equilibrium solution is, from equations 11 and 7,

(12) $R^* - w_1 x_1 = 0$. Equation 12 multiplied by $1/x_1$ is the average revenue net of capital cost expressed as a function of labor input; in other words, it is the competitive industry demand for labor.

In Figure 6, lines r_0, r_1, and r_2 are $(1/x_1) R^*$, given $(w_2)_i = (w_2)_0$, for all $(w_1)_j$, and $(w_1)_j = (w_1)_0$, $(w_1)_1$, and $(w_1)_2$, respectively.[9] For a competitive industry, given a set of factor prices, for

9. The diagram reflects a Cobb-Douglas production function and a linear output demand function. With these assumptions, the expansion paths expressed in terms of net revenue and labor input, r_{ij}, given the factor prices, are linear. That is, given $x_0 = a x_1^\beta x_2^{1-\beta}$, then $(1/x_1) R^* = c_1 - c_2 x_1$, where $c_1 = a_1 a_3 - a_4$ and $c_2 = a_2 a_3^2$. The a_1 and a_2 are constants from the output demand

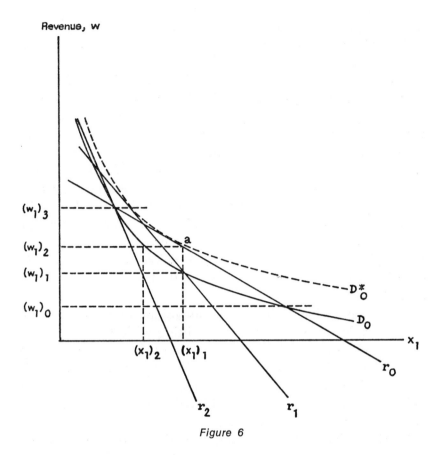

Figure 6

example $(w_2)_0$ and $(w_1)_1$, increases in output and inputs are reflected by movement along r_1; the output from existing firms and from the entry of new firms continues to grow, and inputs continue to be added in the fixed proportions required by the expansion path, until industry profits decline to zero, at $r_1 = (w_1)_1$.[10] With a different wage rate, for example $(w_1)_0$, a different expansion path, r_0, is followed; equilibrium is reached at $r_0 = (w_1)_0$, reflecting both

function; $a_s = a[(1 - \beta)/(w_2)_i^{\beta}]^{i-\beta} (w_1)^{1-\beta}$; and $a_l = (1 - \beta/\beta)^{1-\beta} (w_1)$; given the production function, demand function, and factor prices, the a's all are constants.

10. The description here assumes that all firms have identical production functions, and the industry production function is simply the firm function writ large. It is further assumed that some arbitrary device — for example, capital rationing or informal market sharing enforced by the customers — suffices to keep firm size small and number of firms large.

movement along the industry demand function as output increases and movement along the production function at least-cost factor proportions.

An infinity of expansion paths exists, each path reflecting different factor proportions associated with different wage rates. Given the price of capital, for example $(w_2)_0$, higher wage rates are associated with steeper expansion paths, involving the use of more capital in the least-cost input proportion. The locus of industry equilibria, relating the wage rate to employment at zero profits for the industry — where each wage-employment point reflects movement along an expansion path — is the curve D_0; the subscript identifies the constant price of capital. (Note that D_0 is in fact the $[(1/x_1) R^*]_{0j}$ of the preceding passages; the subscripts reflect the given price of capital and the varying price of labor service.) A union in the industry thus described perceives D_0 as the demand for the labor service of its actual or potential members.

Union behavior, including the imposition of work rules, may now be explored. Assume that the existing wage level is $(w_1)_1$, as a result of past decisions and experience in labor-management negotiations and of labor supply conditions. Employment, and union membership under closed or union shop provisions, is $(x_1)_1$.[11] The union reasonably may be interested in winning a higher wage. If no other restriction is imposed, a higher wage will be accompanied by reduced employment;[12] successful negotiation of the new wage, $(w_1)_2$ for example, would result in employment of only $(x_1)_2$ and unemployment, or contraction of union membership, by the amount $(x_1)_1 - (x_1)_2$.[13] The movement back along the labor demand function reflects capital-for-labor substitution, some contraction of output, and a rather higher product price. Of course, this outcome is no

11. *This assumes, of course, that market labor supply of labor service of variety x_1 is not a constraint. That is, the number of persons, or man-days or other measure of labor service, available at $(w_1)_1$ for example, exceeds $(x_1)_1$. This circumstance probably obtains in most labor markets involving militant and successful unions.*
12. *The most appropriate interpretation of union action is that it transforms the labor supply function from the conventional positive-slope relation to a function infinitely elastic, over the relevant range, at the negotiated wage rate.*
13. *Successful negotiation implies that the collective withholding of labor, threatened by the union, was viewed by the employers as a more costly alternative than granting the wage increase.*

novelty; the adverse employment effects of higher wages result from all conventional analyses and have been discussed widely elsewhere.

However, the union need not accept the contraction in employment if it has sufficient strength to negotiate successfully both the higher wage and constraints on the production process. For example, if rules were won requiring that $(x_1)_1$ be the minimum absolute labor input, the higher wage $(w_1)_2$ could be imposed without forcing the industry to negative profits; the union could have both unimpaired employment and the higher wage. The reasoning proceeds as follows.

At $(x_1)_1$, there are many wage rates higher than $(w_1)_1$ but nonetheless just equal to the industry's average revenue, net of capital costs. In Figure 6, point a on expansion path r_0 is such a point. It relates average revenue net of capital costs, here equal to $(w_1)_2$, to labor input $(x_1)_1$ at input proportions using less capital than does expansion path r_1; the factor proportions are in fact those associated with wage $(w_1)_0$ and the given price of capital $(w_2)_0$. At $(x_1)_1$, if the wage were in fact $(w_1)_0$, the difference between that rate and the average revenue net of capital cost, equal to $(w_1)_2$, is industry profit per unit of labor input. By imposing wage $(w_1)_2$ at minimum labor input $(x_1)_1$, the union transfers all potential industry profit to the work force. The industry is compelled to substitute labor for capital and to curtail output — as a result, the product price rises — until profits are nonnegative. At point a on r_0, the industry profits are indeed nonnegative, by definition of the r_i. By its bar to the traditional employer escape from higher wages — capital for labor substitution — the union in effect imposes an artificial scarcity of capital and then appropriates the resulting quasi-rent.

The exploitive possibilities at any one level of labor input are, of course, limited. Given the conventional industry output demand function and the production function, defined previously, and given the price of capital, the highest wage possible at any selected level of labor input could be found by maximizing revenue net of capital cost with respect to capital input at the selected level of labor input. The curve D^*_0 suggests the locus of such maxima, given the output demand function, the production function, and the price of capital, $(w_2)_0$. The union would maximize its members' wage income at a given employment level by adopting the appropriate restrictions and pressing the wage to the associated point on D^*_0. In general, it could do best by treating D^*_0 as the relevant demand curve for the labor service of its actual or potential members; multiplying by x_1 and maximizing the resulting aggregate wage income with respect to labor input would yield the *maximum maximorum* wage-employment package.[14]

Restrictive work rules may be interpreted as practical approximations of such maximizing union behavior. The specific varieties of the rules illustrate the point. The imposition of a minimum absolute level of labor input, the fixed-quantity rule discussed in the first section of this appendix, is one variety. Coupled with appropriate wage demands, the work rule would become restrictive as the wage is pushed above the conventional unconstrained demand curve for labor (D_0 in Figure 6). In a world of no change, the union reasonably could adopt such a rule in order to enjoy both the highest possible wages and high employment. In a world of even slight change, however, the rule is dangerous or inadequate; small shifts in demand for the output either would force the industry into negative profits or would result in less than the highest possible wage for the selected level of employment.

A more practical constraint would be to require, at the wage rate $(w_1)_2$, for example, that the employers use the factor proportions of expansion path r_0. If output demand is unchanged, the result is identical to the minimum absolute labor requirement rule. If demand conditions do change, as is most likely in the real world, the level of labor input will change, but the simple fixed-proportion requirement continues to be a good solution. It approximates the highest wage possible for the resulting labor input, assuming that the output demand function shifts are not great.

Finally, if the output demand function shifts outward steadily, reflecting, for example, appreciable income elasticity and rising income among the industry's ultimate customers, and if the historic employment level is the chief concern, the union would do best by giving up even fixed proportions. The highest wages at the selected employment level, under such output demand shifts, are possible only by permitting more capital to be used in the production process.

14. *Maximizing wage income is one of a variety of possibilities of rational union action, varying with different assumptions about labor supply and behavior rules of the union; the pioneer and still the best work in this topic is John T. Dunlop,* Wage Determination under Trade Unions *(New York, 1944).*

(The maximization of average revenue net of capital costs with respect to capital input at the selected employment level would yield different levels of optimum capital input as the output demand funcion shifts.) Assuming the resulting factor proportions to be restrictive — that is, other than the least-cost proportions, given the factor prices — the outcome would be the "negotiated production function" discussed in the first part of this appendix.

If the ILWU had continued in force its restrictive practices, this appendix very likely would end with the preceding paragraph. But the union did abandon the rules, and, in view of the strong case for their rationality in most of this section, a brief comment on rule abandonment is appropriate.

The analysis throughout this appendix assumes that the union is able to impose, or win through bargaining, whatever solution it demands. In other words, it always has sufficient strength to impose an alternative — the strike — more costly than the rules, working conditions, or wage rates sought. An adequate analysis of union strength cannot be made here, but it is in order to note that the union's strength may be inadequate, or may be impaired by the attempted imposition of the more restrictive rules-wage packages. In the specific recent history of the ILWU, strength impairment was a likely outcome, through, for example, government intervention on an ad hoc or permanent basis. Under such circumstances, the rational union policy may well include abandonment of restrictive work rules and practices.

B | THE PRODUCTIVITY ESTIMATES: SOURCES, RELIABILITY, AND METHODS

The discussion in Chapters 4 and 5 dealt principally with the results of the estimates of longshore productivity on the Pacific Coast. Data sources, data weaknesses, and details of technique were passed over lightly. This appendix is, in effect, an extended footnote to those chapters, into which most of these essentially technical matters are gathered.

PMA PRODUCTIVITY DATA: ACCURACY AND RELIABILITY

Almost all the productivity estimates in the preceding chapters rely on data contained in the Pacific Maritime Association productivity studies.[1] Underlying the man-hours and tonnages, summarized by commodity, were thousands of reports prepared by hundreds of industry employees in the various ports and docks of the Pacific Coast. The raw data thus gathered were checked, aggregated, and eventually published by the PMA.[1]

Typically, clerks or timekeepers were assigned the task of preparing the productivity study reports in addition to their usual tasks. They were to match direct labor man-hours to specific commodities and to assign to various indirect labor categories the longshore hours on the job not directly used in loading or discharging cargo. The clerks were given detailed instructions on commodity classifications, indirect labor hour categories, and the reporting methods. The PMA productivity study staff were aware that errors did occur. For example, some clerks matched hours and commodities by using the manifests and whatever commodity classification came easiest to them. As a result, the heterogeneous classifications — for example, general cargo — were allocated a good deal of tonnage and hours

---

1. See above p. 114–115 n. 6, for a description of the published studies and names and tenure of the senior PMA staff involved.

that should have been assigned to specific, narrowly defined commodities. Errors also occurred as a result of different methods of hours-to-tonnage balancing. If the preliminary hours-to-goods allocation failed to tally, some clerks prorated the leftover hours, others guessed at the probable omissions, and still others omitted the unassigned hours altogether.

To limit the errors, the PMA productivity study staff audited

Table B-1: Longshore Man-hours Paid, Assessment Tons, and Hours and Tons Reported in PMA Productivity Data, 1960-1963. (hours and tons in thousands)

Year	Longshore hours paid	Hours in productivity data	Percent	Assessment tons	Tons in productivity data	Percent
1960	22,916	19,518	85.2	29,814	24,744	83.0
1961	21,327	18,313	85.9	29,717	25,065	84.3
1962	20,551	17,691	83.2	29,355	23,545	80.2
1963	21,607	17,476	80.9	34,336	27,199	79.2

SOURCES: Assessment tons: see Appendix Table C-2. Hours paid and reported: PMA, *Productivity Study, Longshore Operations, Pacific Coast, 1960–1963*, Part I, Table B, p. 105. Tons reported in productivity data: *Ibid.*, Pacific Coast summaries, annual data in volumes for the respective years.

the raw reports, classified the commodities on a basis comparable for the whole coast and all years, compared hours attributed with hours paid, and so on. In addition, monitors were employed in each of the major port areas to oversee and verify for accuracy the gathering of data at the source. Although there were errors, the staff clearly took substantial steps to correct or minimize them.[2]

Although the PMA sought complete reporting of all cargo handled and all man-hours used on the entire Pacific Coast during the study years, the staff in fact expected rather less than total coverage. As it turned out, usable information was collected for about 80 to 85 percent of labor input and goods handled in the four years (see Table B-1).

The omitted tonnages and man-hours probably are sources of

2. *The descriptions of methods used by the PMA were taken from the reports themselves, and from interviews with Pres Lancaster, Manager of the PMA Contract Data Department, and Max Kossoris, Productivity Study Consultant when the studies were first undertaken.*

error, or bias, in the rates calculated from the reported data. Although the tonnages reported in each of the study years were about the same proportion of total assessment tonnage that reported man-hours were to total hours paid, the similarity is misleading. Assessment tons and reported tons are not strictly comparable. Reported tons are in terms of weight, but assessment tons only in part reflect weight. Part of the cargo is reported in thousands of board feet — specifically, logs and lumber — and part is reported in measurement tons. The latter are used when the cargo is so treated for revenue purposes by the various companies, and reflect the space limitation of the ship's hold in the same way that the measures of weight reflect the ship's weight limitations. Measurement tons, thus, are smaller, by weight, than the 2,000 pound short tons. The misstatement associated with treating 1,000 board feet as one ton has been corrected,[3] but the goods reported in measurement tons remain in the totals. As a result, the tonnages reported in the productivity reports are a higher proportion — by an unknown, but presumably rather small amount — than the table indicates. The implication is that the omitted goods were handled at lower average productivity than the reported goods. Thus, the productivity rates calculated from the reported data are likely to be biased; that is, they reflect a rather higher level of efficiency than actually exists.

However, the biases in reporting very likely have only minimal effect on year-to-year comparisons. The data were gathered and reports prepared by the same people, using the same techniques, looking at the same commodities on the same docks, in each of the years. It appears reasonable to suspect that a tendency to omit hours not easily worked into the reports, or misclassifying commodities, or any other similar source of error in gathering and reporting data, would be consistent and lead to about the same bias in the results in any one year compared with any other of the four years.

Finally, whatever the bias in the rates based on the reported data, it is explicitly considered in most of the productivity estimates. For example, several sets of alternative weights to the tonnage or commodity productivity rates are used, each reflecting different assumptions or facts about the underreporting or misclassification of various commodities.

3. See the notes to Appendix Table C–2.

The wide variability in productivity rates was cited by the industry's productivity study committee as grounds for added mistrust of the 1960 through 1963 studies. For a given commodity, productivity rates calculated from single observations often varied over a range so wide that the highest rate was three or four times larger than the lowest.[4] (An observation is defined as tonnage and man-hours associated with a consignment of the commodity loaded or discharged from a single ship during one call at a port.) The variability is the result of differences in weather conditions, efficiency of gangs, quality of supervision, differences in ships and holds, part of the hold being worked, time of day or week, and similar factors. Regrettably, neither the PMA committee nor the productivity study staff used or published precise measures of dispersion of the observations, rigorous estimates of statistical significance or reliability, or any other quantitative description of the distribution of the observed data. Even worse, this information apparently is permanently unavailable. The raw data reports were destroyed after completing the compilations used in the subsequently published studies.

Nonetheless, an evaluation of statistical reliability of the data is necessary and, at least qualitatively, possible. The PMA conducted pilot studies of productivity in 1959, using three important commodity classifications — canned goods, beer, and general merchandise. Frequency distributions of the observations for these studies were retained and made available. The observations involve only one company at one port, but in other respects the technique is essentially the same as that used in the comprehensive studies of 1960 through 1963. A nonspecialist — a timekeeper — prepared the man-hours and tonnage reports; numerous ships, all hatches, and all parts of the hold were involved; and weather conditions, quality of long-shore gangs, and supervision certainly varied. Relevant data and parameters of the distributions of observations are contained in Table B-2. The ranges are indeed wide, and the likelihood of any single observation being appreciably above or below the mean is substantial. For the general merchandise-loading operation, for example, one out of three observations are above about 0.9 man-hours per ton or below 0.7 man-hours per ton. Assuming that the number

4. *The wide range is noted by most of the industry and PMA spokesmen in their comments about productivity and the studies. The relative magnitudes specifically cited are from an interview with Pres Lancaster.*

of all possible observations of the operation at this place and time period is large and the values are normally distributed, then the probability of any single observation yielding a rate outside the range, 0.7–0.9 man-hours per ton, is about one in three.[5] However, in the productivity studies for 1960–1963, the mean productivity

Table B-2: Characteristics of Distribution of Observations of Productivity Rates, PMA Study, 1959. (Rates = Man-hours/Ton)

	Beer	Canned goods	General merchandise
Total tons	24,293	22,275	210,584
Total man-hours	22,845.5	17,060	170,930.5
Observations (n)	108	116	125
Extreme rates: Highest	1.638	1.769	1.775
Lowest	0.547	0.476	0.341
Mean	0.940	0.767	0.793
Standard deviation (σ)	0.132	0.156	0.107
Standard error of the mean ($\sigma/\sqrt{n}$)	0.013	0.014	0.009

SOURCE: Unpublished data titled "Loading Operations, One Company — One Port, Man-hours per Ton," further identified as PMA Research, March 24, 1959. Data made available by the PMA Contract Data department. Mean, standard deviation, and standard error were calculated from the data.

rates, not single observations, are the values of interest. The range within which the estimated mean will fall, if no real changes in productivity occur, is much smaller than that for single observations. If the 1959 study, discussed above, were repeated for the same company and port, the same or similar longshore gangs and supervisors, the same or similar ships, and with the same production techniques, equipment, and work practices, the probability would be about two out of three that the mean, for general merchandise, would fall be-

---

5. *The mean value is the simple average man-hours per ton. The standard deviation is a measure of dispersion. In a normal distribution — that is, one affected in a random fashion by a large number of variables, each with relatively small weight — about two thirds of the observations fall within one standard deviation above and below the mean. In other words, the standard deviation, σ, is the square root of the average squared differences of the observations from the mean. More precisely, where x_i is any one observation, $\bar{x}$ is the mean, and n the number of observations, then*

$$\sigma = [1/n \sum_{i=1}^{n} (x_i - \bar{x})^2]^{\frac{1}{2}}.$$

tween 0.784 and 0.802 man-hours per ton, and about ninety-nine out of one hundred that it would fall between 0.766 and 0.820 man-hours per ton.[6]

The data used in the productivity studies of 1960–1963 differ chiefly in that the samples of observations are larger and the dispersion is probably a bit greater than that of the 1959 samples. However it appears reasonable to assume that the sample size increase is more than ample to offset the increased range of the observations; in most commodity classifications there are several hundred to a thousand or so observations. About 30,000 productivity study reports were received annually by the PMA staff. In every commodity classification used in subsequent sections of this chapter, the smallest number of observations in the annual sample probably exceeds one hundred. Canned goods and general merchandise, two large categories, probably have sample sizes ten or fifteen times larger in the 1960–1963 data than reported in the 1959 preliminary studies. Given the standard deviation, the standard error of the mean will diminish as the sample size increases. The standard deviation of the larger coastwide samples may be rather larger for some goods, reflecting the effects of different dockside physical facilities, port-to-port differences in work practices, and so on. On the other hand, commodity specialization of ports is an offsetting factor, tending to make the dispersion of the coastwide data more nearly like that of 1959. For example, most of the lumber is discharged at Los Angeles–Long Beach; most of the canned goods are loaded at Oakland and Stockton; only two copra-discharging installations are used on the whole coast; most of the nonferrous ore is discharged at Tacoma and Portland; and so on. Furthermore, company and pier specialization also exist.

All in all, the average productivity rates calculated from the PMA data appear to merit a good deal of confidence when used for year-to-year comparisons. In the 1959 preliminary study the standard errors of the means, relative to the respective means, were 1.38 percent, 1.83 percent and 1.13 percent for beer, canned goods, and general merchandise, in that order. Differences in the mean rates of

---

6. *The standard error of the mean, where σ is the estimated standard deviation in the population of observed productivity rates, and n the number of observations, is $\sigma/\sqrt{n}$, for large samples. (More than one hundred observations is a large sample.) Thus, about two out of three of the estimated means would fall within one standard error of the true mean, and about ninety-nine out of one hundred within three standard errors.*

more than two or three standard errors — that is, differences of more than a few percent of the mean — are probably statistically significant for most commodities, and differences of more than 5 or 6 percent almost certainly could not occur without substantial changes in equipment, work practices or similar variables directly affecting productivity. Typical changes from 1960 to 1963 of the mean rates, calculated by commodity, were much larger — 15 to 20 percent. A reasonable conclusion is that the differences in the rates reflect, with high reliability, significant productivity changes.

METHODS, MORE SOURCES, AND PROBLEMS IN CONSTRUCTING THE EXTRAPOLATED PRODUCTIVITY ESTIMATES

The ideal approach to extrapolating the PMA productivity studies to the years before 1960 and after 1963 would apply the productivity rates for a base year within the study period — for example, 1960 — to the tonnages, by commodity and package, known to have been handled by longshoremen in the relevant years. The ideal may be only approximated.

The PMA studies reported the tonnages, direct labor man-hours, indirect labor man-hours, and productivity rates for the various commodities, by package, and separately for loading and discharging. For example, there were three entries, and productivity rates, for loading canned goods — one for canned goods in cartons, boarded at the dock; one for canned goods in cartons boarded away from the dock, and one for canned goods in unit loads. Most commodities similarly appeared in more than one package classification.

To reconcile the productivity rates to the tonnage data, the tons and man-hours were summed for all packages for loading a given commodity; a similar summation was made for discharging the good. The total man-hours and tons were then used to calculate a single rate for the commodity for loading and another for discharging operations. Two sets of productivity rates, by commodity, were calculated — one set from the 1960 data and one from the 1963 study.

Given the productivity rates, the next step in estimating productivity is the development of detailed data of tonnages handled by longshoremen. The PMA has not gathered disaggregated tonnage figures for the nonstudy years, but the United States government has. The Army Corps of Engineers is charged not only with maintaining the harbors and waterways but also with gathering the basic data describing port activity and all waterborne trade — including commerce on inland waterways, coastwise and other domestic waterways, and foreign trade. The Corps of Engineers reports were used in this study.[7]

In general, the data reported by the Corps of Engineers are good approximations of the tonnages actually handled by PMA and ILWU members. However, some of the Engineers' data were excluded or modified for subsequent use in the productivity estimates. The principal exclusions were domestic internal waterways and intra-port commerce, and tankship cargoes. The latter were approximated by eliminating the quantities reported of all goods known to be tankship cargoes — including, for example, inedible molasses, a wide variety of chemicals, and petroleum and its products. In addition, a number of commodities, bulk goods usually moved by barge and not worked by longshoremen, were also excluded from most of the productivity estimates. Other partial exclusions or modifications are noted in the description of the various productivity estimates and in the last section of this appendix.

The commodity tonnages are reported by the Corps of Engineers only by port, whereas the most reliable productivity rates are those for the entire Pacific Coast. The calculation of coastwide aggregate tonnages required the data for each commodity to be summed over the forty-seven Pacific ports handling oceanborne commerce and separately reported by the Engineers. Further aggregation was necessary in order to match the 234 commodity classifications used by the Engineers with the 70 used by the PMA in the productivity reports. As a result of imperfect overlap, some of the latter had to be combined. In all, the reported tonnages were assigned to 52 commodity classifications for use in subsequent calculations. The Engineers' data were further aggregated to match the productivity data by combining imports and domestic coastwise receipts[8] to a single

---

7. *Published annually: U.S. Army, Corps of Engineers,* Waterborne Commerce of the United States, *in five parts. This study used only Part 4,* Waterways and Harbors: Pacific Coast, Alaska and Hawaii *(Washington, 1957, through 1964).*

8. *"Coastwise" is used by the Corps of Engineers to denote all oceanborne traffic involving U.S. ports at both the shipping and receiving ends of the voyage. It includes the trade between ports in the contiguous states along a single coast — referred to as coastwise trade by people in the industry and in other government agencies — trade between the mainland U.S. and noncontiguous*

Table B-3: Estimated Man-hours Required, Man-hours Saved
by Commodity, and Overall Productivity Change, 1963.
(relative to 1960)

		Inbound		Outbound	
No.	Commodity	Tons	Estimated man-hours	Tons	Estimated man-hours
1	Canned goods	227,328	243,471.0	494,849	549,913.8
2	Rice	80	122.8	407,978	218,175.6
3	Grains, other	16,929	26,001.2	5,753,455	279,318.7
4	Flour	3,435	5,275.8	309,302	220,687.5
5	Citrus			103,128	169,844.2
6	Bananas	310,618	440,083.9	598	813.0
7	Dried fruits and nuts	20,060	27,430.7	122,951	167,582.8
8	Coffee	242,943	244,280.4	1,342	1,824.5
9	Sugar	825,936	100,685.7	4,110	5,587.8
10	Foods, other	463,124	711,311.2	804,225	1,093,406.6
11	Beverages	80,044	138,568.8	126,848	172,459.7
12	Hides	654	856.1	109,434	189,602.7
13	Animal products, inedible	90,699	118,737.6	218,748	43,601.0
14	Animal feeds	6,197	8,112.7	529,613	163,594.2
15	Rubber	45,339	69,502.4	24,173	33,540.4
16	Copra	261,487	183,477.5		
17	Cotton	2,024	2,649.6	346,913	460,659.8
18	Fibers, cordage	34,859	45,459.8	140	179.9
19	Burlap	65,360	65,529.8	4,872	7,317.2
20	Textiles, general	105,650	135,479.7	27,663	35,563.4
21	Logs	103,271	45,281.4	2,453,335	2,538,625.1
22	Lumber	122,498	135,560.6	1,919,129	1,361,328.3
23	Plywood	313,236	277,301.8	47,255	40,710.0
24	Pulp	301,604		581,246	356,067.2
25	Newsprint	673,702	222,381.6	24,484	17,612.5
26	Paper products	56,614	60,514.9	344,717	336,569.2
27	Coke	119	155.7	852,619	87,534.9
28	Glass and products	97,181	133,631.4	8,324	10,122.2
29	Earths	1,580	1,832.3	186,138	285,352.3
30	Salt	487,074	87,641.6	712,496	
31	Iron ore	18	3.5	1,860,476	34,242.0
32	Iron and steel products	1,222,867	646,922.3	120,375	38,228.0
33	Iron and steel pipe	386,364	304,195.5	50,259	46,655.5

Table B-3 (Continued)

No.	Commodity	Inbound Tons	Inbound *Estimated man-hours*	Outbound Tons	Outbound *Estimated man-hours*
34	Iron and steel scrap	5,183	6,785.2	1,338,253	355,987.3
35	Aluminum	17,356	11,567.9	66,601	44,516.6
36	Copper	17,107	15,252.1	90,650	45,863.5
37	Ores, general	458,308	91,463.6	28,815	2,299.5
38	Hardware	108,276	133,482.3	9,230	7,497.8
39	Machinery and vehicles	230,819	197,803.1	262,654	317,657.9
40	Metals and products, other	53,963	48,112.1	90,998	59,942.8
41	Chemicals	236,704	96,695.0	779,775	648,432.6
42	Fertilizer	175,716	179,213.9	133,444	128,602.0
43	Potash	20	8.1	509,412	45,054.0
44	General cargo	499,254	653,593.3	768,473	934,486.0
45	Petroleum and by-products, dry cargo	253,459	284,795.4	257,149	232,659.0
	Totals	8,625,059	6,201,231.3	22,786,649	11,789,719.0

a) Total direct labor man-hours, estimated at 1960 rates   17,990,950

b) Estimated indirect and unattributed longshore hours (at the 1960 proportion)   8,483,884

c) Total longshore hours (a + b)   26,474,834

d) Actual longshore man-hours used   21,953,461

e) Man-hours saved (c less d)   4,521,373

f) Percentage productivity change relative to 1960 (e ÷ d × 100)   20.6%

SOURCES: Calculated from Engineers' tonnage data, with lumber and petroleum tonnage modified to more closely reflect the quantities actually handled by longshoremen; 1960 productivity rates, by commodity, were calculated from PMA, *Longshore Productivity Study, 1960–1963.* Actual longshore hours used are from PMA, Contract Data Department, memo dated February 9, 1966.

inbound tonnage figure, and exports and domestic coastwise shipments to an outbound figure, for each redefined commodity. The substantial amount of data manipulation was accomplished by transferring the Engineers' reported tonnages, for each of the eight years used, to approximately 12,000 keypunched cards, and aggregating, as described above, by computer. The punched cards and aggregation were carefully audited, and the results appear to be highly reliable.[9]

The data, at this point, had been reduced to a set of inbound and outbound tonnages for fifty-two commodity classifications for each of the selected nine years. For most of these commodities, four productivity rates were available — the 1960 and the 1963 rates for loading, and a similar pair for discharging.

The following general method was used to estimate the productivity changes. For each year, direct labor man-hours were estimated by multiplying the tonnage by a base-year rate for each commodity, for loading and discharging separately. The man-hours required for the commodities, at the base-year rates, were summed to a single total for the year. The 1960 proportions that indirect and unattributed longshore hours were to total longshore hours were used to estimate the indirect hours required, and, in effect, allow for bias, at the base-year rates. The difference between estimated total longshore hours and actual longshore hours, relative to actual longshore hours used, is the productivity change in the given year, relative to the 1960 base year.

Table B-3 provides a detailed illustration of the approach for a single estimate for one year, 1963. Tonnages shown are those reported by the Corps of Engineers, with only one exception — petroleum. The figures shown for petroleum are the domestic dry-cargo tonnages; these figures understate the amount actually handled by about 30 percent for the years near 1960, but they are the best estimates available.

states, territories, or possessions — chiefly Alaska, Hawaii, and Puerto Rico — and domestic intercoastal trade.

9. *Comparison of a 1 percent sample of the cards, drawn at random, with the published data turned up no keypunching errors. Further, all aggregated tonnages that departed more than a few percentage points from the year-to-year trend were completely rechecked by a subroutine on the computer and verified by comparison with the original published figures. The program or keypunching errors discovered in this audit were corrected. The tonnages, by commodity and year, used in estimating productivity appear, rounded to the nearest thousand, in Appendix Table C-5.*

Indirect labor time, as the table suggests, is a large fraction of total longshore hours and requires some explanation at this point. In the PMA productivity study reports, the hours ascribed to rigging the ship, readying cargo, idle time, and dead time varied between 27 and 30 percent of direct labor hours in the four study years. In the 1960 data, the proportion was 29.4 percent. However, estimating the direct labor requirements for 1960 with the method illustrated in Table B-3, and adding indirect hours — the 29.4 percent — estimated at the productivity study proportion to direct hours, yields an estimate of total longshore hours smaller than actual hours paid. The difference — unattributed hours — is about 2,841,000 hours. Part of the difference, about 500,000 hours, consists of hours paid but not worked — vacations and similar fringe benefits.[10] The remaining two million or so man-hours presumably reflect bias. That is, the calculated productivity rates reflect, in the aggregate, a rather higher degree of efficiency than actually exists.

The difference between my estimate of direct labor man-hours and paid longshore man-hours in 1960 was about 7,547,900 hours. Assuming that the indirect hours, other hours paid but not worked, and the bias are related to direct labor hours, the 1960 relation is the correction necessary to adjust the estimated direct hours to total longshore hours for the various years.[11] The 1960 proportion of indirect and unattributed hours to estimated direct hours was 0.471564; applying this proportion to the estimated direct labor hours for 1963 yields the estimate in line *b* of Table B-3. Adding indirect and unattributed hours to the direct labor hours results in the adjusted estimated total longshore hours shown in line *c* of the table. Actual

10. *Hours paid exceeded hours worked by about one-half million man-hours for each of the four productivity study years. From PMA, Longshore Productivity Study, 1960–1963, Part I, Table B, p. 105, and memorandum of total hours from the PMA Contract Data Department, dated February 9, 1966.*

11. *Indirect hours are in fact a function of direct hours, and any contraction in the former associated with a reduction of the latter is properly regarded as an increase in efficiency. The inclusion of hours paid but not worked — associated with fringe benefits of various kinds — very likely understates the productivity change for the later years and overstates it for the earlier years. Hours paid but not worked tend to increase over time, as the fringe benefits grow more liberal. With respect to bias, the simplest assumptions are that it reflects unreported indirect time or that it affects all commodity rates in proportion to their contribution to total man-hours. Either assumption justifies the method selected for adjusting direct labor hours to total longshore hours.*

Table B-4: Commodity Weight in Total Tonnage, Forty-five Commodities, Engineers' and PMA Data, 1960.
(in percent)

		Loading		Discharging	
No.	Commodity	Engineers' data	PMA data	Engineers' data	PMA data
1	Canned goods	3.47	4.03	3.44	2.15
2	Rice	1.36	.84	0	a
3	Grains, other	29.52	34.13	.02	a
4	Flour	2.03	2.09	.05	a
5	Citrus	.56	.59	0	a
6	Bananas	.01	a	2.93	4.06
7	Dried fruits and nuts	.72	.62	.17	.04
8	Coffee	.01	a	2.21	2.82
9	Sugar	.02	a	7.58	10.46
10	Foods, other	2.84	2.19	3.46	3.65
11	Beverages	.71	.04	.94	.58
12	Hides	.41	.40	.01	a
13	Animal products, inedible	1.07	.58	.84	a
14	Animal feeds	.97	.27	.06	a
15	Rubber	.11	a	.46	.54
16	Copra	0	.05	3.94	5.72
17	Cotton	2.13	2.29	.01	a
18	Fiber, cordage	.01	a	.18	.27
19	Burlap	.01	.02	.52	.75
20	Textiles, general	.12	.10	.96	.11
21	Logs	1.94	1.59	1.38	.32
22	Lumber[b]	14.20	12.47	8.56	1.70
23	Plywood	.24	.11	2.12	2.17
24	Pulp[c]	2.20	2.30	3.08	.06
25	Newsprint	.22	.06	5.50	7.03
26	Paper products	1.10	1.06	1.40	.41
27	Coke	2.78	2.46	.02	a
28	Glass and products	.05	a	.92	.83
29	Earths	1.03	.29	.01	.18
30	Salt[c]	2.38	.17	4.43	4.96
31	Iron ore	4.79	5.11	.16	1.41
32	Iron and steel products	1.11	.52	14.87	12.63
33	Iron and steel pipe	.18	.09	4.78	5.39
34	Iron and steel scrap	7.30	3.59	.10	a

Table B-4 (Continued)

		Loading		Discharging	
No.	Commodity	Engineers' data	PMA data	Engineers' data	PMA data
35	Aluminum	.30	.28	.04	.06
36	Copper	.57	.42	.27	a
37	Ores, general	.21	.33	4.32	4.54
38	Hardware	.03	.01	.82	.49
39	Machinery and vehicles	1.18	.67	3.20	2.56
40	Metals and products, other	.36	.07	1.27	1.08
41	Chemicals	3.42	2.26	4.46	1.21
42	Fertilizers	.78	.19	1.52	1.38
43	Potash	2.97	3.23	0	a
44	General cargo	3.04	13.57	6.67	20.57
45	Petroleum and by-products, dry cargo	1.54	.91	2.34	.07
	Total	100.00	100.00	100.00	100.00

[a] Not reported separately by the PMA.

[b] Engineers' tonnages modified to more accurately reflect the quantity actually handled by longshoremen (Appendix B, pp. 259–260 for discussion.)

[c] Pulp tonnage, discharging, and salt tonnage, loading, were not used in any productivity estimate (see pp. 122–124 for discussion.)

SOURCES: Calculated from data in Appendix Table C-5 and from PMA, *Longshore Productivity, 1960–1963.*

longshore hours paid are shown on the next line, and the total man-hours saved and relative productivity increase follow.

Productivity changes, 1957–1964. The preceding illustration uses only one of many more or less plausible combinations of tonnages and productivity rates. At the heart of the matter is the search for the most accurate weights with which each commodity productivity rate enters the aggregate. The Engineers' data provide one set of weights; its principal strength is immediate applicability, without further assumptions or exercise of judgment, to non-PMA data for a wide range of years. Use of the unmodified Engineers' data is the best protection against the suspicion that the weights are being manipulated, perhaps subconsciously, to bring about one or another preferred result. On the other hand, the PMA productivity study reports provide, in some respects, a more plausible set of commodity weights — more accurately, four similar sets — in that the tonnages and commodity composition are known to have been handled by longshoremen. The principal weakness, and an important one, is the persisting doubt about the true composition of the annual cargo volume, which comes from the absence in the reports of a considerable quantity of tons and man-hours.

Table B-4 compares the two principal sets of weights for a single year, 1960. A first and accurate impression is that, with few exceptions, the two major weighting schemes are much alike; so much so that there is no doubt that they both describe the same activity and that the oceanborne dry cargo reported by the Corps of Engineers is a good approximation of the goods actually handled by PMA and the union's members. On the other hand, the few discrepancies, discussed below in detail, may be significant. A large number of productivity estimates were undertaken in order to evaluate or reconcile these discrepancies.

All together, a large number of sets of estimates of productivity were made for the eight selected years. The results of eighteen such estimates are presented in Table B-5.[12] The different estimates use three basic sets of commodity weights — Corps of Engineers, PMA data for 1960, and PMA data for 1963. Within each, alternative treatments of general cargo and the goods not included in the PMA reports were used, as were two sets of productivity rates, 1960 and 1963. In every estimate the year-to-year productivity changes for any commodity, other than general cargo, are the same. For example, in each of the estimates, the productivity change in 1963 relative to 1960 for loading citrus was 17.9 percent; for loading canned goods, 9.7 percent, and so on. However, the weight with which these relative productivity changes enter the aggregate does vary.

Tonnages excluded or modified. The clearest approach to the many estimates and their results is in terms of the discrepancies between Engineers' and PMA reported tonnages. First, the PMA figures for wood pulp in discharging and salt in loading operations are vastly smaller than the Engineers' data (Table B-4). Further, the

---

12. *Other estimates were made using, for example, total shoreside hours in place of longshore hours, various rates for general cargo with the PMA weighted estimates, and so on. The results of these estimates do not differ in any significant way from those presented in Table B-4.*

PMA studies omit or grossly underreport cement, pulpwood, gypsum, limestone, unmanufactured shells, and a number of other similar commodities. These are usually bulk goods, low in value relative to their weight; they are known or assumed not to have been handled by longshoremen. Accordingly, the first set of estimates — identified as the "basic list" (I.A.1.a. through c and I.B.1.a. through c in Table B-5), excludes these goods.[13] The only other modification of Engineers' tonnages in this list is the estimation of dry-cargo petroleum products by using the 1960 proportion of dry cargo to total tonnage. On the whole, this set of relative tonnages is reasonable, and has the virtue, noted earlier, of minimum manipulation.

To test the consequences of possible error in excluding the various bulk goods, all the tonnages were put back in, weighted by the all-goods average bulk-cargo loading and discharging rates. The resulting estimates of productivity change for the various years — the extended basic list estimates (I.A.2 and I.B.2 of Table B-5) — differ almost not at all from the estimates made excluding the goods.

A more important discrepancy between the Engineers' and PMA reported tonnages involves lumber. The PMA reports accord a significantly smaller weight to lumber, especially for discharging operations, than do the Engineers' data. Further, lumber is important in terms of man-hours as a result of large tonnages involved and labor-intensive methods required for handling. By every method of estimating man-hour requirements or productivity, lumber is the first or second largest user of man-hours among the identified commodities. Equally serious, its relative importance, according to the Engineers' figures, has declined sharply over time. Nearly a million fewer outbound tons, representing about 800,000 fewer man-hours at the 1960 rates, were reported in 1963 or 1964 than in 1957 or 1958. The decline in lumber discharged is less dramatic, but, relative to total tonnage, it is significant. Finally, analysis of the disaggregated data — man-hours and tonnages by port or region — establishes conclusively that PMA members and union longshoremen could not have handled all the lumber reported in the Engineers' figures. For

13. The forty-five commodities of the "basic list" are identified in Table B-3, pp. 240–241, and, in greater detail, in this Appendix, pp. 259–267. The tonnages appear in Appendix Table C-5, pp. 274–277, with lumber and petroleum products reported separately.

Table B-5: Eighteen Estimates of Productivity Changes, Pacific Coast Longshoring, 1957-1964.
(in percent deviation from the 1960 base year)

	1957	1958	1959	1960	1961	1962	1963	1964
I. *Engineers' Weights*								
A. *1960 Productivity Rates*								
1. *Basic List*								
a. average general cargo rate	−6.85	−7.04	−4.68	0	2.08	8.24	20.41	31.91
b. general cargo at zero	−8.21	−7.79	−5.63	0	3.88	10.76	21.84	33.00
c. general cargo at breakbulk	−6.58	−6.90	−4.48	0	1.76	8.08	20.21	31.79
2. *Extended basic list*	−8.11	−7.34	−5.30	0	2.24	8.51	20.95	31.60
3. *Revised basic list*								
a. average general cargo rate	−4.01	−9.46	−5.60	0	3.55	8.54	20.60	34.00
b. general cargo at zero	−5.23	−10.60	−6.80	0	5.79	11.14	22.26	35.50
c. general cargo at breakbulk	−3.76	−9.26	−5.35	0	3.15	8.08	20.36	33.81
B. *1963 Productivity Rates*								
1. *Basic list*								
a. average general cargo rate	−5.94	−6.89	−5.07	0	2.01	7.83	18.52	29.83
b. general cargo at zero	−6.96	−7.53	−5.99	0	3.58	9.78	19.47	30.42
c. general cargo at breakbulk	−5.36	−6.63	−4.69	0	1.25	7.05	18.08	29.52

2. *Extended basic list*	−6.65	−7.07	−5.43	0	2.11	7.86	18.92	29.66
3. *Revised basic list*								
a. average general cargo rate	−2.86	−8.70	−5.59	0	3.20	8.08	18.42	31.67
b. general cargo at zero	−3.84	−9.63	−6.73	0	5.11	10.29	19.49	32.54
c. general cargo at breakbulk	−2.49	−8.34	−5.18	0	2.44	7.20	17.95	31.31
II. *PMA Weights*								
A. *1960 Productivity Rates*								
1. 1960 PMA weights	−4.14	−12.24	−8.22	0	6.51	10.18	22.16	31.26
2. 1963 PMA weights	−5.20	−12.89	−8.18	0	5.79	8.45	19.67	34.83
B. *1963 Productivity Rates*								
1. 1960 PMA weights	−3.23	−11.49	−8.08	0	6.02	10.01	20.89	35.43
2. 1963 PMA weights	−4.44	−12.39	−8.17	0	5.38	8.18	18.29	33.19

example, for 1963 the Engineers reported that the southern California area received about 1,257,000 tons of lumber; [14] for the same year, the PMA productivity study reported only 68,000 tons discharged for the area. At the 1963 productivity rate for discharging lumber, calculated from the PMA data, an additional 900,000 direct labor longshore man-hours would have been required to handle the good. However, only 263,000 total longshore hours, including indirect and hours paid but not worked, were not accounted for in the productivity study reports for the area and year. In brief, use of the Engineers' tonnages for lumber very likely results in biased estimates of year-to-year productivity change.

Accordingly, the tonnages for lumber were modified, with PMA assessment data, to more closely approximate the goods handled by longshoremen. Fortunately, the assessment procedures adopted by the PMA apply different rates to bulk tonnages, goods reported in thousands of board feet, and all other cargo. As a result, data are available for a long period of time for these three varieties of cargo. The goods reported in board feet consist wholly of logs and lumber. Board feet were converted to short tons at the productivity study rate — 1,000 board feet = 1.8 short tons — and the log tonnage, as reported by the Engineers, was subtracted, leaving the total lumber tonnage handled by PMA members. The tonnage was prorated to loading and discharging at the average proportions for the two operations in the 1960–1963 productivity study rate. There is no doubt that the modified lumber tonnage more accurately reflects the appropriate weight for the good in the cargo handled by members of both the PMA and ILWU.

Modified lumber tonnage is the principal change in the estimates identified as the "revised basic list" — used in I.A.3, I.B.3 of Table B-4 and all the estimates using the tonnage weights from PMA productivity studies. The only other change — a minor refinement — is the substitution of dry-cargo petroleum products and inedible molasses tonnage actually reported for domestic commerce in place of the basic list estimate. This modification understates the tonnage handled by longshoremen, but not by much. The estimates using the revised list are very likely the most reliable.

14. *Corps of Engineers,* Waterborne Commerce, *1963, pp. 1–10. The figure is the sum of the tonnages for commodities 405, 413, 417, and 421 for San Diego, Long Beach, and Los Angeles.*

General-cargo weights and rates. The most disconcerting, and probably the most serious, discrepancy between the two sets of tonnage weights has to do with general cargo. Far more tons, and a much heavier relative weight in the total, are assigned to general cargo in the PMA productivity studies than results from the Corps of Engineers data. The discrepancy is the result in part of imperfect reconciliation of Engineers and PMA classifications, and, in larger part, or incorrect assignment of tons and man-hours by the clerks gathering the basic PMA data. As a consequence, the commodity productivity rates calculated from PMA data are biased and choice of the rates appropriate for general cargo is rather difficult.

Table B-6 illustrates the problem, using the data for just one year, 1963. The difference between the PMA and Engineers tonnages, by commodity, in thousands and rounded, and direct labor man-hours, estimated by commodity, are shown. The tonnage differences represent the goods actually handled by PMA and ILWU members, but not included in the productivity study reports, or goods attributed to general cargo but for which specific commodity classifications existed in the reporting scheme. The larger tonnage in the Engineers data requires more man-hours, estimated by commodity rates, but the increase in required hours appears to be disproportionate to the increase in tons. If it were assumed, unreasonably, that the commodity rates were not biased and that the identity and quantity of goods reallocated from general-cargo to specific commodity classifications were such that the man-hours required before and after the allocation were the same, then the unattributed tons must have been handled at very high productivity rates — about one-half man-hour per ton for loading, and only one-tenth man-hour per ton for discharging. In other words, they must have been largely bulk goods. But this is very unlikely; there are not enough unreported tons of goods capable of being handled by bulk methods. Further, comparisons by major port area of missing man-hours and probable missing tons indicates that the unreported tons must have included large quantities of nonbulk goods.

The most reasonable conclusion is that the reallocation of goods from general cargo to specific commodities leads to the attribution of fewer man-hours to the tonnage reported as general cargo in the PMA studies than without the reallocation. The implication is that the commodity productivity rates are biased; that is, the identified

Table B-6: Tonnage Differences, PMA and Engineers Data, and Estimated Man-hours, by Commodity, Pacific Coast, 1963. (in thousands of tons)

		Loading		Discharging	
No.	Commodity	Engineers less PMA tons	Estimated man-hours required at 1960 rates	Engineers less PMA tons	Estimated man-hours required at 1960 rates
1	Canned goods	112.5	125,019	96.5	85,371
2	Rice	122.9	65,724	0.1	149
3	Grains, other	−232.2	−11,273	16.9	25,225
4	Flour	100.7	71,850	3.4	5,075
5	Citrus	8.7	14,328		
6	Bananas	0.6	816	0.9	972
7	Dried fruits and nuts	51.5	70,195	17.9	21,546
8	Coffee	1.3	1,768	27.1	26,879
9	Sugar	4.1	5,574	−27.4	−1,918
10	Foods, other	362.9	493,391	262.4	391,659
11	Beverages	113.9	154,856	49.8	76,086
12	Hides	32.9	57,002	0.6	569
13	Animal products, inedible	109.4	21,806	90.7	85,932
14	Animal feeds	176.9	54,643	6.2	5,874
15	Rubber	16.5	22,894	14.3	21,530
16	Copra			50.5	26,969
17	Cotton	48.9	68,934	2.0	1,895
18	Fibers, cordage	0.1	129	8.8	10,100
19	Burlap	−2.1	−3,154	4.3	3,825
20	Textiles, general	26.3	33,811	103.2	78,429
21	Logs	496.0	513,243	99.5	49,606
22	Lumber	227.9	161,660	−4.8	−3,474
23	Plywood	31.6	27,223	84.5	60,449
24	Pulp	67.1	41,105	7.0	
25	Newsprint	10.8	7,769	75.9	16,821
26	Paper	137.7	134,445	26.5	14,708
27	Coke	−49.7	−5,103		
28	Glass	8.3	10,093	45.9	42,621
29	Earths	132.3	202,818	−8.1	−8,504
30	Salt	−11.5		80.7	2,462
31	Ore, iron	−43.6	−803	−13.0	−2,461
32	Iron and steel products	77.2	24,517	377.8	163,669

Table B-6 (Continued)

No. Commodity	Loading		Discharging	
	Engineers less PMA tons	Estimated man-hours required at 1960 rates	Engineers less PMA tons	Estimated man-hours required at 1960 rates
33 Iron and steel pipe	—4.1	—3,806	—12.2	—6,888
34 Iron and steel scrap	970.6	258,188	5.2	4,927
35 Aluminum	10.4	6,951	9.9	4,994
36 Copper	44.4	22,464	17.1	8,578
37 Ores, general	23.7	1,891	254.0	50,690
38 Hardware	6.2	5,037	54.9	67,681
39 Machinery and vehicles	114.5	138,478	55.8	47,133
40 Metals products, other	78.3	51,578	—19.2	16,277
41 Chemicals, other	413.4	343,769	200.4	81,865
42 Fertilizer	126.9	122,296	29.4	29,985
43 Potash	37.3	3,299		
45 Petroleum and petroleum products	182.9	166,388	231.3	259,897
Total	4,144.4	3,491,813	2,312.7	1,734,681
44 General cargo	—2,010.7	—2,445,072	—1,199.3	—1,570,052
Totals 1–43, 45 plus General Cargo	2,134.7	1,046,741	1,113.4	164,629

SOURCES: Corps of Engineers tonnages, see Appendix Table C-5; PMA data from PMA, *Long shore Productivity Study, 1960–1963*. Tonnage differences and man-hour estimates were calculated from the data.

goods reflect a rate of efficiency greater than actually existed, or the general-cargo rate reflects lower than the true efficiency for the relevant goods. Both are probably the case. First, no reasonable set of tonnages, applied to the calculated commodity productivity rates, accounts for all the hours actually used in the productivity study years. Secondly, the bias in the commodity rates very likely resulted from assigning odd tonnages and unallocated man-hours to general cargo.[15]

Several approaches to deal with the problem are plausible and have been tried here. First, the bias may be ignored on the grounds that it affects year-to-year comparisons only slightly. The estimates identified as Engineers' tonnages using the aggregate general-cargo rates in fact use this approach. Secondly, the productivity rate for the general cargo in the Engineers' data may be changed. The goods allocated to other categories apparently were handled more efficiently than the tonnages remaining. Hence, a lower productivity rate is appropriate to the markedly reduced remaining tonnage. A number of estimates were made, using the break-bulk general-cargo rates as an available, plausible lower rate. These estimates still assume biased rates, and a general-cargo productivity rate not necessarily applicable to the tonnage. Nonetheless, they do indicate the direction and magnitude of change when heavier weight is given general cargo. A third approach recognizes the impossibility of distinguishing between unattributed and misclassified tonnages. It abandons general cargo altogether as a separate classification. The hours required for general cargo are treated simply as another variety of missing hours. In effect, general-cargo tonnage enters at the average productivity rate for the relevant year. The approach assumes that all rates are biased and that the bias does not significantly affect the year-to-year comparisons.

Finally, the problem may be tackled by reweighting the tonnages to match the relative weights in the PMA data. The tonnages

15. *The temptation to do so was probably great. Most of the specific commodities may be identified with specific employers and, at the time the reports were submitted by the clerk, with specific longshore gangs. Unusually low efficiency associated with a specific commodity, for example, could be noticed and would be of great interest to an employer. On the other hand, general cargo was known to be heterogeneous; it could be almost anything, handled by any employer, at widely varying rates of efficiency.*

are appropriate to the productivity rates by this method, but the unattributed hours, and hence the commodity rate biases, are large.

The choice, from the four annual sets of data, of the appropriate productivity rates is the final conceptual problem. Like lumber tonnage, but unlike the problem of general cargo, an intelligent choice in this matter — selection of base-year rates — is possible.

The index number problem is familiar. In building or using a price index, or indexes of production, the choice of a base year not only makes a difference in the results but, usually, the differences are irreconcilable. The difficulty arises from the correlation between the weights used and the variable measured. In price indexes, for example, price changes usually are highly correlated with quantities of the goods sold or consumed. Thus, the weights used reflect the importance of the various good or service prices and are partly a result of the price change itself. In the estimates of productivity made in this study, this problem takes the form of a possible causal relation between productivity-rate change and tonnage handled for the various goods. For example, if more efficient handling leads to larger quantities being handled, then the choice of recent year weights, assuming efficiency increases with time, would result in smaller measured productivity changes than the estimates using earlier year weights. Even worse, neither the early or late year weights result in good measures of productivity change; the former surely overstates, and the latter understates.

Fortunately, in the productivity estimates of this sudy, the problem is not serious. Differences in the estimates using two base years — one at each end of the four-year study period — are not great, in most cases within a few percentage points of each other. Further, the changes in productivity rates and tonnages handled appear not to be significantly casually related. Apart from the rise in exports of logs and iron ore — largely the result of shifts in the demand for the goods in Japan — most of the substantial commodity changes during the eight years studied appear to be erratic, up for some years, down for others, and not a function of time or productivity change.

Of the four possibilities, the best measurement of productivity change would use the 1960 rates and base year. The choice implies that the 1963 tonnage, for example, would not have been substantially different if there had been no change in productivity, and that the estimates actually measure the difference between the man-hours required had there been no productivity change and actual man-hours used. Perhaps equally important, the 1960 rates are the most reliable, and hence, desirable, of the entire group of four annual sets.

Rather surprisingly, the results of the various productivity estimates are very similar. All indicate that productivity fluctuated, with no trend, before 1960. Productivity was significantly higher in 1960 than in the preceding years, and it rose steadily every year thereafter. The similarity among the estimates is reassuring. The use of any one as an approximation of the productivity changes for the relevant years would not err greatly.

In choosing among the estimates, a few comments with respect to possible year-to-year bias are appropriate. General cargo is most likely a source of such bias in both directions in time away from 1960. In the earliest years, the commodity classifications used by the Corps of Engineers were a bit less precise than in later years, and larger tonnages are reported as "commodities, not elsewhere classified." These goods were included in general cargo in the early years, but some of them are most likely attributed to more narrowly defined commodity classifications in subsequent periods. In the later years some goods that were handled in relatively small amounts in 1960, and accordingly classified with general cargo, grew in importance. The amount of both kinds of bias is probably small; the estimates eliminating general cargo as a separate classification certainly overcorrect for it. All other methods would include the bias, and, the heavier the weight accorded general cargo, the more important is the bias.

All in all, perhaps the most reliable estimate, and the one generally used for reference in the later chapters of this study, is the one using Engineers' tonnage weights, the revised basic list of commodities, general-cargo tonnage at average general-cargo rates, and the 1960 productivity rates — identified in Table B-5 as I.A.3.a. Engineers' tonnage weights are preferred because they involve the least manipulation; the revised basic list is preferable because it most closely approximates the goods actually handled by longshoremen. Although the choice is difficult, the use of the average general-cargo rate, rather than ignoring general cargo altogether or assigning some heavier weight, appears preferable. It uses more information than does the first alternative, is less subject to the general-cargo bias of the second, and involves less apparent manipulation of rates and weights than either. Finally, the 1960 productivity rates are more reliable, therefore preferable, than the others.

On the other hand, the publication of many different estimates of productivity, although possibly confusing, performs a positive role. The many estimates emphasize the impossibility of fine precision in measuring productivity change with the sort of data available for this industry. It would be misleading, because it appears so precise, to state that productivity in 1964, for example, was 31.91 percent above 1960; equally plausible or better estimates would be 34.83 percent, 34.00 percent, and so on. However, it is perfectly appropriate to assert that productivity in 1964 was about 33 percent above 1960, give or take a few percentage points. Finally, the many estimates are sufficiently close to each other, and the year-to-year changes so great, that the direction and approximate magnitudes of productivity change are unmistakable.

RELATIONS BETWEEN THE VARIOUS MEASURES OF PRODUCTIVITY AND AGGREGATION OVER COMMODITIES

The relations between average productivity, relative change in average productivity (usually as a percent of base-year productivity), man-hours saved, differences between mean rates cited in various tables in the chapters, appendixes and appendix tables, and the aggregation to an overall measure of productivity change are as follows:

(1) In conventional usage, average productivity is tons per man-hour. Define base-year productivity, $\frac{t_0}{m_0} = p_0$ and in the current year, $\frac{t_1}{m_1} = p_1$, where t is tonnage and m represents man-hours.

(2) The change in average productivity, relative to the base year is

$$\frac{(p_1 - p_0)}{p_0} = \frac{p_1}{p_0} - \frac{p_0}{p_0} = \frac{p_1}{p_0} - 1.$$

(3) The mean rates in some of the tables are man-hours per ton, $\frac{m}{t}$ or, for the base year, $\frac{1}{p_0}$, and the current year, $\frac{1}{p_1}$.

(4) The difference between mean rates is $\dfrac{1}{p_0} - \dfrac{1}{p_1}$, and

(5) man-hours saved, the difference between man-hours required at the base-year rate and man-hours used in the current year, is

$$\left(\frac{m_0}{t_0}\right)t_1 - \left(\frac{m_1}{t_1}\right)t_1 = \left(\frac{1}{p_0} - \frac{1}{p_1}\right)t_1$$

(6) Man-hours saved relative to man-hours actually used is

$$\left(\frac{1}{p_0} - \frac{1}{p_1}\right)\frac{t_1}{m_1}.$$

(7) But, $\dfrac{t_1}{m_1} = p_1$, thus, rewrite (6) as $\left(\dfrac{1}{p_0} - \dfrac{1}{p_1}\right)p_1$, or

(8) $\dfrac{p_1}{p_0} - \dfrac{p_1}{p_1} = \dfrac{p_1}{p_0} - 1$, the change in average productivity relative to the base year, as in (2) above.

(9) The difference in mean rates relative to a mean rate was used as an approximate test of significance of the difference. When the current year mean rate is used, this is also the productivity change relative to the base year. Explicitly,

$$\frac{\dfrac{1}{p_0} - \dfrac{1}{p_1}}{\dfrac{m_1}{t_1}} = \left(\frac{1}{p_0} - \frac{1}{p_1}\right)\frac{t_1}{m_1}, \text{ and, from (6) through (8) is the}$$

productivity change relative to the best year.

For any given commodity, i, define the difference between the base- and current-year mean rates,

(10) $\dfrac{1}{p_0} - \dfrac{1}{p_1} = x_1$, and $i = 1, \ldots, n$, commodities.

(11) From (5) and (6), man-hours saved is $x_i(t_1)_i$, and productivity change relative to the base year is $\dfrac{x_i(t_1)_i}{(m_1)_i}$.

(12) To aggregate, weight the relative productivity change for commodity i by its relative contribution to total man-hours,

$$\frac{x_i(t_1)_i}{(m_1)_i} \cdot \frac{(m_1)_i}{M_1}; \text{ where } M_1 = \sum_{i-1}^{m}(m_1)_i.$$

(13) Sum for all commodities,

$$\sum_{i-1}^{n} \left[\frac{x_i(t_1)_i}{M_1} \right]; \text{ or, } \frac{1}{M_1} \sum_{i-1}^{n} \left[x_i(t_1)_i \right].$$

Rewriting, $\sum_{i-1}^{n} \left[x_i(t_1)_i \right]$, the aggregate man-hours saved, reflecting current year commodity (and where relevant, package) composition, as

(14) $\left(\dfrac{1}{P_0} - \dfrac{1}{P_1} \right) T_1$, where T_1 is total current year tonnage, then

(13) becomes

(15) $\left(\dfrac{1}{P_0} - \dfrac{1}{P_1} \right) \left(\dfrac{T_1}{M_1} \right) = \dfrac{P_1}{P_0} - 1$, the aggregate productivity change relative to the base year.

COMMODITY CLASSIFICATION RECONCILIATION

The PMA and Engineers commodity classifications were reconciled as indicated in Table B-7. The names of the classifications are condensed, and the numbers in parentheses are the Engineers classification numbers. The use of two, or, in rare cases, more numbers to identify a commodity indicates that the Corps of Engineers used the numbers concurrently — usually to distinguish exports or imports from other branches of trade in the good — or that the classification number was changed during the eight-year period for which productivity estimates were made.

The forty-five redefined commodities of the table were the "basic list" of goods tonnages used in most of the productivity estimates. To more closely approximate tonnage worked by longshoremen, or to eliminate unreliable productivity rates, further consolidations or eliminations were made.

Some of the basic list commodities appear predominantly, or solely, as outbound or inbound cargoes. As a result, classifications for which PMA reported no data, or for which the Engineers' data indicated that only a few hundred to a few thousand tons were involved, were combined with related or residual classifications. Specifically, for loading operations: bananas, coffee and sugar were added to foods, other; copra and glass were added to general cargo;

fibers, cordage, was added to textiles, general. On discharging operations: rice, other grains, and flour were added to foods, other; copper was added to metals and metal products; hides, inedible animal products, animal feeds, unmanufactured cotton, coke, and iron and steel scrap were added to general cargo.

In all the productivity estimates, salt is excluded from the outbound tonnages. Nearly all of the half-million tons of outbound shipments of salt are loaded at Redwood City on San Francisco Bay, and, according to local officials, no longshoremen are used. The few thousand tons reported in the PMA studies originated in other ports. No adjustment was attempted to allow for the insignificant number of man-hours involved.

Similarly, inbound wood pulp is excluded in all estimates from the commodity tonnages. Almost all of the 100,000 to 250 thousand tons of wood pulp discharged each year is unloaded at a small port on the San Joaquin River by industrial employees, not longshoremen. No adjustment was made to account for the few thousand remaining tons discharged each year.

In addition to the above partial exclusions, a number of goods were entirely excluded — both the inbound and outbound tonnages — from the productivity estimates. The excluded goods are, for the most part, not handled by longshoremen in appreciable quantities. In all, seven classifications were created for these goods, chiefly to account for all of the oceanborne tonnage. The effect of omitting the tonnage from the estimates, even if they were worked by longshoremen, was estimated and found to be negligible. The excluded goods were inedible molasses, pulpwood, cement, gypsum, limestone, sand and gravel, coal tars and coal-tar products, benzol or benzene, industrial alcohols, sodium hydroxide, inedible vegetable oils and fats, watercraft and merchant vessels, Department of Defense special category goods, U.S. articles returned, unmanufactured shells, rafted logs, liquid sulfur, slag, sulfuric acid, water, ice, waste materials, L.C.L. freight, government materials used in waterway improvement, and "low value shipments."

Table B-7: Commodity Classifications, Reconciliation of PMA and Corps of Engineers Data.

No. Classification used in present study	PMA classification	Corps of Engineers classification
1 Canned goods	Canned goods	Meat, canned (013) Animal oils, edible (020) Condensed and evaporated milk (033) Fish, canned (043) Vegetables, canned (123) Fruits, canned (135) Fruit juices (136) Vegetable oils, edible (150) Molasses, edible, and syrups (185) Beverages and syrups, not elsewhere classified (195)
2 Rice	Rice	Rice (101)
3 Grains, other	Barley Wheat Grains, other	Corn (100) Barley and rye (102) Wheat (103) Oats (104)
4 Flour	Flour-bran	Wheat flour (107) Flour and preparations, other (109)
5 Citrus	Citrus	Fresh fruit[a] (130)
6 Bananas	Bananas	Bananas, fresh (132)
7 Dried fruits and nuts	Dried fruit–nuts	Dried fruit (133) Nuts (140)
8 Coffee	Coffee	Coffee, raw or green (160)
9 Sugar	Sugar	Sugar (180)
10 Foods, other	Packaged foods Ventilated foods Chilled fresh fruits and vegetables Chill cargo, other Frozen, fish–meat–poultry Freeze cargo, other Pineapples Beans–peas (including cocoa beans)	Meat, fresh or frozen (010) Meat, otherwise prepared (017) and (018) Dried milk (035) Cheese (037) Dairy products, other (039) Fish, fresh or frozen (040) Fish, otherwise prepared (045) and (047) Shellfish (049)

Table B-7 (Continued)

No.	Classification used in present study	PMA classification	Corps of Engineers classification
			Eggs (050)
			Edible animal products, other (055)
			Vegetables, fresh or frozen (120)
			Vegetables, other (125) and (127)
			Fruits, fresh or frozen (130)
			Fruits and preparations, other (137) and (138)
			Cocoa beans (161)
			Tea (165)
			Cocoa (167)
			Spices (170)
			Groceries and foods, other (199)
11	Beverages	Beverages	Liquors and wines, including beer (190)
12	Hides	Hides	Hides and skins, raw (060)
13	Animal products, inedible	Tallow	Tallow, inedible (080)
			Animal products, inedible, other[b] (095) and (098)
14	Animal feeds	Feeds	Grain sorghums (108)
			Animal feeds, other (110)
15	Rubber	Rubber, including crude and scrap	Rubber, crude (200)
			Rubber, synthetic (201)
			Rubber, scrap and reclaimed (203)
16	Copra	Copra	Copra (233)
17	Cotton	Cotton	Cotton, unmanufactured (300)
18	Fibers, cordage	Fibers–cordage	Hemp, unmanufactured (324)
			Sisal, henequen and jute, unmanufactured (326)
			Vegetable fibers, other (328)
19	Burlap	Burlap–bagging	Burlap and jute bagging (331)

Table B-7 (Continued)

No. Classification used in present study	PMA classification	Corps of Engineers classification
20 Textiles, general	Textiles, general	Cotton semimanufactures (310) Cotton manufactures (320) Wool, semimanufactures and manufactures (350) Vegetable fiber semi-manufactures and manufactures, other (335) Man-made or synthetic fibers and manufactures (380) and (381) Textile products, other (390)
21 Logs	Logs–timbers	Logs (400)
22 Lumber	Poles–piling Lumber Pencil slats	Posts (405) Lumber (413) Railroad ties (417) Wood manufactures, other (421)
23 Plywood	Plywood	Plywood, veneers (415) and (416)
24 Pulp	Pulp	Wood pulp (441)
25 Newsprint	Newsprint	Standard newsprint paper (450)
26 Paper products	Paper, general Paper, heavy Wallboard–linerboard Paper scrap	Paper base stocks, not elsewhere classified (445) Paperboard (457) Paper and products, other (460) and (475)
27 Coal and coke	Coke, both coal and petroleum coke	Coke, including petroleum coke (504)
28 Glass and products	Glass	Glass and glass products (530)
29 Earths	Earth[e]	Clays and earths (540) Nonmetallic minerals, not elsewhere classified[d] (555)
30 Salt	Salt	Salt (553)
31 Iron ore	Ore, aluminum–iron	Iron ore[e] (600)

Table B-7 (Continued)

No. Classification used in present study	PMA classification	Corps of Engineers classification
32 Iron and steel products	Iron and steel products, including castings and forgings	Pig iron (601)
		Iron and steel semifinished products (603)
	Iron and steel, basic metal	Iron and steel castings and forgings (605)
	Iron and steel, sheets	Rolled and finished steel mill products (604) and (609)
33 Iron and steel pipe	Iron and steel pipe[f]	Iron and steel pipe, tubes and tubing (608)
34 Iron and steel scrap	Scrap, general, and scrap, bulk	Iron and steel scrap (602)
35 Aluminum	Aluminum, general	Aluminum metal (618)
36 Copper	Copper, general	Copper, refined in crude forms (622)
		Copper, semifabricated forms (624)
		Copper alloy, semifabricated forms and scrap (632)
37 Ores, general	Ores, general	Manganese (613)
		Chrome (614)
		Copper ore and concentrates (620)
		Nickel ore and concentrates (652)
		Zinc ore (670)
		Other nonferrous ores (682)
		Aluminum ore[g] (617)
38 Hardware	Hardware	Tools and basic hardware (606)
39 Machinery and vehicles	Machinery Automobiles	Electrical Machinery (700)
	Vehicles, general	Automobiles and trucks (787)
		Vehicles, other[h] (797)
40 Metals and products, other	Wire and cable	Household utensils (607)
	Other metal–metal products	Metal manufactures, other (611) and (612)
		Ferroalloys (615)
		Zinc metal and forms (672)

Table B-7 (Continued)

No. Classification used in present study	PMA classification	Corps of Engineers classification
41 Chemicals	Borates Chemicals, other	Industrial chemicals, other (828), (829) and (830) Chemical specialties (844) and (846) Miscellaneous chemical products (860)
42 Fertilizers	Nitrates Fertilizers, other	Ammonium sulphate fertilizer (849) Other nitrogeneous fertilizer (850) and (851) Phosphates (852) and (853) Superphosphates (854) Fertilizers, other (859)
43 Potash	Potash	Potash (855)
44 General cargo	General Cargo[1] Household goods Mail Ordnance Seeds	Animals, edible (005) Leather and manufactures (065) Furs and manufactures (075) Animals, inedible (090) Rubber tires (205) Rubber manufactures, other (207) Naval stores (210) Drugs, herbs (220) Soybeans (231) Castor beans (234) Flaxseed (232) Oilseeds (235) and (236) Vegetable tanning and dyeing materials (250) Seeds, not elsewhere classified (260) Tobacco, unmanufactured (280) Tobacco manufactures (285) Vegetable products, inedible not elsewhere classified (297)

Table B-7 (Continued)

No. Classification used in present study	PMA classification	Corps of Engineers classification
		Wool, unmanufactured (340)
		Cork (430)
		Building Stone (526)
		Brick and tile (543)
		Clay products, other (547)
		Dry sulphur (550)
		Aluminum ore (617)
		Lead ore (640)
		Lead metal (642)
		Tin ore and scrap (660) and (662)
		Tin metal (665)
		Precious metals and manufactures (690)
		Aircraft and parts (790) and (793)
		Medicines and pharmaceuticals (810)
		Synthetic resins (837)
		Carbon black (845)
		Pigments, paints and varnishes (847) and (848)
		Dynamite (862)
		Soaps and preparations (865)
		Commodities, not elsewhere classified (900) and (901)
45 Petroleum and by-products, dry cargo	Oil and oil products	Gasoline to and including natural gasoline[j] (505 to and including 522)

[a] Exports from southern California only.

[b] The Engineers' published data did not include a separate category for tallow for the earlier years; the commodity was included in inedible animal products. The classification — inedible animal products, other — was retained in order to make the year-to-year data as comparable as possible.

[c] Includes asbestos, chalk, feldspar, mica, and similar minerals.

[d] For loading only. (See text, pp. 122–124, for explanation of commodity classification differences between loading and discharging operations.)

[e] Although the PMA productivity study ostensibly includes aluminum ore with iron ore, it appears more likely, from comparison of the two sets of data by port or region of the

Table B-7 (Continued)

Pacific coast, that aluminum ore was probably treated as general cargo in loading operations, and as general ore in discharging.

[f] Includes angles, bars, beams, rails, and rods.

[g] Discharging only.

[h] Machinery was combined with vehicles because it appeared that PMA's general vehicles included goods classified by the Engineers' under agricultural machinery, construction machinery, and similar headings.

[i] In the published commodity descriptions, PMA general cargo includes "relatively small amounts of" bamboo, boats, bones, building materials, carpets, cement, coal, coconuts, charcoal, coke residue, crockery, DDT, heavy lifts, hung meat, lacquers, latex, lead, lead ore, limestone, marble, mulch, oyster seed, paints, light paper products, peat moss, plastics, nonmetallic pipes, rattan, rubber tires, sand, tin, tin scrap, soap and detergents, steel mesh, tobacco, wool, and other goods. PMA's household goods, mail, ordnance, and seeds were also included in general cargo because they did not closely match any of the Engineers' classifications.

[j] Only a small fraction of the tens of millions of tons of these goods are dry cargo handled by longshoremen. Two alternatives were used to approximate the petroleum products tonnage actually loaded or discharged by longshoremen and PMA members. One was to apply a fraction, estimated for a base year, to total petroleum and products tonnage to deflate to estimated dry-cargo tonnage. The 1960 dry-cargo tonnage was estimated by adding the known domestic dry-cargo volume — published by the Department of Commerce — to the foreign dry-cargo tonnage approximated by accounting for all other dry cargo and for all tankship cargo, and assuming the discrepancy to be the otherwise unidentifiable petroleum dry-cargo tonnage. The second alternative was to substitute the dry-cargo petroleum products tonnage in domestic trade for total petroleum and products. This understates the true tonnage by its exclusion of the dry-cargo petroleum in foreign trade, but it is a reasonable approximation; the excluded tonnage is relatively small — one hundred thousand tons or so.

ESTIMATES OF CONTAINER TONNAGE

The container tonnages included in the Afterword are my own rough estimates. The companies will not release figures for their own tonnage, and neither government nor industry groups gather such data. The estimates for 1964 and 1966 are basically the Corps of Engineers tonnages for the three branches of domestic trade, adjusted downward to exclude goods not suited to containers — for example, lumber, vehicles, and goods handled in bulk. The 1968 and 1969 figures are estimates based on the simple extrapolation of modest growth in domestic trade, and, for foreign trade, on sailing schedules and average loads per container and containers per ship. The Japanese four-company consortium, for example, has had one ship departing every ten days, with an east-west reported average of about 785 containers per ship. On the average, each container carries about 15 tons of cargo, inbound and outbound combined. By simple arithmetic, each round trip amounts to about 23,550 tons, and the consortium would carry, at these average rates, about 850,000 tons in one year. The estimates by carrier and by port, prorated for less than full-year service, were combined and compared with port figures, where available. For example, Oakland reported that 1,531,000 tons of containerized cargo were handled in 1968, and that 2.4 million were expected to pass through the port in 1969; Los Angeles handled about one million tons in 1968, and Seattle expected about 1.5 million tons in 1969.[16]

16. Journal of Commerce, *Vol. 300, No. 21,955 (June 9, 1969), pp. 4A, 11A. The chief sources of data are U.S. Army, Corps of Engineers,* Waterborne Commerce of the United States, *various years; the* Journal of Commerce, *especially the containerization supplements of Vol. 296, No. 21,683 (May 13, 1968) and Vol. 300, No. 21,955 (June 9, 1969).*

C / TABLES

Table C-1: Tons and Man-hours,
PMA Member Companies, 1948-1954.
(thousands of tons and man-hours)

Year	Assessment tons[a]	Longshore and clerks man-hours	Tons per man-hour
1948	14,600	16,900	0.864
1949	17,400	18,300	0.951
1950	19,800	23,300	0.850
1951	24,700	27,300	0.905
1952	24,800	25,800	0.961
1953	23,300	25,800	0.903
1954	20,600	24,100	0.855

[a] As reported by member companies for assessment purposes: weight tons of 2,000 pounds, measurement tons of forty cubic feet, lumber at 1,000 board feet.

SOURCE: Pacific Maritime Association data reported in *Study of Harbor Conditions in Los Angeles and Long Beach; Hearings, October 19, 20 and 21, 1955*, U.S. House Committee on Merchant Marine and Fisheries, 84th Congress, 1st Session (Washington: 1955), p. 99.

Table C-2: Man-hours and Bulk, Nonbulk, and Total Tonnage,
PMA Member Companies, 1952-1965.

Year	Nonbulk	Bulk, dry	Total tons	Total man-hours	Tons per man-hour
	Tonnage[a]				
1950	16,668,152	2,915,514	19,583,666	NA	NA
1951	20,104,032	6,085,563	26,189,595	NA	NA
1952	18,206,846	7,696,854	25,903,700	26,834,400	0.9653
1953	19,299,938	5,230,816	24,530,754	27,057,000	0.9066
1954	17,163,182	4,440,305	21,603,487	26,427,000	0.8175
1955	18,816,243	5,593,419	24,409,662	27,295,300	0.8943
1956	18,731,877	9,422,033	28,153,910	28,898,900	0.9742
1957	18,724,885	12,395,160	31,120,045	29,216,100	1.06
1958	17,102,134	7,920,978	25,023,112	28,672,300	0.8727
1959	18,274,818	8,095,602	26,370,420	29,776,373	0.8856
1960	19,041,443	10,772,116	29,813,559	29,853,699	0.9987
1961	18,065,208	11,652,088	29,717,296	27,729,840	1.0717
1962	19,353,961	10,000,791	29,354,752	26,666,824	1.1008
1963	21,105,528	13,230,436	34,335,964	27,817,828	1.2343
1964	23,123,360	13,505,833	36,629,193	27,725,016	1.3212
1965	25,900,047	16,813,165	42,713,212	30,098,443	1.4191

[a] Tonnage reported by member companies for assessment purposes. Bulk tonnage consists almost wholly of tons of 2,000 pounds of weight. Nonbulk tonnage includes some goods reported by weight tons of 2,000 pounds, some reported by measurement tons of forty cubic feet, and some — lumber and logs — reported by board feet. In the above figures, lumber and logs were converted to tons of 2,000 pounds by the formula: 1,000 board feet x 1.8 = 1 ton.

SOURCES: Pacific Maritime Association Contract Data (Research) Department; tonnage data in memo dated June 16, 1966; man-hours data taken from PMA *Annual Reports* for 1952 through 1958 and from memo dated February 9, 1966, for 1959 through 1965.

Table C-3: Pacific Coast Average Tons per Man-hour
Two Estimates for Bulk Tonnage, 1952-1965.

Year	Tons per man-hour		Index (Col. 1, with 1953 = 100)
	(1) Bulk-handling man-hours at zero	(2) Bulk-handling man-hours estimated at 1960 rates	
1952	0.6785	0.7176	95.1
1953	0.7133	0.7405	100.0
1954	0.6495	0.6709	91.0
1955	0.6894	0.7173	96.6
1956	0.6482	0.6910	90.9
1957	0.6409	0.6971	89.8
1958	0.5965	0.6295	83.6
1959	0.6137	0.6471	86.0
1960	0.6378	0.6847	89.4
1961	0.6515	0.7079	91.3
1962	0.7258	0.7814	101.7
1963	0.7587	0.8341	106.4
1964	0.8340	0.9190	116.9
1965	0.8605	0.9626	120.6

SOURCE: Calculated from tonnage and man-hour data in Appendix Table C-2. (Column 2 was calculated by first estimating the man-hours required, at the 1960 productivity rate, for bulk tonnage for each year. The remaining man-hours were then applied to the nonbulk tonnage.)

Table C-4: Difference in Mean Productivity Rates, By Commodity, Pacific Coast, 1960-1963.

| No. Commodity Name | Man-hours per ton | | | |
| | Outbound | | Inbound | |
	Difference in rates	Productivity change	Difference in rates	Productivity change
		percent		*percent*
1 Canned goods	.098366	9.71	.186343	21.06
2 Rice	.307800	135.61	a	
3 Grains, other	.011541	31.19	a	
4 Flour	.049840	7.51	a	
5 Citrus	.249543	17.86	b	
6 Bananas	a		.337107	31.22
7 Dried fruits and nuts	.144595	11.87	.163770	13.61
8 Coffee	a		.013657	1.38
9 Sugar	b		.051905	74.15
10 Foods, other	.065232	5.04	.043294	2.90
11 Beverages	a		.203326	13.31
12 Hides	.234126	15.63	c	
13 Animal products inedible	.069351	53.36	c	
14 Animal feeds	.217185	236.82	c	
15 Rubber	.231160	19.99	.027330	1.82
16 Copra	b		.167624	31.39
17 Cotton	.293824	28.42	c	
18 Fibers, cordage	d		.041579	3.29
19 Burlap	.243499	19.35	.112995	12.70
20 Textiles, general	—.360904	—21.92	.522378	68.74
21 Logs	.293903	39.67	—.060081	—12.05
22 Lumber	.032888	4.86	.382972	52.92
23 Plywood	—.025557	—2.88	.169905	23.75
24 Pulp	—.044021	—6.70	e	
25 Newsprint	.165661	29.92	.108471	48.95
26 Paper products	—.029878	—2.97	.513881	92.59
27 Coke	.028318	38.09	c	
28 Glass and products	c		.446521	48.09
29 Earths	.226953	17.38	.109883	10.47
30 Salt	e		.149430	489.85
31 Iron ore	.008857	92.76	f	
32 Iron and steel products	—.245097	—43.56	.094887	21.86

Table C-4 (Continued)

| | Man-hours per ton | | | |
| | Outbound | | Inbound | |
No. Commodity Name	Difference in rates	Productivity change	Difference in rates	Productivity change
		percent		*percent*
33 Iron and steel pipe	.350689	60.71	.222772	39.46
34 Iron and steel scrap	.072914	37.76	c	
35 Aluminum	—.038266	—5.42	.162027	32.12
36 Copper	.044265	9.59	g	
37 Ores, general	—.107867	—57.48	.010245	5.41
38 Hardware	.126593	18.46	.314636	34.27
39 Machinery and vehicles	.254018	26.59	.186773	27.87
40 Metals and products, other	.076674	13.17	.389918	77.73
41 Chemicals	.051411	6.59	.018617	4.78
42 Fertilizers	.073466	8.25	.093087	10.04
43 Potash	.040623	84.95	a	
44 General cargo	.203479	20.10	.361710	38.18
45 Petroleum and by-products, dry cargo	—.029312	—3.14	.219497	24.28
General cargo:				
Aggregate	.203470	20.10	.361710	38.18
Break-bulk	.098690	6.90	.168480	12.09
Unit Loads	.275931	90.70	.249562	125.60
Bulk	—.006302	—11.53	.246809	128.08

[a] These commodities were combined with foods, other; only small tonnages, or no tonnages for some goods, were reported in the PMA data.

[b] Not reported in PMA data.

[c] Combined with general cargo.

[d] Combined with textiles, general.

[e] Omitted; most of the tonnage is not handled by longshoremen.

[f] Combined with ores, general.

[g] Combined with metals and metal products, other.

SOURCE: Calculated from data in PMA, *Longshore Productivity Study, 1960–1963*.

Table C-5: Tonnages Handled, by Commodity, Pacific Coast Oceanborne Commerce, Dry Cargo, 1957-1964.
(in thousands of tons of 2,000 pounds)

No. Outbound commodity	1957	1958	1959	1960	1961	1962	1963	1964
1 Canned goods	926	828	743	681	542	533	495	485
2 Rice	292	209	310	267	295	324	408	392
3 Grains, other	6326	4511	4258	5800	5180	4387	5753	4919
4 Flour	300	419	271	398	342	334	309	287
5 Citrus	125	110	121	110	134	95	103	114
6 Bananas	1	1	1	1	1	1	1	1
7 Dried fruits and nuts	161	146	97	141	105	117	123	123
8 Coffee	6	4	3	2	1	1	1	2
9 Sugar	3	14	4	4	5	3	4	5
10 Foods, other	621	580	642	558	575	701	804	885
11 Beverages	113	136	120	139	142	127	127	121
12 Hides	60	58	44	81	86	91	109	130
13 Animal products, inedible	158	147	176	211	218	198	219	269
14 Animal feeds	144	242	162	191	305	542	530	545
15 Rubber	20	24	22	22	14	12	24	37
16 Copra	0	0	0	0	0	0	0	0
17 Cotton	394	233	186	419	314	236	347	299
18 Fibers, cordage	0	0	0	2	1	0	0	0
19 Burlap	3	2	2	2	4	4	5	4
20 Textiles, general	31	25	24	24	18	18	28	23
21 Logs	218	292	304	381	1388	1228	2453	3132
22 Lumber[a]	2234	1998	2199	2300	1969	2127	1919	2102
23 Plywood	19	28	55	48	45	49	47	61
24 Pulp	317	235	275	432	424	472	581	610
25 Newsprint	241	187	142	43	37	18	24	23
26 Paper products	213	177	195	216	261	298	345	430
27 Coke	1173	450	455	547	639	551	853	1372
28 Glass and products	9	8	9	10	8	10	8	12
29 Earths	120	130	162	203	219	162	186	219
30 Salt	502	444	500	468	620	631	712	470
31 Iron ore	1130	552	572	942	975	1083	1860	2275
32 Iron and steel products	425	160	133	218	451	189	120	443
33 Iron and steel pipe	0	47	39	35	28	24	50	29

Table C-5 (Continued)

No. Outbound commodity	1957	1958	1959	1960	1961	1962	1963	1964
34 Iron and steel scrap	1169	514	898	1434	1790	892	1338	1544
35 Aluminum	17	16	26	59	44	72	67	77
36 Copper	97	79	25	112	117	101	91	88
37 Ores, general	22	10	8	41	28	15	29	39
38 Hardware	9	8	7	6	6	5	9	11
39 Machinery and vehicles	268	176	207	232	217	229	263	279
40 Metals and products, other	84	59	58	70	70	55	91	69
41 Chemicals	757	699	616	672	652	723	780	772
42 Fertilizers	199	152	222	153	157	166	133	120
43 Potash	308	286	404	583	557	595	509	709
44 General cargo	647	565	672	597	547	527	768	869
45 Petroleum and by-products, dry cargo[b]	472	451	405	322	287	292	257	280
Total	20334	15412	15774	19177	19818	18238	22883	24676
46 Inedible Molasses	4	0	0	0	4	1	25	35
47 Pulpwood	3	4	1	2	3	4	3	56
48 Cement	644	715	591	622	452	344	356	349
49 Nonmetallic Minerals	106	326	54	124	44	131	341	74
50 Tankship Chemicals	10	8	304	356	340	370	493	495
51 Watercraft	636	480	448	315	202	273	285	238
52 Sundry excluded goods	0	0	5	9	1	209	131	135
Engineers' tonnages for:								
22 Lumber	3237	3293	3286	3246	2808	2834	2954	2976
45 Petroleum and petroleum products	19827	19550	22822	25972	23329	23198	22237	20514

Table C-5 (Continued)

APPENDIX TABLE C-5; PART II

No. Inbound commodity	1957	1958	1959	1960	1961	1962	1963	1964
1 Canned goods	332	365	296	341	318	303	227	341
2 Rice	2	4	0	0	0	0	0	0
3 Grains, other	6	1	10	2	1	15	17	1
4 Flour	5	5	5	5	3	4	3	7
5 Citrus	0	0	0	0	0	0	0	0
6 Bananas	248	243	242	291	324	309	311	292
7 Dried fruit and nuts	24	18	16	17	20	17	20	17
8 Coffee	208	195	218	219	215	239	243	211
9 Sugar	848	612	833	752	846	740	826	759
10 Foods, other	251	322	355	343	328	371	463	407
11 Beverages	72	76	81	93	63	73	80	96
12 Hides	1	1	1	1	1	1	1	1
13 Animal products, inedible	50	71	64	83	97	84	91	102
14 Animal feeds	67	57	20	6	12	8	6	20
15 Rubber	71	64	66	46	41	41	45	53
16 Copra	291	305	348	391	383	349	261	274
17 Cotton	1	1	1	1	1	1	2	1
18 Fibers, cordage	18	21	28	18	18	32	35	35
19 Burlap	52	60	57	52	52	59	65	58
20 Textiles, general	68	80	85	95	95	100	106	112
21 Logs	182	125	113	137	161	92	103	47
22 Lumber[a]	143	128	140	147	126	136	123	134
23 Plywood	177	209	312	210	218	277	313	355
24 Pulp	341	434	417	306	130	128	302	482
25 Newsprint	674	515	568	546	604	658	674	716
26 Paper products	143	129	210	139	52	50	57	70
27 Coke	0	0	0	2	0	0	0	0
28 Glass and products	45	59	104	91	85	94	97	123
29 Earths	5	2	3	1	1	2	2	3
30 Salt	406	389	446	440	466	517	487	614
31 Iron ore	0	3	16	16	0	0	0	0
32 Iron and steel products	1316	775	1055	1476	851	1135	1223	1385
33 Iron and steel pipe	(3)	254	393	474	332	376	386	379

Table C-5 (Continued)

APPENDIX TABLE C-5; PART II

No. Inbound commodity	1957	1958	1959	1960	1961	1962	1963	1964
34 Iron and steel scrap	10	26	10	10	10	3	5	6
35 Aluminum	9	8	16	4	9	12	17	23
36 Copper	17	17	18	27	11	17	17	20
37 Ores, general	620	384	387	429	361	402	458	833
38 Hardware	60	74	113	81	91	95	108	101
39 Machinery and vehicles	259	287	349	318	185	195	231	297
40 Metal and products, other	147	65	67	126	106	62	54	68
41 Chemicals	325	359	396	443	425	339	237	281
42 Fertilizers	99	139	156	151	171	185	176	244
43 Potash	0	0	0	0	3	0	0	0
44 General cargo	692	613	656	662	428	441	499	550
45 Petroleum and by-products, dry-cargo[b]	406	369	372	267	231	203	254	218
Total	8691	7864	9043	9259	7875	8165	8625	9736
46 Inedible molasses	388	359	342	431	398	540	485	507
47 Pulpwood	742	918	621	1031	1233	1079	1449	1218
48 Cement	424	475	329	359	376	318	310	305
49 Nonmetallic minerals	703	1004	1115	1090	912	1048	1445	1478
50 Tankship chemicals	7	20	271	419	371	379	379	432
51 Watercraft	77	65	18	67	70	150	153	94
52 Sundry excluded goods	0	0	15	1	0	0	0	4
Engineers' tonnages for:								
22 Lumber	1271	1714	1648	1650	1185	1458	1559	1603
45 Petroleum and by-products, dry-cargo	30437	19437	32284	39797	39208	40590	36464	36414

[a] Estimated from PMA assessment tons data.
[b] Domestic commerce dry cargo only.
[c] Combined with iron and steel products (1957 only).

SOURCE: Adapted from U.S. Army Corps of Engineers, *Waterborne Commerce of the United States*, various annual issues. (See Appendix B, pp. 259–267, for full source citation and explanation of commodity classifications.)

Table C-6: Dockwork Man-hours Used and Man-hours Saved,
Nonbulk Cargo, by Commodity, Pacific Coast, 1963
(for PMA Reported Tonnages Only).
(in thousands of man-hours)

Commodity	Hours required at 1960 rates[a]	Actual hours[b]	man-power savings
LOADING			
A. *Goods Usually Palletized*:[c]			
Canned goods	77.5	18.8	58.7
Rice, nonbulk	17.9	0.3	17.6
Grain, nonbulk	3.8	2.9	0.9
Flour	19.3	5.7	13.6
Citrus	45.8	24.3	21.5
Foods, other	123.7	73.3	50.4
Animal products, inedible	2.7	0.8	1.9
Animal feeds, nonbulk	4.3	2.7	1.6
Paper and paper products	31.9	19.4	12.5
Textiles	1.5	1.8	—0.3
Chemicals, fertilizers (nonbulk)	88.5	56.3	32.2
Earths	28.9	18.1	10.8
General cargo: break-bulk	586.3	402.8	183.5
Subtotal	1,032.1	627.2	404.9
B. *Goods Often Not Palletized*:[c]			
Logs	8.8	1.2	7.6
Lumber	15.0	7.7	7.3
Cotton	88.0	36.5	51.5
Hides	38.6	25.0	13.6
Pulp	1.8	1.7	0.1
Newsprint	0.8	0.4	0.4
Iron and steel mill products	7.0	1.2	5.8
Iron and steel scrap, nonbulk	5.8	2.4	3.4
Aluminum	1.2	0.8	0.4
Copper	0.1	0.1	—
Metal products, machinery, vehicles	13.2	6.8	6.4
Petroleum products	10.4	6.9	3.5
Plywood	1.3	0.8	0.5
General cargo: cribs, vans, unit loads	56.3	35.6	20.7
General cargo: Containers	11.8	2.3	9.5
Subtotal	260.1	129.4	130.7
Total loading, nonbulk goods	1,292.2	756.6	535.6

Table C-6 (Continued)

Commodity	Hours required at 1960 rates[a]	Actual hours[b]	man-hour savings
DISCHARGING			
A. *Goods Usually Palletized*[c]			
Coffee	63.0	44.6	18.4
Sugar, nonbulk	1.0	0	1.0
Canned goods	43.0	24.8	18.2
Foods, other	102.2	82.9	19.3
Copra, nonbulk	0.3	0.1	0.2
Rubber	17.2	16.0	1.2
Textiles (including jute, burlap)	25.2	18.2	7.0
Paper	12.2	3.7	8.5
Glass	18.6	9.7	8.9
Earths	2.2	1.2	1.0
Hardware, metals and products	31.5	17.9	13.6
Chemicals	4.3	2.3	2.0
Fertilizers	36.0	21.9	14.1
General cargo: break-bulk	511.7	387.9	123.8
Subtotal	868.4	631.2	237.2
B. *Goods Often Not Palletized*[c]			
Bananas	20.9	0	20.9
Logs and Lumber	24.5	13.3	11.2
Plywood	37.6	26.9	10.7
Newsprint	28.8	22.6	6.2
Vehicles	32.4	16.5	15.9
Iron and steel pipe	80.4	36.5	43.9
Iron and steel mill products	120.7	63.2	57.5
Ores, nonbulk	0.3	0.5	—0.2
General cargo: cribs, unit loads	6.4	2.5	3.9
Containers	3.6	0.1	3.5
Subtotal	355.6	182.1	173.5
Total discharging, nonbulk goods	1,224.0	813.3	410.7
Grand total, loading and discharging	2,516.2	1,569.9	946.3

[a] Hours estimated by applying the 1960 dockwork man-hours per ton, by commodity, to the 1963 tonnage reported in the PMA productivity study.

[b] Dockwork hours reported in the 1963 productivity study.

[c] Goods listed under "A" usually require palletization, or unitized packaging, in order to be loaded to or discharged from the ship. Some of the goods listed under "B" may be palletized, but they are often, or almost always, handled by special gear, loaded or discharged by direct transfer, and so on.

SOURCE: Calculated from the data in the PMA productivity studies.

Table C-7: Direct Labor Man-hour Savings, by Package and Commodity and by Commodity only, 1963 at 1960 Productivity Rates, Pacific Coast.

		Loading		Discharging	
		By Package and		By Package and	By
No.	Commodity	Commodity	Commodity	Commodity	Commodity
1	Canned goods	44,177	37,605	15,506	24,374
2	Rice	32,825	87,754	—	a
3	Grains, other	44,772	69,081	—	a
4	Flour	5,738	10,397	—	a
5	Citrus	10,243[b]	23,557	—	a
6	Bananas	—	a	106,003	104,402
7	Dried fruits and nuts	7,635	10,339	28	360
8	Coffee	—	a	2,607	2,947
9	Sugar	—	a	22,633	44,291
10	Foods, other	−19,447	28,787	7,335	8,689
11	Beverages	8	841	5,490	6,140
12	Hides	17,858	17,911	—	c
13	Animal products, inedible	3,685	7,580	—	c
14	Animal feeds	8,659	76,601	—	c
15	Rubber	1,736	1,780	243	847
16	Copra	—	c	35,665	35,369
17	Cotton	77,006	87,560	—	c
18	Fibers, cordage	—	d	421	1,085
19	Burlap	688	1,704	10,178	6,904
20	Textiles, general	−226	−505	689	1,306
21	Logs	496,867	575,256	107	−228
22	Lumber	126,587	55,620	71,192	48,752
23	Plywood	−1,137	−401	47,151	38,857
24	Pulp	−24,175	−22,631	—	e
25	Newsprint	608	2,270	64,876	64,844
26	Paper products	−13,542	−6,185	17,920	15,468
27	Coke	7,588	25,551	—	c
28	Glass and products	—	c	18,144	22,907
29	Earths	8,021	12,210	879	1,066
30	Salt	—	e	49,589	60,728
31	Iron ore	36,259	16,865	—	f
32	Iron and steel products	1,493	−10,588	85,293	80,189

Table C-7 (Continued)

No. Commodity	Loading		Discharging	
	By Package and Commodity	Commodity	By Package and Commodity	By Commodity
33 Iron and steel pipe	15,897	19,077	80,641	88,775
34 Iron and steel scrap	37,432	26,810	—	c
35 Aluminum	—1,238	—2,151	573	1,215
36 Copper	1,490	2,049	—	g
37 Ores, general	—328	—550	5,372	2,226
38 Hardware	24	380	10,923	16,802
39 Machinery and vehicles	32,432	37,645	29,964	32,685
40 Metals and products, other	616	974	18,132	28,542
41 Chemicals	56,151	18,837	1,130	676
42 Fertilizers	613	478	10,855	13,619
43 Potash	18,698	19,178	—	c
45 Petroleum and by-products, dry cargo	—1,309	—2,143	319	922
Total, identified tonnage	1,034,404	1,229,543	719,858	754,759
General cargo:				
Break-bulk		198,234		192,765
Containers		34,400		1,844
Other unit loads		19,300		1,700
Bulk		—171		39,688
Total, general cargo	268,794	251,763	280,720	235,997
Total, direct labor	1,303,098	1,481,306	1,000,578	990,756

[a] Combined with foods, other.

[b] This figure is apparently an error; by their methods of calculating man-hour savings, the PMA should have recorded about 25,000 man-hours saved for citrus.

[c] Combined with general cargo.

[d] Combined with textiles, general.

[e] Omitted.

[f] Combined with ores, general.

[g] Combined with metals and products, other.

SOURCES: Columns 1 and 3: Pacific Maritime Association, *Longshore Productivity Study, 1960–1963*, Part I, pp. 106–113. Columns 2 and 4: Calculated from data in PMA, *Longshore Productivity Study, 1960–1963*, Part II, all Pacific Coast, full year, commodity detail tables.

Table C-8: Age Distribution, Registered Longshoremen, by Registration Status, Pacific Coast, July 1964.

Age	Fully Registered ("A")	Limited Registered ("B")	Total
Over 75	29	0	29
66–74	222	4	226
60–65	1,569	14	1,583
55–59	1,729	36	1,765
50–54	2,082	56	2,138
45–49	1,708	120	1,828
40–44	1,274	259	1,533
35–39	984	370	1,354
30–34	698	377	1,075
25–29	411	558	969
20–24	91	532	623
18–19	1	24	25
Total	10,798	2,350	13,148

Source: PMA Records.

SOURCES AND OTHER READINGS

SOURCES AND OTHER READINGS

This study was based almost wholly on primary sources — union, industry and government studies, reports, publications, and other material. Most of the industry and union material is unpublished; it consists of typed, multilithed, or mimeographed transcripts, summarized minutes, reports, tables of data, and the like. The government material consists chiefly of Congressional committee hearings and voluminous data published by several agencies. These primary sources are:

INDUSTRY AND UNION DOCUMENTS AND PERIODICALS

International Longshoremen's and Warehousemen's Union and Pacific Maritime Association. *Arbitration Awards* of Messrs. Fielding, Kagel, Kidd, Meehan, Morse, Roderick, Sloss, Thomas and others. San Francisco, Los Angeles, Portland, and Seattle: 1935–1965. (Mostly typescript.)

————— *Coast Labor Relations Committee Minutes.* Summarized minutes. San Francisco, 1935–1965. (Mimeographed, typescript.)

————— *Conference of Arbitrators, ILWU and PMA.* Summarized minutes. San Francisco, 1961–1965. (Mimeographed.)

————— *Documents between ILWU–PMA from May through September 1960 — up to Caucus, October 3.* San Francisco, 1960. (Mimeographed and typescript.)

————— *Joint Negotiating Committee Minutes.* Summarized minutes. San Francisco, 1955–1966. (Typescript.)

————— *Pacific Coast Longshore Agreement* with various *Supplements, Memoranda of Understanding,* and *Changes.* San Francisco, 1937–1959. (Mostly Mimeographed.)

————— *Pacific Coast Longshore Agreement, 1961–1966.* San Francisco, 1962.

————— ————— *The ILWU–PMA Supplemental Agreement on Mechanization and Modernization: effective January 1, 1961.* San Francisco, November 15, 1961. (Mimeographed.)

————— ————— *Fourth Amendment to ILWU–PMA Supplemental Agreement on Mechanization and Modernization* (with supplements). San Francisco, December 19, 1966. (Mimeographed.)

International Longshoremen's and Warehousemen's Union. *Deregistration of "B" Men, San Francisco, 1963–1964.* San Francisco, December 3, 1964. (Mimeographed.)

————— *Age Distribution of Longshoremen, Clerks and Walking Bosses as of 1949.* San Francisco, October 23, 1953. (Mimeographed.)

———— *Ages of Longshoremen and Clerks, by Year Entered Industry.* San Francisco, March, 1966. (Typescript.)

———— *The Dispatcher.* San Francisco: published biweekly. Especially useful were volumes XXIII–XXV of 1965–1967.

————*Estimated Status of M & M Funds.* San Francisco, April 4, 1966. (Mimeographed.)

———— *Longshoremen, Clerks and Bosses, Registered But Not Pensioned.* San Francisco, June 29, 1960. (Mimeographed.)

———— *Proceedings of the Biennial Convention.* San Francisco, 1948–1951, 1955–1962.

———— *Proceedings of the Longshore, Shipclerk and Walking Boss Caucus.* San Francisco, 1955–1966. (Typescript.)

———— *Table of Increases in Wage Package, 1961–1966.* San Francisco, April 4, 1966. (Mimeographed.)

———— *Union Negotiating Committee Minutes.* Summarized. San Francisco, 1955–1965. (Typescript.)

Pacific Maritime Association. *Annual Report.* San Francisco, 1950–1965.

———— *History of Tonnage, 1950–1965.* San Francisco, June 16, 1966. (Typescript.)

———— *Loading Operations, One Company — One Port, Manhours per Ton.* San Francisco, March 24, 1959. (Typescript.)

———— *Longshore Manhours, Pacific Coast. 1954–1965.* San Francisco, June 30, 1966. (Typescript.)

———— *Monthly Research Bulletin.* San Francisco, 1952–1956.

———— *Productivity Study, Longshore Operations, Pacific Coast, 1960–1961.* In two parts. San Francisco, 1963.

———— *Productivity Study, Longshore Operations, Pacific Coast, 1961–1962.* In two parts. San Francisco, 1964.

———— *Productivity Study, Longshore Operations, Pacific Coast, 1960–1963.* In two parts. San Francisco, 1965.

Pacific Shipper. San Francisco, weekly issues, 1964, 1965.

The Waterfront Worker. San Francisco, 1934, 1935.

GOVERNMENT PUBLICATIONS AND DOCUMENTS

National Longshoremen's Board, *Proceedings,* August 8–24, 1934, San Francisco. (Typescript.)

U. S. Congress, House of Representatives, Committee on Merchant Marine and Fisheries, *Labor-Management Problems of the American Merchant Marine; Hearings, June 20–July 20, 1955.* 84th Cong., 1st sess. Washington, 1955.

———— ———— ———— ———— *Labor-Management Problems of the American Merchant Marine; Hearings, March 12, 1956.* 84th Cong., 2nd sess. Washington, 1956.

———— ———— ———— ———— *Study of Harbor Conditions in Los Angeles and Long Beach, Hearings, October 19, 20, and 21, 1955.* 84th Cong., 1st sess. Washington, 1955.

———— ———— ———— ———— *West Coast Maritime Industries Survey; Hearings, October 1–14, 1954.* 83d Cong., 2nd sess. Washington, 1954.

———— ———— Joint Economic Committee. *Subsidy and Subsidy-Effect Programs of the U. S. Government.* 89th Cong., 1st sess. Washington, 1965.

———— Department of the Army. Corps of Engineers. *Waterborne Commerce of the United States,* Part 4, *Waterways and Harbors, Pacific Coast, Alaska and Hawaii.* Calendar years 1955–1964. Washington, 1956–1965.

———— Department of Commerce. Bureau of the Census. *United States Foreign Trade: Waterborne Foreign Trade Statistics,* Summary Report FT 985. Washington: Monthly and annual issues, 1955–1965.

———— ———— ———— *U. S. Foreign Waterborne Commerce Review.* Washington: annual issues, 1955–1965.

———— ———— Federal Maritime Board and Maritime Administration. *Manual of General Procedures for Determining Operating Differential Subsidy Rates.* Washington, 1957.

———— ———— Maritime Administration. *Domestic Oceanborne and Great Lakes Commerce of the United States.* Washington: annual issues, 1954–1965.

———— ———— ———— *United States Seaports: Alaska, Pacific Coast, and Hawaii; Port Series,* Part 1. Washington, 1961.

———— ———— Office of Business Statistics. *Business Statistics, 1965.* Washington, 1965.

———— Department of Labor. Bureau of Labor Statistics. *Wage Chronology: Pacific Longshore Industry, 1934–65,* Bulletin 1491. Washington, 1966.

OTHER PUBLICATIONS OF PRIMARY DATA

International Shipping and Shipbuilding Directory, 1965. London: Benn Brothers, Limited, 1965.

Lloyd's Register of Shipping: Vol. I (Register of Ships), Vol. III (Register Book, Owners). 1965–1966. London, 1965.

St. Clair, Frank J., editor-in-chief. *Moody's Transportation Manual.* With supplements. New York: Moody's Investor Service, Inc., 1965 and 1966.

Standard and Poor's. *Standard Corporation Descriptions.* New York: Standard and Poor's Corporation, 1965 and 1966.

A number of books and articles provide useful background or supplementary material dealing with the industry, the union, the modernization and mechanization agreement, or work rules in other industries. The following is a selected list of such books, articles, and similar publications.

BOOKS AND DISSERTATIONS

Armstrong, James Chester. "A Critical Analysis of Cargo Handling Cost in the Steamship Industry." Master's thesis. University of California, Berkeley, 1947.

Baker, Elizabeth Faulkner. *Printers and Technology*. New York: Columbia University Press, 1957.

Barnes, Charles B. *The Longshoremen*. New York: Survey Associates, Inc., The Russell Sage Foundation, 1915.

Chaudhuri, P. C. *Port and Dock Workers: Report of an Enquiry into Demands of Labour*. Faridabad: Ministry of Transport and Communications, Government of India, 1957.

Cross, Ira B. *A History of the Labor Movement in California*. Berkeley: University of California Press, 1935.

Cunningham, Brysson. *Cargo Handling at Ports*. New York: John Wiley & Sons, 1924.

Dunlop, John T., editor. *Automation and Technological Change*. Englewood Cliffs, N. J.: Prentice–Hall, 1962.

Dunlop, John T. *Wage Determination under Trade Unions*. New York: The Macmillan Company, 1944.

Eliel, Paul. *The Waterfront and the General Strike*. San Francisco: Industrial Association, 1934.

Francis, Robert C. "A History of Labor on the San Francisco Waterfront." Doctoral dissertation. University of California, Berkeley, 1934.

Goldblatt, Louis, and Otto Hagel. *Men and Machines*. San Francisco: International Longshoremen's and Warehousemen's Union. Pacific Maritime Association, 1963.

Gorter, Wytze, and George H. Hildebrand. *The Pacific Coast Maritime Shipping Industry, 1930–1948*. 2 vols. Berkeley: University of California Press, 1952, 1954.

Goodman, Jay Selwyn. "One Party Union Government: The ILWU Case." Master's thesis. Stanford University, 1963.

Haber, William G., and Harold M. Levinson. *Labor Relations and Productivity in the Building Trades*. Ann Arbor: University of Michigan Press, 1956.

Hallinan, Vincent. *A Lion in Court*. New York: G. P. Putnam's Sons, 1963.

International Longshoremen's and Warehousemen's Union, *The ILWU Story: Three Decades of Militant Unionism*. 2nd ed. San Francisco: 1963.

Jacobs, Paul. *Dead Horse and the Featherbird*. Santa Barbara: Center for the Study of Democratic Institutions, 1962.

Jensen, Vernon H. *Hiring of Dock Workers*. Cambridge, Mass.: Harvard University Press, 1964.

Kampelman, Max M. *The Communist Party vs. the CIO: A Study in Power Politics*. New York: F. A. Praeger, 1957.

Kaufman, Jacob J. *Collective Bargaining in the Railroad Industry*. New York: King's Crown Press, 1954.

Larrowe, Charles P. *Shape-Up and Hiring Hall*. Berkeley: University of California Press, 1955.

Leiter, Robert D. *Featherbedding and Job Security*. New York: Twayne Publishers, 1964.

Levinson, Harold M. *Determining Forces in Collective Wage Bargaining*. New York: John Wiley & Sons, 1966.

Liebes, Richard Alan. "Longshore Labor Relations on the Pacific Coast, 1934-1942." Doctoral dissertation. University of California, Berkeley, 1942.

Munson, Fred C. *Labor Relations in the Lithographic Industry.* Cambridge Mass.: Harvard University Press, 1963.

National Research Council, Maritime Cargo Transportation Conference, *Cargo Ship Loading: An Analysis of General Cargo Loading in Selected U. S. Ports.* Washington: National Academy of Sciences, National Research Council, 1957.

———— ———— *Inland and Maritime Transportation of Unitized Cargo.* Washington: National Academy of Sciences, National Research Council, 1963.

———— ———— *Longshore Safety Survey.* Washington: National Academy of Sciences, National Research Council, 1956.

———— ———— *Maritime Transportation of Unitized Cargo.* Washington: National Academy of Sciences, National Research Council, 1959.

———— ———— *The SS Warrior: An Analysis of an Export Transportation System from Shipper to Consignee.* Washington: National Academy of Sciences, National Research Council, 1954.

———— ———— *San Francisco Port Study.* Washington: National Academy of Sciences, National Research Council, 1964. (2 vols.)

Perlman, Selig. *A Theory of the Labor Movement.* New York: The Macmillan Company, 1928.

Port of New York Authority, *Port Development Expenditure Survey: United States, Puerto Rico, Canada; January 1, 1946 to December 31, 1962.* New York: October, 1963.

Porter, Arthur R. *Job Property Rights.* New York: King's Crown Press, 1954.

Quin, Mike [Paul William Ryan]. *The Big Strike.* Olema, Cal.: Olema Publishing Company, 1949.

Richardson, Reed C. *The Locomotive Engineer, 1863–1963; A Century of Railway Labor Relations and Work Rules.* Ann Arbor: University of Michigan Press, 1963.

Schneider, Betty V. H., and Abraham Siegel. *Industrial Relations in the Pacific Coast Longshore Industry.* Institute of Industrial Relations: University of California, 1956.

Slichter, Sumner H. *Union Policies and Industrial Management.* Washington: The Brookings Institution, 1941.

Slichter, Sumner H., James J. Healy, and E. Robert Livernash. *The Impact of Collective Bargaining on Management.* Washington: The Brookings Institution, 1960.

Swados, Harvey. *A Radical's America.* Boston: Little, Brown and Company, 1962.

Ulman, Lloyd. *The Rise of the National Trade Union.* Cambridge, Mass.: Harvard University Press, 1955.

Ward, Estolv E. *Harry Bridges on Trial.* New York: Modern Age Books, 1940.

Webb, Sidney and Beatrice. *Industrial Democracy.* London: Longmans, Green, and Co., 1897.

Weinstein, Paul A., editor. *Featherbedding and Technological Change*. Boston: D. C. Heath and Company, 1965.

Whyte, W. Hamilton. *Decasualization of Dock Labour*. Bristol: J. W. Arrowsmith, 1934.

ARTICLES

Arrow, Kenneth J., Hollis B. Chenery, Bagicha S. Minhas, and Robert M. Solow. "Capital-Labor Substitution and Economic Efficiency," *Review of Economics and Statistics*, XLIII (1961), 225–250.

Barnett, George E. "The Printers," *American Economic Association Quarterly*, third series, X (1909), 433–819.

Daykin, Walter L. "Arbitration of Work Rules Disputes," *Arbitration Journal*, XVIII (1963), 36–45.

———— "Work Rules in Industry," *Labor Law Journal*, XII (1961), 380–386.

Fairley, Lincoln. "The ILWU-PMA Mechanization and Modernization Agreement," *Labor Law Journal*, XII (1961), 664–680.

———— "The ILWU-PMA Mechanization and Modernization Agreement: An Evaluation of Experience Under the Agreement; The Union's Viewpoint," *Proceedings of the Sixteenth Annual Meeting, Industrial Relations Research Association* (1963), 34–47.

———— "The West Coast Longshore Agreement," *Dissent*, IX (1962), 186–190.

Glazier, William. "Automation and the Longshoremen: A West Coast Solution," *The Atlantic Monthly*, CCVI (1960), 57–61.

Gomberg, William. "Featherbedding: An Assertion of Property Rights," *The Annals of the American Academy*, CCCXXXIII (1961), 119–129.

Gulick, Charles A., and Melvin K. Bers. "Insight and Illusion in Perlman's Theory of the Labor Movement," *Industrial and Labor Relations Review*, VI (1953), 510–531.

Horowitz, Morris A. "The Diesel Firemen Issue on the Railroads," *Industrial and Labor Relations Review*, XIII (1960), 550–558.

Horvitz, Wayne L. "The ILWU-PMA Mechanization and Modernization Agreement: An Experiment in Industrial Relations," *Proceedings of the Sixteenth Annual Meeting, Industrial Relations Research Association* (1963), 22–33.

Jacobs, Paul. "Harry, the Gag Man," *The New Leader*, XLVII (July 6, 1964), 12–13.

Kaufman, Jacob J. "Logic and Meaning of Work Rules on the Railroads," *Proceedings of the Fourteenth Annual Meeting, Industrial Relations Research Association* (1961), 378–388.

———— "The Railroad Labor Dispute: A Marathon of Maneuver and Improvisation," *Industrial and Labor Relations Review*, XVIII (1965), 196–212.

Killingsworth, Charles C. "The Modernization of West Coast Longshore Work Rules," *Industrial and Labor Relations Review*, XV (1962), 295–306.

Kossoris, Max D. "Working Rules in West Coast Longshoring," *Monthly Labor Review*, LXXXIV (1961), 1–10.

—————— "1966 West Coast Longshore Negotiations," *Monthly Labor Review*, LXXXIX (1966), 1067–1075.

Lancaster, Pres. "Meeting the Problem of Automation and Job Security," in Jerome W. Blood, ed., *The Personnel Job in a Changing World*. New York: American Management Association, 1964, 57–68.

Leontief, Wassily. "The Pure Theory of the Guaranteed Annual Wage Contract," *Journal of Political Economy*, LIV (1946), 76–79.

Livernash, E. Robert. "The General Problem of Work Rules," *Proceedings of the Fourteenth Annual Meeting, Industrial Relations Research Association* (1961), 389–398.

Simler, Norman J. "The Economics of Featherbedding," *Industrial and Labor Relations Review*, XVI (1962), 111–121.

Stieber, Jack. "Work Rules and Practices in Mass Production Industries," *Proceedings of the Fourteenth Annual Meeting, Industrial Relations Research Association* (1961), 399–412.

Swados, Harvey. "West Coast Waterfront: The End of an Era," *Dissent*, VIII (1961), 448–460.

Weinstein, Paul A. "Featherbedding: A Theoretical Analysis," *Journal of Political Economy*, LXVIII (1960), 379–389.

Weir, Stanley. "The ILWU: A Case Study in Bureaucracy," *New Politics*, III (1964), 23–28.

INDEX

"A" men: definition, 36; average annual hours, 169; eligible for share of wage guarantee fund, 187–188

Abatement, of M&M fund contributions, 104–105

Age of longshoremen: median, various years, 165–167; distribution, 166–167, 282; reasons for high average, 166; proportion of young men, 168; mandatory retirement, 182; reduced for normal retirement, 182; grounds for preferential job assignment, 186; a motive to induce change, 191

Aggregation, commodity rates, described, 258–259

Agreement, ILWU-PMA: of 1960, summary of provisions, 1; of 1960, ratification, 100; of 1960, duration, 100; of 1966, ratification, 180; of 1966, duration, 180, 188

Alameda, port facilities, 14

Alaska: commerce with mainland, 5; number of ILWU members, 15; use of unit loads in trade, 86

Alaska Steamship Company: principal routes, 8; parent corporation, 9; number of ships, 11

Aluminum, large sling loads, 145

American Export Isbrandtsen Lines: subsidized ships in Pacific trade, 10; included in revenues and profits data, 174, 176

American Mail Line, parent corporation, 10, 11

American President Lines: ships in Pacific Coast trade, 8, 11; subsidized ships, 10–11; subsidiary, 10, 11; joint venture, 12; led in 1948 strike settlement, 21; included in revenues and profits data, 172–174, 176

Arbitration: awards used as sources, 30n;

1957 wage and hours settlement, 85; contingency to settle 1960 negotiations, 94; number each year, 146, 203; "instant" described, 192. *See also* National Longshoremen's Board

Arbitrator: 1960 southern California appointment, 98; former union officials, 98, 192; determines working conditions, 146. *See also* Bulcke, Dodd, Fielding, Hazel, Kagel, Kerr, Kidd, Morse, Murray, Roderick, Rosenshine, Sloss, Stalmaster, Thomas, Watkins, Ziskind

Army, U.S.: gathers data for productivity study, 19; threat to load cargo, 20. *See also* Engineers, U.S. Army

Ashley, Thomas L., U.S. Congress, House of Representatives, 80

Astoria, port facilities, 14

Atlantic ports: effect of 1965 strike, 174–175; share in total U.S. trade, 176

Attrition of work force: post-1960, 164; forecast, 195. *See also* Retirement, Deaths

"B" men: union membership, 36; work opportunity, 36, 169; grievances, 36–37, 169; analogous to probationary status, 37, 169; role as buffer, 169; average annual hours, 169; promoted, 1963, 169; proportion of total work force, 169; excluded from wage guarantee fund, 187–188; new registrations, 199–200

Bananas: important import, 5; special handling methods, 46, 82, 134, 150; increased efficiency, 148, 149

Beer, productivity rates, 236

Belly packing. *See* Hand carrying

Benefits. *See* Death benefits, Disability benefits, Pensions, Retirement, Vested benefit, Wages

Bethlehem Steel Corporation, 9